Political Ontology, Community,
and Institutions

SUNY series in Contemporary Italian Philosophy
―――――
Silvia Benso and Brian Schroeder, editors

Political Ontology, Community, and Institutions

Roberto Esposito in Dialogue with Contemporary Thinkers

Edited by

Laura Cremonesi, Rita Fulco, and
Valentina Surace

With an unpublished interview
with Roberto Esposito

SUNY PRESS

Cover image: Disegno di una Fortezza, Leonardo da Vinci, Biblioteca Ambrosiana.

Published by State University of New York Press, Albany

© 2025 State University of New York

All rights reserved

Printed in the United States of America

No part of this book may be used or reproduced in any manner whatsoever without written permission. No part of this book may be stored in a retrieval system or transmitted in any form or by any means including electronic, electrostatic, magnetic tape, mechanical, photocopying, recording, or otherwise without the prior permission in writing of the publisher.

Links to third-party websites are provided as a convenience and for informational purposes only. They do not constitute an endorsement or an approval of any of the products, services, or opinions of the organization, companies, or individuals. SUNY Press bears no responsibility for the accuracy, legality, or content of a URL, the external website, or for that of subsequent websites.

EU GPSR Authorised Representative:
Logos Europe, 9 rue Nicolas Poussin, 17000, La Rochelle, France
contact@logoseurope.eu

For information, contact State University of New York Press, Albany, NY
www.sunypress.edu

Library of Congress Cataloging-in-Publication Data

Names: Cremonesi, Laura, editor. | Fulco, Rita, 1972– editor. | Surace, Valentina, editor.
Title: Political ontology, community, and institutions : Roberto Esposito in dialogue with contemporary thinkers, with an unpublished interview with Roberto Esposito / edited by Laura Cremonesi, Rita Fulco, and Valentina Surace.
Other titles: Roberto Esposito in dialogue with contemporary thinkers, with an unpublished interview with Roberto Esposito
Description: Albany : State University of New York Press, [2025] | Series: SUNY series in Contemporary Italian philosophy / Silvia Benso and Brian Schroeder, editors | Includes bibliographical references and index.
Identifiers: LCCN 2024042780 | ISBN 9798855802085 (hardcover : alk. paper) | ISBN 9798855802108 (ebook)
Subjects: LCSH: Esposito, Roberto, 1950– | Political science—Philosophy. | Public institutions—Philosophy. | Social institutions—Philosophy. | Communities—Philosophy.
Classification: LCC JA71 .P6124 2025 | DDC 320.01—dc23/eng/20241223
LC record available at https://lccn.loc.gov/2024042780

Contents

Acknowledgments   vii

Introduction   1
    Laura Cremonesi, Rita Fulco, Valentina Surace

Part One:
Politics and Institutions

1. From the Impersonal to Instituting Thought:
   Esposito's Departure from Deleuze   23
   Stefania Achella

2. From Biopolitics to Common Immunity: The Role of
   Michel Foucault in the Philosophy of Roberto Esposito   41
   Laura Cremonesi

3. Conflict and Institution: Roberto Esposito and Claude Lefort   57
   Mattia Di Pierro

4. *Polis* and *Polemos*: Esposito between Hannah Arendt and
   Simone Weil   75
   Rita Fulco

5. The Political in Roberto Esposito and Carl Schmitt   95
   Francesco Marchesi

Part Two:
Political Ontology and Community

6. On Bodies: Perspectives of a Dialogue between Esposito and Nancy — 111
   Daniela Calabrò

7. The Impersonal between Ethics and Politics: Roberto Esposito and Emmanuel Levinas on the Third Person — 131
   Silvia Dadà

8. Assurance and Community: The Far Proximity between Esposito and Heidegger — 145
   Sandro Gorgone

9. Roberto Esposito and Reiner Schürmann: A Political Ontology after Heidegger — 163
   Alberto Martinengo, translated by Sarah De Sanctis

10. Immunity and Community: A Note of Discord between Roberto Esposito and Jacques Derrida — 181
    Valentina Surace

11. From the Neuter to the Instituting Praxis: The Role of Blanchot in Roberto Esposito's Thought — 197
    Massimo Villani

Appendix: Institutions, Conflicts, Common Immunity: In Dialogue with Roberto Esposito — 213
   Interview by Laura Cremonesi, Rita Fulco, and Valentina Surace, translated by Tijana Okič

Contributors — 227

Index — 233

Acknowledgments

We had the privilege and joy of jointly leading a panel within the Fourth International Conference of the Society for Italian Philosophy, which was held online November 5–7, 2021. This event was originally supposed to take place in 2020 in Turin but was postponed due to the COVID-19 pandemic. Our panel, which had been selected from an international call, was titled "Some Political Intersections of Roberto Esposito's Thought: Deleuze, Derrida, Arendt, and Simone Weil." It was an opportunity for the three of us to discuss our lines of research, even though we already shared friendship and work, in different ways and places. Subsequently, thinking back to the panel, on the one hand, and to Silvia Benso's passion for Italian thought, on the other, we felt it was important to try to broaden the topic of our talks—that is, the comparison between Roberto Esposito's thought and twentieth-century philosophy—to other Italian scholars who, like us, had had the opportunity to collaborate, work, or discuss with Roberto Esposito. And that is how the idea of this volume originated.

Our thanks therefore go, first and foremost, to all those who collaborated on the volume, for the effort and time they put into writing it.

We owe a special thanks to Silvia Benso, since without her enthusiasm, trust, and constant and patient attention, this book would not have its current form. Silvia Benso's passion for Italian philosophy prompted us to think together of a panel to participate in the interesting and unique event that is the International Conference of the Society for Italian Philosophy, which has been held regularly since 2016 and is chaired with dedication and professionalism by Silvia Benso. She carries out this commitment together with other scholars, whom we thank; in particular: Antonio Calcagno, Peter Carravetta, Pierre Lamarche, Elvira

Roncalli, and Brian Schroeder, who are members of the SIP Steering Committee.

Thanks to Michael Rinella, who followed all stages of this project, right from the presentation, with admirable professionalism and attention. Thanks also to Tijana Okič, friend and PhD colleague at the Scuola Normale Superiore in Pisa (Italy), for her generous willingness to take care of the translation and revision of the interview.

Of course, our most heartfelt and deepest thanks go to Roberto Esposito, not only for the clarity and breadth of his teaching, from which each of us as well as each contributor to this volume has benefited, but, above all, for giving time and attention to answer our questions, allowing us to publish an unpublished interview. In our opinion, this interview is very important because of the topics discussed, which reveal a turning point in Esposito's thought. We therefore thank him for his generosity, of which the friendly welcome he gave us is a great manifestation.

Laura Cremonesi, Rita Fulco, and Valentina Surace
Pisa, Messina, Reggio Calabria, June 2023

Introduction

Life and Institutions: Roberto Esposito's Path of Thought as a Path of Dialogue

RITA FULCO

The important interview "Institutions, Conflicts, Common Immunity: In Dialogue with Roberto Esposito," published for the first time in this volume, traces the main themes of Roberto Esposito's most current thinking. In answer to my first question, Esposito begins by describing his "impersonal" relationship with philosophy: "Thought—for me, but I'd say for anyone—is rather a necessity, a shockwave imposing itself irrespective of one's will. In many ways, as claimed by some Arab Aristotelians who, without much success, spoke about the 'agent intellect,' to think is not the expression of an internal choice but, rather, a 'foreign' element coming from the outside, absorbing us, sometimes despite ourselves. [. . .] For me, in particular in recent years, the thought machine, precisely because I wasn't controlling it, has been an important tool, necessary for survival and, within certain limits, important for what, in a somewhat pompous way, is defined as the 'life of the spirit'" (*infra*, 214). Reflecting on these words seems important to me, at least for two reasons: first, Esposito rarely explicitly describes his relationship with philosophy; second, this statement, at first glance, seems to be at odds with the method Esposito follows in his reflections, which are always "in dialogue" with other philosophers and, consequently, derive from a very specific choice of his own. To fully understand what Esposito says, one must consider his statements as the very origin of his method of thinking: even before his dialogue with the philosophers, Esposito practices listening, that is, he seeks to be open to a "correspondence" with thought itself in the forms it takes in individual philosophers.

This "corresponding" opens the way for a dialogue that can, later on, either become a common path or turn into distancing. Describing his relationship with philosophy, Esposito tries to illuminate a side of the philosophical reflection that generally remains in the shadows, namely, *inspiration*. Like poetry or literature, philosophy requires listening to an "elsewhere" that inspires reading, confrontation, dialogue, and, finally, translation into writing.

In this interview, Roberto Esposito puts himself more personally at stake than he has done elsewhere. As far as I know, Esposito had never spoken of thought as the "life of the spirit." It will be interesting to see whether this theme will develop in his forthcoming writings.

Esposito's viewpoint also emerges in relation to dramatic issues we have tried to discuss, for example, that of war. Esposito speaks of war with his usual clarity and lucid realism, but he cannot hide the melancholic character of some of his reflections, that is, the "nostalgia" for a more just world that, however, clashes with a negative anthropology: "I think that war is unlikely to disappear from history. Not because it is part of politics but, if anything, because it is part of our anthropology, at least the one we have known thus far, as Freud argued on more than one occasion. Far from deriving from war, politics has to aim at containing its invasiveness, transforming military conflict into a civic one" (*infra*, 216). Equally clear is his discussion on the opposition between extremism and radicalism, phenomena that, for Esposito, should not be confused: "Regarding the difference or, rather, opposition between extremism and radicalism, it is a matter of overturning, subverting a common place which assimilates two quite different phenomena. [. . .] Radicalism, as the word itself implies, refers to the deepest roots, to rootedness in the context of origins and the articulation of its polarities. Extremism, to the contrary, implies a separation from the roots and the divergence of seemingly opposing poles, which does not allow for the common horizon containing them to be recognized" (*infra*, 218).

In the second part of the interview, Esposito, prompted by Laura Cremonesi, returns to the subject of the different paradigms of political ontology, *destituent* and *constituent*, and his proposal of an *instituting* paradigm. The search for and elaboration of the instituting paradigm constitutes one of the most recent lines of research of Esposito, who does not hide the difficulties encountered on this path. However, the instituting paradigm had already emerged in the 1920s. It is no coincidence that an important part of Esposito's work—as he emphasizes—has a genealogical character. Indeed, he focuses first on Roman law and then on Spinoza, Machiavelli, and Hegel, who are the main interlocutors of his latest book, *Vitam instituere: Genealogie dell'istituzione* (2023): "Genealogy, like—for other reasons—archaeology, is necessary in order to come closer to one part of the present which we are unable to see if we read it head on, directly. The tradition that accumulates upon it as an impenetrable layer prevents the phenomena from being directly grasped. The only way to get around or penetrate it is to reopen the relation with the origin which precedes that tradition, whilst knowing that it is inaccessible" (*infra*, 221). Choosing the genealogical method is also a conscious choice of the risk of anachronism. Anachronism, however, must also be assessed in relation to its philosophical productivity, in light of authors such as Carlo Ginzburg: "History does not follow one single thread, it proceeds neither forwards nor backwards, but forms a constellation in which past, present, and future entangle in a new and unknown figure dominated by anachrony. Only the conscious assumption of the anachronism can, in principle at least, contest the dominion of what happened over what didn't, but which continues to suddenly appear in its absence in the present" (*infra*, 222).

In the last part of the interview, Valentina Surace notes that the pandemic was a fundamental juncture in which the past, present, and future came to a "showdown." Considering Esposito's latest volume dedicated to the issue of immunity, *Common Immunity: Biopolitics in the Age of the Pandemic* (2023), Surace focuses on the issue of *biopolitics*, which is understood both affirmatively and negatively, as thanatopolitics. The question of immunity is central to establishing a balance that does not lead to the dissolution of the community that is to be protected: "Just as there are no individual bodies without immunological mechanisms of defense, there are no societies either. Of course, in order for these to have a positive effect, one must have a sense of proportion. If the immunological apparatus grows more than it should, it risks fighting against the body, biological or social, which it ought to defend, leading it thus to collapse" (*infra*, 224).

In this context, rethinking the role of conflict is necessary, as it always risks degenerating into violent conflict, both within society, as social conflict—or even civil war—and as war waged against the external enemy. From this point of view, the purpose of institutions is fundamental, as they aim "to shape" the conflict: "It can also be said that the political is the space in which material conflicts are symbolized, becoming conflicts of power and mutual recognition between the sides. You are right, a political conflict can always escalate into a violent conflict. To contain such possibility, one needs precisely institutions, destined to keep it within certain limits compatible with the survival of social systems" (*infra*, 225).

According to Esposito, it is crucial to find a rational balance in the evaluation of problematic concepts such as conflict but also in the evaluation of more "politically correct" concepts, that is, those of responsibility, reception, and hospitality. To make these into watchwords without considering the real situation, the conjuncture, the need that emerges, from time to time, from the here and now, is to vote politics to failure. A criticism such as anarchism does not take into account the need to give a shared form to civilized living: "One thing is to criticize the authoritarian or exclusionary modalities of the principle of sovereignty; quite another though is to imagine a society without power. At the end of such reasoning, there is anarchy. Are we certain it is better than democracy?" (*infra*, 225).

It is no coincidence that the framework of this volume is precisely the relationship between philosophy and politics. In the global age, reflecting on the status of politics is increasingly urgent. In particular, it is necessary to *philosophically* reflect on actuality. Politics and thought, in fact, cannot be disjointed: in the background of political action, there is always an ontology, that is, the question of what power is to be exercised and what are the ways in which it is to be exercised. It is not by chance that political conflict manifests itself in multiple forms, as does the instituting processes that attempt to shape it.

From his earliest works, Roberto Esposito questions the crisis of politics and why thought is unable to convincingly respond to it. He does so by distancing himself not only from political theology but also from those paradigms—*destituent* and *constituent*—that have lost nowadays much of their analytical and propositional capacity. However, his proposal is not only critical. Esposito's thought relates to our present through the creation of new categories—among the most recent, those of instituting thought and common immunity—capable of opening a breach in an apparently increasingly closed horizon. His aim is to propose what Foucault called an "ontology of actuality." Therefore, dealing with Esposito's thought means, first and foremost, dealing with our present.

This is the main goal of this volume, which focuses on Roberto Esposito's dialogue with major contemporary thinkers.

Dialoguing with other thinkers characterizes the style of Esposito's philosophy. His focus on some of their categories is a method in which Esposito consciously and willingly chooses to allow his own thought to emerge and develop. It is a way of doing philosophy "in common" with those who preceded him and with his contemporaries, always gazing toward the present. Since the publication of one of his first books, *Categories of the Impolitical* (2015), Esposito has outlined the concept of *impolitical* in conversation with many thinkers, such as Carl Schmitt, Maurice Blanchot, Hannah Arendt, and Simone Weil. Moreover, Esposito dedicates a whole volume to Arendt and Weil, *The Origin of the Political: Hannah Arendt or Simone Weil?* (2017). In his reflection on the community (*Communitas: The Origin and Destiny of Community*, 2009), the relationship between *being* and *politics* is elaborated through discussions with Martin Heidegger, Jean-Luc Nancy, and Jacques Derrida. In *Immunitas: The Protection and Negation of Life* (2007), some of Esposito's most interesting themes are related to Michel Foucault. Together with Gilles Deleuze, Foucault is also Esposito's privileged interlocutor in *Bios* (2004), a fundamental work in which Esposito develops his original idea of *affirmative biopolitics*. In *Third Person: Politics of Life and Philosophy of the Impersonal* (2007), Esposito offers his own interpretation of Emmanuel Levinas's concepts of *subject* and *person*. In *Two: The Machine of Political Theology and the Place of Thought* (2013), *Politics and Negation: Towards an Affirmative Philosophy* (2018), *Instituting Thought: Three Paradigms of Political Ontology* (2020), and *Common Immunity* (2023), the dialogue with Foucault and Deleuze, on the one hand, and the dialogue with Heidegger and other thinkers, such as Reiner Schürmann, on the other, led Esposito to rethink the questions of the *negative* and *conflict*, while attention to French thought focused on some "instituting thinkers," among others, on Claude Lefort. Lefort's thought is also important in the other two volumes, which completed Esposito's triptych on the question of institutions, namely, *Institution* (2022) and *Vitam instituere* (2023).

A few more words are called forth by this last work, which, for reasons of time—it was, in fact, published in 2023—is not considered by most of the authors in this volume. However, it confirms and strengthens the theses that are pursued by each, completing Esposito's reflection on institutions. This book concludes the research that Esposito started with *Pensiero istituente* and continued with *Istituzione*. In *Vitam instituere*,

Esposito does not merely confront the philosophers closest to institutional semantics but, rather, tries to consider the history of philosophy from an instituting perspective. In what sense? The attempt is to overturn the hermeneutic process that generally starts from the thought of certain philosophers to reach a certain conclusion. Esposito, instead, considers the philosophical tradition from a different perspective, by rereading the authors with whom he has dealt—in particular, Machiavelli, Spinoza, and Hegel—and "projecting" the instituting perspective on their philosophy.

This perspective is used as a magnifying glass to provide a new interpretation, questioning the role of the thought of these classical authors in the development of the theory of institutions. Esposito constructs a genealogy that is understood as a search for an origin that would not be attainable with the traditional tools of historiography or philology. In the background of this path, we find the Latin locution *vitam instituere*.

Highlighting its importance for his own research, Esposito describes it in the following words, with which I would like to conclude: "It recalls, in its essential terms, on the one hand, the dual side of life, at once instituting and instituted, and, on the other hand, the potentially vital dimension of institutions. This intersection between law and life appears extremely opaque, like a tangle that is too tight to be unraveled. Therefore, it is approached in the genealogical mode—that is, indirectly, not head-on: *vitam instituere* is both the remote matrix from which we come and the still indistinct goal toward which we move." (*Vitam instituere*, VIII [my translation]).

Politics and Institutions

Valentina Surace

The first part of the book is devoted to Esposito's political thought and the philosophers who played a relevant role in his reflection on politics. This part clearly shows how the movement of Esposito's thought has referred, in its constitution and modification, to some contemporary authors who had different levels of relevance in each of these phases.

Thinkers such as Michel Foucault and Gilles Deleuze have long accompanied Esposito's thought and particularly his reflection on the category of biopolitics. However, in Esposito's more recent work and in his project of instituting thought, he seems to have taken some distance from these two authors in favor of another side of French philosophy, represented by Maurice Merleau-Ponty and Claude Lefort. References to Simone Weil and Hannah Arendt, in contrast, marked the first phase of Esposito's political reflection, centered on the origin of the political and the impolitical, but they also emerged again in the questions raised by the creation of the instituting paradigm. Carl Schmitt, instead, seems to play a more constant role, since he deeply influences Esposito's general conception of politics.

The chapters by Stefania Achella and Laura Cremonesi focus on the long-standing relationship Esposito's thought has had with two important figures in contemporary French thought: Deleuze and Foucault. For different reasons, towards these two authors, Esposito's thought performs a similar movement from strong closeness to progressive distancing. In both cases, it can be said that the volume *Bios* represents the moment of greatest adherence to the philosophies of these two, which complete each other in creating an affirmative biopolitics, whereas the new Esposito's research on instituting thought represents a strong distancing from both: from Deleuze, because Esposito sees in his political ontology the origin of that constituent paradigm from which, in *Instituting Thought*, he intends to take a distance; from Foucault, because he does not seem to play a central role in any of the three paradigms of political ontology: although he is a thinker of conflict, in his philosophy, a real problematization of institutions—always seen only in their repressive aspect—is lacking.

As Achella notes in her chapter "From the Impersonal to Instituting Thought: Esposito's Departure from Deleuze," at the core of the movement that leads Esposito to the progressive distancing from Deleuze is the question of the negative. One of the things that, in the last decades of the twentieth century, brought Deleuze to the center of attention in contemporary philosophical-political thought was his ability to elaborate an entirely affirmative ontology, with an almost complete elision of the negative. In this vein, as Achella notes, Deleuze's thought is the "most radical attempts to overcome the Hegelian dialectic" (*infra*, 24): in his ontology, it is not the power of the negative that confers dynamism on being and ensures any possibility of change and conflict. In fact, the function of the negative is replaced by repetition, understood as the affirmative proliferation of differences. In this abolition of the negative, life is also taken; as Achella writes: "Deleuze struggles against the negative in all its forms, down to the most natural, and for this reason most radical, form of it: death" (*infra*, 28). It is precisely this thought on life—allowing the conceptualization of a power of life capable of counteracting the deadly effects of biopower——that draws Esposito's attention in *Bios*, in which Deleuze's vitalism completes the uncertainties of Foucauldian conceptualization of biopower, allowing the delineation of affirmative biopolitics. If Deleuze still has a central place in Esposito's *A Philosophy for Europe: From the Outside*, he loses his relevance in the works that Esposito dedicates precisely to the question of the negative, that is, *Politics and Negation*. In this book, Esposito focuses on the philosophical and political risks that a total elision of the negative can entail and states the necessity, for philosophical thought, to make itself capable of taking the negative into account. In this new philosophical horizon, Deleuze's entirely affirmative thought has minor relevance. It is true that Deleuze, as well as Foucault, is at the origin of some affirmative figures of negation (difference, in Deleuze; the conflict between power and resistance, in Foucault). However, Esposito asks, is Deleuze's thought truly capable of avoiding the risk of affirming the inexistence of negation? Does difference "abolishes an existing negation? Or does [the] difference reveal the inexistence of the negation? [. . .] At stake in this alternative is the ontological status of the negative. Does the negative exist or not?" (Esposito, *Politics and Negation*, 142).

The answer to this question is clearly expressed in *Instituting Thought*: the constituent paradigm, which finds its origin precisely in Deleuze's political ontology, fails precisely because of its inability to think the negative and to crush reality and politics on the same plane, preventing it from giving rise to an effective political praxis.

As Achella concludes, the dismissal of Deleuze's thought and the affirmation of the necessity of confronting the negative reopens, inevitably, the dealing with Hegel. In Esposito, this follows a "wholly unusual path" (*infra*, 34): it is from the tradition of Italian Thought and Italian philosophers such as Machiavelli and Gramsci that, in *Living Thought*, Esposito returns to a Hegelian perspective and "perceives the capacity of the negative to set being in motion" and, conversely, the risk, in Deleuze, that the absence of the thought of the negative is "translated from ontological into a political effect of impossibility to act and transform" (*infra*, 35).

A similar movement—from strong adherence to a certain distancing—also inhabits Esposito's relationship to Foucault's thought and is described in Laura Cremonesi's chapter, "From Biopolitics to Common Immunity: The Role of Michel Foucault in the Philosophy of Roberto

Esposito." The moment in which Esposito most intensely discusses Foucault's categories is represented by *Bios*: in this text, in fact, the Foucauldian category of biopolitics turns out to be central. In discussing it, Esposito takes part in that strong renewal of Italian Thought that, in the late 1990s and early 2000s, revolved precisely around a reflection on biopolitics. With other Italian authors of this period, Esposito highlights a twofold aspect of the Foucauldian category: its hermeneutical fecundity for the understanding of our current time and recent past, on the one hand, and its insufficiency, on the other. For many reasons, in fact, the Foucauldian category of biopolitics turns out to be insufficiently elaborated by Foucault and, to be made a real and effective tool for understanding our present, it needs to be integrated. In *Italian Thought*, this integration follows different paths. In Esposito's thought, the aim is to propose an affirmative category of biopolitics. To do so, the first step is to highlight the multiple interpretive alternatives that Foucault's thought leaves open—in particular, that of the relationship between biopolitics and sovereignty—and the theoretical and political consequences that each of them leaves unresolved. Once this indeterminacy of the category is shown, Esposito can then propose a double integration of it: on the one hand, with the immunitary paradigm, which together with biopolitics allows us to better grasp the features of modernity and the thanatopolitical risk inherent in the politics on life; on the other hand, with the thought of other authors, including Deleuze, who allow us "to emphasize that 'vitalism' that can be foreseen in Foucault's pages on biopolitics and in his reference to life's ability to resist, which Foucault himself does not fully develop" (*infra*, 49).

Although it represents Esposito's greatest closeness to Foucault's philosophy, *Bios* does not fail to highlight the indeterminacies of Foucauldian political categories and the need to turn to other authors to develop the full potential inherent in them. Nonetheless, the category of biopolitics still plays a central role in Esposito's philosophy, as shown by works such as *From the Outside* and the more recent *Common Immunity*: both of these books emphasize how the category of biopolitics is still relevant in understanding the most important crisis that Europe and the entire world have faced in recent years, the one generated by the COVID-19 pandemic.

As for Deleuze, for Foucault, too, the point of greatest distancing is represented, in Esposito, by the opening of the project of instituting thought: if Deleuze plays a prominent role in it—still, in a critical way—Foucault's absence stands out instead. Although he is an author capable of thinking about affirmative figures of negation, he does not seem to play any role within the three paradigms. While Foucault is a thinker of conflict, he is certainly not a thinker of institutions, which he has always seen as centers for the diffusion of power relations. Instead, according to Esposito, as even the pandemic crisis has shown, thinking about the positive role of institutions and a new link between institutions and life is the most urgent political and philosophical task.

In Esposito, the distancing from the thought of Foucault and Deleuze coincides with a new interest in another side of French thought, different from both the destituent and the constituent paradigms but rooted instead in the French phenomenology of Merleau-Ponty: this is the thought of Lefort, whose role in Esposito's recent reflection is outlined by Mattia Di Pierro in his "Conflict and Institution: Roberto Esposito and Claude Lefort."

As early as the 1970s, Di Pierro notes, Lefort expressed a critique of the constituent paradigm and, in particular, of Deleuze's political thought that, in many respects, anticipated that carried out in these years by Esposito in his work on instituting thought. Indeed, Lefort had already seen the risk of "crushing of social and political reality on a plane of complete immanence and a bipolar conception that sharply divides event and form, instituting and instituted, where the latter term indicates only the negation of the former" (*infra*, 65). Instead of being crushed on this plane of indistinction with the political, the social must be thought of as an inextricable web of praxis and meanings. In this way, Lefort succeeds in "preventing both a radical divergence and a complete superposition (between the political and ontology). There is neither Heidegger's irreducible distance nor Deleuze's absolute superposition between the political and ontology—one instead finds a conflictual tension that simultaneously connects and distances them" (Esposito, *Instituting Thought*, 149).

At the roots of Lefort's political ontology are two major lines of thought: the first, already mentioned, is represented by Merleau-Ponty, who elaborates a conception of institution—itself derived from Husserlian phenomenology—understood as a whole of permanence and change. Each new event is, for Merleau-Ponty, both a rearticulation and a change of previous elements. This idea is taken by Lefort to a political level: society institutes itself in a "succession of contingent and precarious refoundation, a continuous instituting movement in which unity and separation coexist" (*infra*, 67).

Instead, the second line can be identified in Machiavelli, which is why, as Di Pierro notes, Esposito's interest in Lefort and his interpretation of Machiavelli goes back to long before the elaboration of the instituting thought. According to Esposito, as becomes clear in his recent book, *Vitam instituere*, which traces a genealogy of instituting thought, it is Machiavelli who inaugurated a modern thought on institutions because he was the first to emphasize the primacy of the instituting moment over the instituted and to place conflict at the core of order. Conflict and order are not two opposite dimensions but are always interconnected. By leaving conflict open, institutions ensure the health of political bodies. This insight from Machiavelli is a central moment in Lefort's instituting thought and political ontology: the internal division that crosses every society must be maintained as the source of the necessary vitality of the social and, as Di Pierro underlines, "the political is nothing but the explanation, the interpretation, that a society gives itself of its own division" (*infra*, 67).

In Esposito's more recent reflection, this side of French philosophy represented by Merleau-Ponty and Lefort has thus gained increasing importance because it seems to have the capacity to resolve some of the questions that the reflections of Foucault and Deleuze left open.

The presence of Arendt and Weil certainly appears evident in Esposito's early political thought, as Rita Fulco notes in her "*Polis* and *Polemos*: Esposito between Hannah Arendt and Simone Weil": "This dialogue 'in the margins' with Weil and Arendt is a milestone in the progression of Esposito's philosophy" (*infra*, 76). "In the margins" certainly does not mean that this dialogue is marginal; instead, it means that it is consistently situated on the edge of every moment of Esposito's reflection, from the 1996 book devoted to the two philosophers, *The Origin of the Political: Hannah Arendt or Simone Weil?* to the recent project of instituting thought. The very question raised by the volume, that of "the origin of the political," or that of the relationship between origin and actuality is, as Fulco shows, a central element of Esposito's philosophy.

This is demonstrated precisely by one of his most recent articles, the tribute he paid to Jean-Luc Nancy after his death (Esposito, "What Is Philosophy?"). In different ways, contemporary philosophy in fact seems to have given this same answer to the question of philosophy's contemporary task: this consists of finding the tools to think about the relationship between origin and actuality. "A philosopher—this is a first answer to the question of what philosophy is—is the one who inhabits the interstice between different and even opposing temporalities, experiencing the antinomic impact that arises from the copresence of the archaic and the present. Philosophy is the ability to sustain this friction, giving voice to the dilemmas it entails" (Esposito, "What Is philosophy?").

After all, Fulco argues, if Arendt and Weil interrogate the origin of the political, it is to gain an understanding of their present, marked by totalitarianism. They both try to understand whether totalitarianism is internal or external to the sphere of politics and power, a mere contingency or a destiny already inscribed in our political categories and political logic. While both agree in seeing at the origin of Western history and politics *polemos*, a war that culminates in the destruction of the *polis*, they diverge in their interpretation of the relationship between this same origin and actuality. For Weil, force, which is coessential to politics and power, cannot be countered by law and politics—a possibility that Arendt considers open instead—but can only find in itself an inner limit. Unless, Fulco notes, a spiritual education, a true *metanoia*, or a conversion of the mind enters into play. It is necessary to change the mind "because, though it seemed infallible, it has failed, transforming power that should have been at the service of life into a terrible instrument of death" (*infra*, 83). This divergence appears more nuanced, Fulco continues, in Arendt's later works and in the centrality they give to thought as an instrument of critique and change of our present.

However, it is precisely this last inflection of Weil's philosophy that makes Esposito think, as Fulco writes, "that Simone Weil can illuminate our time, but only by contrast—starting from what we have lost sight of. Esposito refers, in particular, to the fact that for Simone Weil human existence has a root in the supernatural; for her, there is a relationship between reality and transcendence, between politics and spirituality. This relationship is difficult to recognize in our current situation, in which politics is secularized, that is, removed from faith as well as from thought" (*infra*, 88–89). Instead, Arendt's presence appears more constant in Esposito's reflection, and her political thought is also widely discussed in Esposito's more recent books because, as Fulco points out, "Arendt's political philosophy is part and parcel of 'instituting paradigm' that Esposito does not find developed, for example, by Michel Foucault" (*infra*, 86-87). Indeed, Arendt recognizes the importance of the instituting process, despite a marked emphasis on the continuous creation of the *novum*.

Another thinker permanently present in Esposito's political reflection is Schmitt, on whom Francesco Marchesi focuses in his chapter

"The Political in Roberto Esposito and Carl Schmitt." Although not always explicitly evoked as an object of reflection in Esposito's work, Schmitt's presence is never lost because, as the author states quite neatly, "Roberto Esposito's conception of politics is the conception of politics of Carl Schmitt. Politics, or better "the political," is for both these authors the conflict, or the 'Two,' that dwells in every concrete political order" (*infra*, 95). As Marchesi notes, this interpretation of Schmitt that Esposito makes his own comes from the Italian philosophical current of workerism (*operaismo*) of the 1970s and, in particular, from the work of Mario Tronti. It remains stable throughout Esposito's whole philosophical journey, although it is inevitable to observe some interpretive oscillations in the three phases of Esposito's political thought, which Marchesi identifies as "the antifoundational theory of democracy and community in the impolitical years, the rejection of any kind of political form in the biopolitics period, and the (also Machiavellian in Esposito's view) identification between order and conflict in his works on Machiavelli and in his recent institutional turn" (*infra*, 95). At each of these stages, the two Schmittian theses on the role of decision and the figure of enmity never fail in shaping the main features of Esposito's political reflection, which allows Marchesi to conclude that, from *Categories of the Impolitical* to the works on instituting thought, despite the differences and theoretical innovations that mark this trajectory of Esposito's—clearly highlighted in the previous chapters—"The concept of political is essentially enmity as a tool of building a, necessarily empty, political form (sovereignty, immunity, institution)" (*infra*, 97) constituting an important constant in Esposito's political-philosophical project.

Political Ontology and Community

Laura Cremonesi

The second part of this volume includes theoretical essays that investigate the ontological concepts on which Esposito's political theory is based, showing how they are explored in relation to key twentieth-century thinkers. In particular, these essays focus on the concepts of body, person, the impersonal, immunity and community, the conjuncture between being and politics, and the idea of the negative, which are analyzed with reference to the modern era and the pandemic event.

In her chapter, "On Bodies: Perspectives of a Dialogue between Esposito and Nancy," Daniela Calabrò demonstrates the urgency of rethinking the concept of the body, in which life is given (*bios*), as well as its relationship with technology. Calabrò notes that in the era of biotechnology and therapeutic eugenics, artificial insemination and the end of life, a body is always connected to other bodies, both organic and inorganic, in a sort of latent promiscuity, of exchange between vital and nonvital, between self and other. In this sense, our theoretical perspective always concerns practices of grafting or intrusion. Since the body is conceived as a constant fluctuation between inside and outside, immunization and contamination, the identity paradigm of the subject is entirely deconstructed. According to current biomedical approaches, the concept of *life-form* replaces the traditional concept of "subjectivity." Within this context, Calabrò focuses on the long-distance dialogue between Esposito and Jean-Luc Nancy to show that today, the human is not projected into the world, but the world is introjected into the human. As Esposito writes in *Immunitas*, "technique has now taken up residence in our very limbs." His remarks recall Nancy's thinking in *The Intruder*, namely, that between me and me, "there is an incision's opening, and the irreconcilability of a compromised immune system." For Calabrò, it seems that Esposito definitively silences the category of body, as it is unsuitable to respond to a globalized and interconnected, fluid and even cyborg world. He prefers the notion of flesh, as the common mode of being of that which seeks to be immune, whereas Nancy aims to go beyond the concept of flesh, which is closely linked to the Christian tradition. However, both Esposito and Nancy describe the subjects as hopelessly partitioned and exposed, and both agree that when the body loses absolute ownership of itself through technology, the *proper* mode of our "being body" consists of being "improper." In this sense, Esposito's analysis converges with Nancy's thinking, although the focus on the biopolitical and immune side is most salient in Esposito's work. After all, what the pandemic has shown is that when community and immunity come into contact, the life of the individual is protected only by the life of the collective. Hence, we must conceive of common immunity to protect human beings not "from" each other but "with" each other and "for" each other.

Being with the other and for the other is at the center of reflections of Silvia Dadà, who, in "The Impersonal between Ethics and Politics: Roberto Esposito and Emmanuel Levinas on the Third Person," investigates the underground influence of Emmanuel Levinas's thought on Esposito's philosophy. In particular, she compares Esposito's "political impersonal" with Levinas's "ethical impersonal," demonstrating that the concept of the impersonal emerges because they consider the concept of person inadequate to describe the complexity of the human being, as it is an "exclusionary device," which acts performatively by excluding what is not a person. Esposito proposes the "third person" as an alternative to the concept of person. His third person does not include the identity of the subject but instead draws on the Levinasian concept of *illeité*, which has two modes: "internal" and "external." The "internal impersonal" concerns the third person who is at the bottom of the face-to-face relationship with the other. The "external impersonal" concerns justice, since the ethical relationship runs the risk of wronging the Other's Other, that is, the third party. Dadà identifies several points of contact between Esposito and Levinas. First, both use the category of the impersonal not to abandon that of person but to deconstruct it; both intend to overcome the idea of the modern subject, Levinas, by describing it as vulnerable and responsible, Esposito, in turn, by valuing the most dynamic aspects of life (*bios*). Dadà does not fail to note that there are also profound differences between the two perspectives. The most obvious one concerns biopolitics, since, unlike Esposito, Levinas considers it to always be negative. For Dadà, however, Esposito's criticism of Levinas's failure to escape the aporia between the logic of two and the logic of three is paradoxically the point of greatest closeness between the two thinkers for two reasons. First, Levinas does not reduce the logic of three to the logic of two but rather affirms the need to continually relate them to one another, as justice bridges ethics and politics. Second, in his recent work *Instituting Thought*, Esposito describes institutions as dynamic structures that continually question themselves because of the ethical principle of responsibility and in the name of justice. Therefore, he goes beyond affirmative biopolitics, but he maintains the category of the impersonal.

A certain continuity in Esposito's thought is also highlighted by Sandro Gorgone, whose chapter "Assurance and Community: The Far Proximity between Esposito and Heidegger" focuses on the concept of immunity. Gorgone observes that the demand for global immunization that was driven by the pandemic led to a redefinition of the relationship between community and immunity, with a view to their possible overlap, which Esposito describes as "communal immunity." In his recent writings, Esposito recognizes the immune mechanism not only as the center of contemporary biopolitics but also as a general horizon of meaning in the philosophical texts of modernity. Gorgone focuses on Esposito's interpretation of the question of community in Heidegger's existential analytics and the roots of the contemporary immune mechanism in the Heideggerian diagnosis of modernity. The immune paradigm can be interpreted in an ontological-existential sense as a presupposition of the relationship between identity and otherness, which underlies the community bond. Gorgone notes that it is precisely in the Heideggerian thematization of being-with (*Mitsein*) contained in the existential analytic of *Being and Time* that, according to Esposito, lies the possibility of a conception of the communal and community in an immune sense. The being of *Dasein* is, to use Nancy's expression, "singular-plural"; it is, as being-with, essentially in-view of others. The "with" (*cum*) is not an object of sharing but the ecstatic openness that makes everyone constitutively lacking. Following Nancy's lead, Esposito clarifies that the exposition of the world and the arrangement of the "between us" are the two constitutive features of the ontology of being-in-common. Moreover, Gorgone shows how, for Esposito, the immune system does not primarily exert a defensive and exclusionary function but is at the origin of the very definition of the bodily self and its relations with the outside world, that is, the construction of the self as the interweaving of identity and otherness. Esposito indeed interrogates the mechanism of immunological tolerance and, more generally, the semantic spectrum of the concept of tolerance, which is fundamental to all modern thought and liberal-democratic culture. As Gorgone notes, another Heideggerian context in which it is possible to trace the immune mechanism is that of the diagnosis of the modern as an affirmation of subjectivity and simultaneous reduction of the world to image. Esposito, like Heidegger, believes that assurance (*Sicherstellen*) is the fundamental characteristic of representation by which the real is reduced to an object and placed at the disposal of the subject; it is the main characteristic of the modern age, in which, consequently, there is a priority of immunity over community. In conclusion, Gorgone points out that, for Esposito, Heidegger effectively recognizes the intrinsically violent nature of insurance processes, which was tragically being realized in the politics of the Nazi regime. Later, it would impose itself as a decisive biopolitical device even in postwar liberal democracies.

The crucial role that Heidegger plays in Esposito's last works is similarly recognized by Alberto Martinengo, who, in his "Roberto Esposito and Reiner Schürmann: A Political Ontology after Heidegger," points out that Heidegger's influence takes two forms: "direct," in the analysis of Heideggerian texts, and "mediated," through broader interpretations and discussions. Martinengo highlights the relevance of the post-Heideggerian tradition, most notably Reiner Schürmann, who describes the "political" as the domain that most clearly shows a metaphysical principle's scope of rule. Martinengo attributes Schürmann's originality to two key elements. First, he argues that the acting (*praxis*), in a complete reversal of Aristotelianism, is the principle of Heidegger's ontology: *esse sequitur agere*. The second element of Schürmann's originality is the demonstration that Heidegger's thought is divided between a desire to transcend metaphysics and a relapse into a kind of metaphysics of the second order. He notes, moreover, this same rupture in Heidegger's political thought. Schürmann's reading of Heidegger, which is linked to the reopening of the philosophical and political discussion surrounding Heidegger's work after the publication of the first *Black Notebooks*, is decisive for the construction of Esposito's "political ontology," which expresses the essential relationship between *being* and *politics*; this means that each political conception has an ontological relevance and, vice versa, each ontology has a political structure. The relationship between being and politics, which can be reduced to three kinds, namely, destituting, constituting, and instituting, has recently become the "*Sache des Denkens*" for Esposito. Although the space devoted to Schürmann in *Instituting Thought: Three Paradigms of Political Ontology* is very circumscribed, for Martinengo, Schürmann's perspective is crucial for Esposito, as he is one of the interpreters of Heidegger who takes the destituting paradigm to its extreme consequences. In the wake of Schürmann, Esposito considers Heidegger as a model to be opposed to defining the instituting paradigm. Moreover, Heidegger represents the turning point toward ontological-political postfoundationalism. At the end of his analysis, Martinengo concludes by observing that Esposito finds Heidegger's deconstruction of the illusion of politics as a doing wholly unsatisfactory because it excludes the possibility of philosophically guiding political action.

The intersection of philosophy and politics is crucial in the reflections of Valentina Surace, who, in "Immunity and Community: A Note of Discord between Roberto Esposito and Jacques Derrida," points out that currently, Esposito and Jacques Derrida's ideas are more relevant than ever because, in the "COVID-19 era," immunity has become practical politics as well as a genuine cornerstone of society. The concept of immunity, along with the concept of community, is an interpretive key to the political paradigm for both Esposito and Derrida, who nevertheless explore it from different perspectives, arriving at results that are equally divergent. Both thinkers emphasize the negative aspects of immunity, especially its dynamics of rejection, and the positive aspects of autoimmunity, without which hosting the other is impossible. However, Esposito thinks that the autoimmune can become a political resource to rethink the commune; instead, Derrida remains distrustful of the community. Reflecting on the pandemic event, Esposito thinks that "after being activated, by necessity, the immunitary principle needs to activate the communitary principle." Derrida, by contrast, was convinced that it was necessary to deconstruct the communitary principle as such, which characterizes the political categories associated with our ideas of democracy. He thought that an autoimmunitary threat pervades every community, affording them an opportunity for another chance. Esposito and Derrida recognize that the immunitary paradigm characterizes immuno-democracies, in which citizens expect protection rather than participation, and they agree that its logic is ambivalent: excessive immunity leads to death, yet the immunitary system protects the body, whether individual or social. Beyond the troublesome distinction between *biopolitics* and *deconstruction*, Surace sees that both Esposito and Derrida reveal that the notion of immunity problematizes the boundary between inside and out, identity and alterity, and life and death, pushing us to consider it a threshold or passage. As we are fundamentally exposed beings, nothing can save us from contamination by the other. In this respect, we should think more about institutions to come. Esposito thinks of a planetary democracy in which differences unite the world. Derrida regarded it as "a link of affinity, suffering, and hope."

Rethinking institutions is what Esposito does in his most recent works, in which, as Massimo Villani notes in his "From the Neuter to the Instituting Praxis: The Role of Blanchot in Roberto Esposito's Thought," Esposito rediscovers the instituting function of the negative in the wake of Hegel. Esposito sees institution as a process in which the contradiction between order and conflict is held within a form. According to Villani, Maurice Blanchot operates as a catalyst in Esposito's approach to Hegel. In particular, the exploration of Blanchot's notion of the neuter leads Esposito, as if by backlash, toward the necessity of determinate negation. Villani explains that Blanchot plays a strategic role in Esposito's research at three key points. The first occurrence of Blanchot in Esposito's work is in *Categories of the Impolitical*, where Esposito picks up on what young Blanchot (1930) asserts about the political that is beyond history, challenging the idea of a coincidence between the rational and the real. The second occurrence is in *Third Person*, where Esposito resorts to the mature Blanchot (1950), who is radically antidialectical (and anti-Hegelian), to overcome the impasses of the impolitical in the direction of a theory of the impersonal. Esposito explores Blanchot's neuter, which dismantles the notion of person that constitutes the fundamental pivot of the theological-political machine. The third occurrence is in *Politics and Negation*, which is a sort of hinge between the impersonal and the instituting thought. Here, Esposito recovers the instituting force of the negative, recognizing that an affirmative thought cannot renounce confrontation with the negative, risking exhausting itself in a politically ineffective exercise. Esposito thinks of a dialectical and productive tension between negative and affirmative: each of these two polarities dissolves into abstraction if it does not meet the opposition of the other. However, Villani observes that in the book in which Esposito attempts to delineate an instituting thought, Blanchot is absent. The only trait of Blanchot's reflection that will be retained in this last phase is that relating to the impersonal, as institutions are the product of impersonal forces. Blanchot's negative turns in two opposite directions: it rejects all the binary oppositions on which metaphysics was founded, forcing experience into aporia, in the literal sense of block. Instead, the negative that Esposito seeks to rethink is a process that denies itself. Realizing that the only affirmative mode of negation is "the negation of negation," Esposito directs his thinking toward Hegel's "work of the negative."

It is clear from this brief reconstruction that the contributions that make up the second part of the volume, which refer to and complement one another, focus on the fundamental theoretical tools that Esposito uses to critically interpret the times in which we live and to politically inhabit the world.

Conclusion

In this volume we have tried to show how Esposito developed his philosophy through a profound dialogue with other European thinkers. The essays also demonstrate the fruitful contrast between his thinking and theirs. This contrast has given rise to elements of great philosophical novelty in Esposito's reflections. Consequently, everyone has tried to focus on the peculiarity of his hermeneutic operation, which has helped to give a new meaning to the relationship between philosophy and politics. For Esposito, philosophy and politics are inseparable, even when he turns his attention to metaphysical or ontological questions.

By following the development of his thought, one understands how necessary and urgent it is today to give new meaning to the horizon of the political. The only way to do this is to explicitly and decisively bring the present into philosophical reflection. Or rather, using Foucault's terms, to try to think an "ontology of actuality." The horizon within which any political action is situated is, in fact, always ontological: What is power? How can it best be exercised? In short, questions of essence, of being, remain at the center of gravity of the different modes within which particular political actions are exercised. It is not by chance that political conflict takes different forms, which correspond to the instituting processes enacted by the multiple answers that can be given to the question of the being of power and politics.

To question the crisis of politics is therefore to ask why philosophy does not respond to this crisis. Perhaps it is not enough to distance ourselves from political theology. It is also necessary to rethink and distance ourselves from paradigms that no longer manage to provide answers to the need for proposals for building a more just world. These now "dumb" paradigms seem to include the destituent paradigm and the constituent paradigm, although in the recent past many hopes have been raised by their proposals.

It is necessary to think of new categories that have the creative power of a new beginning, but starting from what already exists. Esposito proposed those of "instituting thought" and "common immunity." Our attempt to think with Esposito of an "ontology of actuality" testifies to the hope of being able to open a window in the great wall that politics seems to have built between itself and human beings. In fact, they often suffer politics much more than they determine it, as should be the case in a society that is de facto and not only de jure democratic.

For us, as for Esposito, thinking or philosophizing means first and foremost engaging with our present. We hope, therefore, that this volume can be a tool for putting the inseparable and, we believe, necessary link between philosophy and politics back on the agenda. We hope that it can contribute to a view of the present that not only grasps its criticality but also glimpses its possibilities for change, in the direction of a broader and more inclusive social justice, which is linked to a deep respect for the common world we coinhabit.

Part One
Politics and Institutions

One

From the Impersonal to Instituting Thought

Esposito's Departure from Deleuze

Stefania Achella

Roberto Esposito's relationship with Deleuzian thought is long-standing. The Italian philosopher begins to engage more intensely with Gilles Deleuze as early as *Bios*, where the themes of the political and the community were addressed from the perspective of life. Like all enduring relationships, it undergoes a major repositioning, from an initial adherence, albeit with a consistent critical distance, to then a slow distancing, due to the Italian philosopher's increasing attention to the role of negation. If, therefore, Esposito stands on Deleuze's side in the texts of the first decade of the new century, from *Bios* (2004) to *A Philosophy for Europe: From the Outside* (2016), starting from *Politics and Negation* (2018) and then even more markedly in the analyses on the institution, the distancing from the French philosopher acquires a clear-cut delineation.

What interests Esposito from the outset are the devices put in place by the French philosopher, the conceptual constellation that develops from the centrality of life: it is not only the reference to positions of thought such as that of "conversion," or the analysis on "animality." The goal is much broader: to understand how life deals with law. This is why for Esposito, as we shall see, Deleuze's early writing constitutes an important point of departure.

The engagement with Deleuze, however, goes far beyond just the speculative questions posed in his philosophy. It is set in a broader context: in the spread of growing interest since the 1990s, also in Anglo-Saxon countries, in continental radical thought, which prompts the consideration of so-called *French Theory*—the post-structuralist evolution of French philosophy—being considered an essential pivot for denouncing the ontological core of neoliberal politics.[1]

Along a path similar to that taken in the same years by Toni Negri, Esposito gives life to *Italian Theory*—later to abandon the overly compromised term *theory* in favor of *thought,* a term more central to the Italian tradition,[2] as Esposito explains in *Living Thought: The Origins and Actuality of Italian Philosophy* (2012). He thus sees in French post-structuralism the possibility of reacting to the spread of a neocapitalist rhetoric that had tried to pull critical thinkers such as Foucault and Deleuze to its side. That is to say, in order to reopen to the possibility of political struggle, it is necessary to seek "a space of manoeuvre," a place where thought can be repositioned. This place that coincides with a space of negation, with a non-being, therefore requires a rethinking of the relation between politics and being. After the decline of Heidegger's philosophical proposal, in which being and non-being appeared to be opposed, it now becomes necessary to rethink negation, the "non" of non-being. In negation there is an opening to transcendence, to overcoming the real, to make change possible.

This is the theme that marks Esposito's thinking since *A Philosophy for Europe* and leads him to repeatedly grapple with Deleuze. And for Esposito, challenging Deleuze's thought becomes a way of coming to terms with the "negative."

Background: The Deleuzian Struggle against the Negative

Reacting to that "virus" of Hegelianism injected into an entire generation that still laps at Deleuze, the effect of Alexandre Kojève's well-known courses at the École Pratique des Hautes Études, the French philosopher endeavors to create one of the most radical attempts to overcome the Hegelian dialectic.[3] Deploying along an axis from Spinoza to Nietzsche, Deleuze builds his anti-Hegelian armada. It is in Spinoza, in fact, that for the first time the relationship between substance, attributes, and modes passes not through negation but through total affirmation. It is in Spinoza that cause is presented as immanent. The abolition of any hierarchy, including that of the personality of God, eliminates any principle beyond that which is present in the effect. Contrary to the Hegelian interpretation, which sees Spinoza as his forerunner in placing negation at the heart of determination (*omnis determinatio est negatio*), for Deleuze every act of transcendence, and thus every negation, does not end in determination but rather in annihilation.

The effort of thought must therefore consist in exorcising and banishing the point of negation as the transcendent plane that authorizes the establishment of the principle of authority. Antidualism does not aim to overthrow the hierarchy of terms, as happens in Hegel, by bringing duality back to the unity of the knowing subject or spirit. Rather, the main goal is to question dualism itself. The action fielded by Deleuze is different from the recovery that the Italian tradition would make, first with Labriola and then with Gramsci, of the Hegelian dialectic from a Marxist perspective.[4] This tradition in fact sees, in the Hegelian dialectic, a genetic method rather than a closed system, and reads in this form of process the expression of the imperfect nexus between theory and praxis: immanence is the ground plane on which the noncoincidental remand between discourse and action is played out, whose imperfection also determines the potentiality of change. Deleuzian discourse develops in a different direction, with Spinoza as its starting point, deconstructing the Hegelian system down to its first principle. For Deleuze, the assimilation of difference through the process of overcoming that establishes a superior, superordinate affirmative truth implies the elimination of difference itself. It is therefore around the role of negation that these traditions would separate definitively.

From this divarication, it is not difficult to understand the appeal Deleuze had on a wing of political radicalism that intended to analyze the potential of the political beyond the universalist framework of Marxism. And it is not difficult to see how the heart of the matter develops around the question of negation. In the Hegelian dialectic, negation is the principle that sets being in motion, the cut that determines, through rupture, the initiation of a process of understanding and the constitution of a thinking subjectivity. If we remove, as Deleuze does, the power of the negative, how do we confer dynamism on being? Are not change and conflict in danger of foundering in the quiet waters of an indistinct being?

The Deleuzian solution is novel. The function of negation is replaced by that of repetition, which succeeds in subverting in its deferral the sameness of being. Being is expressed in multiple modes, yet these modes do not thereby negate each other nor establish hierarchy among themselves. The philosopher writes: "It is not the negative which is the motor. Rather, there are positive differential elements which determine the genesis of both the affirmation and the difference affirmed. It is precisely the fact that there is a genesis of affirmation as such which escapes us every time we leave affirmation in the undetermined, or put determination in the negative."[5]

Repetition, states Deleuze, is neither opposition nor mediation.[6] The Hegelian theater of representation must be opposed by the theater of repetition. It is Kierkegaard and Nietzsche who invent this new scenario, where language comes before words, gestures before organized bodies. This is "the whole apparatus of repetition as a 'terrible power.'"[7] This repetition, "which saves above all from the one which enchains,"[8] isn't a mere quantitative repetition.[9]

In this sense, Deleuze can state that "difference and repetition have taken the place of the identical and the negative, of identity and contradiction."[10] The right of the different, the heterogeneous, is at the heart of the Deleuzian rejection of Hegelianism.[11] It arrives at a complex repetition, capable of holding within itself the multiformity of the real without creating the generalization of the concept. The force that relates to another force does not aim to deny it, but rather to affirm its own difference, its being other. The element of opposition proper to dialectical force is contrasted with the enjoyment of active force that makes *deferring* the place where an unconditional yes to life is consummated.

To understand this process well, it is enough to return to the pages that Deleuze—in *Proust and Signs*—devotes to the *Recherche*, in which in repetition there is not the confirmed starting identity but something absolutely new, unthought-of. Repetition "lets being be commemorated in its being-ness."[12]

As a classic *concept of reflection*, difference submits itself to the demands of representation by making itself "*organic* representation." To this Deleuze opposes an "*orgiastic* representation."[13] The effect he will create is an inversion: differences do not register as a differentiation of the univocal, as a scandal with respect to the original unity, but are distributed.[14] The universality of the genus as well as the singularity of the individual do not occur as a result of the structuring operated from the outside through a concept that applies to objects like an umbrella, that collects and thereby individualizes them, but the movement of individualization and differentiation occurs from within, from the dynamic, immanent, and infinite foundation within each object.

In this sense, the orgiastic dimension of representation refers back to the movement of dissolution of the Apollonian order brought from the outside, through an inebriation in which the inner depths of things are revealed. Although Deleuze's reference here is Nietzsche, one cannot help but think of "the bacchanalian revel where not a member is sober"[15] of which Hegel speaks in the *Phenomenology* and about which the masters of French Hegelianism had long wondered. Yet for Deleuze, the Hegelian orgy remains false precisely because, through the dual negation of non-contradiction, it sanctions the primacy of identity over difference, of measure over delusion.[16]

The Play of Immanence and the Power of Conflict

With respect to the reference to a thought that ultimately encounters liberation only in contingency, the question remains whether, and in what way, it is possible to preserve the conflictual potential that is instead explicit in the Hegelian dialectic. How, in this context, can we find an answer capable of being productive with respect to the questions of time, without limiting ourselves, as "beautiful souls," to the absence of solutions? Undoubtedly, the Deleuzian critique, which comes at a time when the historical defeat of the Marxist revolutionary ideal appears evident, puts forth indisputable reasons. The critique of the illusion exercised on the proletariat, whereby the idea of contradiction could have served as a path to liberation, finds its confirmation in that historical horizon. Contradiction is shown to be the weapon of the bourgeoisie. The framework that originates from the Aristotelian distinction between form and matter, being and entities, power and act, served for a world made up of objects and subjects structured in a hierarchical and ordered relationship. Discarding Hegel, what matters for Deleuze is the cut that forms take on as reality and that they never defer to a universal, separate, substantial truth. Once the transcendent plane of substance has been unhinged, there remains a chaotic matter-flux in which no process of identification takes place, only—as Duns Scotus does[17]—individuation. The term "haecceity," as Esposito highlights, is relating to a mode of individuation that is different both from the individual already constituted, and, even more, from the person, because it refers indiscriminately to a human being, a state, or a time—like a heat wave, or a brightness of yellow, or five o'clock in the evening. In any case, it is not an ontological substance but a mode of existence that, without being presupposed, results instead from the encounter between forces, affects, and occurrences that precede it and cause it.[18]

Thus, the production process must amount to an individuation, not an identification: *A Life*. "It is only when immanence is no longer immanence to anything other than itself that we can speak of a plane of immanence. No more than the transcendental field is defined by consciousness can the plane of immanence be defined by a subject or an object that is able to contain it."[19] Pure immanence is "A LIFE, and nothing else."[20]

A life as haecceity or singularity "is not suspended from the thread of events, waiting for that ultimate event, death, to manifest itself, but is patient construction driven by an endless question: what can, today, this life be."[21] The death that Kojève, through Heidegger, had reintroduced into Hegelian thought is definitively expelled. Deleuze struggles against the negative in all its forms, down to the most natural, and for this reason most radical, form of it: death. Of this life that does not know death, because it does not question itself about it, far away, transcendent, from this plane of immanence, it can be said that it is, that it is now.

Honeymoon

Deleuzian topics of immanence and the negative accompany Roberto Esposito's philosophical itinerary in the structuring of his philosophical-political proposal. In his early political writings in particular, Esposito uses Deleuze's philosophical categories for a deconstructive discourse with respect to the Western tradition.

It is in *Bios* that the issue of life erupts for Esposito, and it is no coincidence that in this text, in which he grapples with the idea of a fully affirmative ontology, Deleuze appears in a central position, particularly with his last writing *L'immanence: Une vie*, whose point of arrival, as we have seen, is—to borrow Esposito's words—"a kind of philosophical affirmation of life."[22] Compared to the philosophy of life coming from the nineteenth and twentieth centuries that had made clear the knot of "power *over* life," with Deleuze the prospect of "a power *of* life"[23] unfolds.

It is around this concept that the research behind *Bios* revolves. As Esposito writes:

> Here the move from the determinate article to that of the indeterminate [a life] has the function of marking the break with the metaphysical feature that connects the dimension of life to that of individual consciousness. There is a modality of *bios* that cannot be inscribed within the borders of the conscious subject, and therefore is not attributable to the form of the individual or of the person.[24]

Already foreshadowed here is the reasoning that will return shortly thereafter in *Third Person*. Deleuzian philosophy, at this height of Esposito's theoretical work, has on the one hand the affirmative valence of immanent life, and on the other the functional deconstructive objective of deconstructing the concept of person *versus* that of impersonal. Life is not referable to an individual but is impersonal and at the same time possesses its own singularity, "as that of a newborn, who is similar to all the others, but different from each of the tonality of the voice, the intensity of a smile, the sparkle of a tear."[25] It is here that it sets in motion, through the Deleuzian concept of difference, the logic of "an impersonal singularity (or a singular impersonality), which, rather than being imprisoned in the confines of the individual, opens those confines to an eccentric movement that 'traverses men as well as plants and animals independently of the matter of their individuation and the forms of their personality.' "[26]

Eschewing the alternative between personalization and depersonalization, Deleuze's deconstructive operation "is not to be understood as something that affects life—an attribute that makes life the subject of immanence—but as life itself, removed from the exclusionary thresholds engraved on it by the devices of the subject and the person."[27] In the critique of the person in the traditional sense, built on the duality at the origin of political theology, Deleuze marks a fundamental turning point, in which the entire theory of the impersonal can be summarized: the animal-becoming prospected by Deleuze "becomes 'propagation by epidemic, by contagion, [which] has nothing to do with filiation by heredity.' "[28] Becoming animal in fact denotes the human being's emergence from an anthropocentric model and assumption of what lies outside his species boundaries. Closing on this Deleuzian perspective in his 2007 book, Esposito points out how "the third person, this figure that has yet to be fathomed, points to this unicum, to this being that is both singular and plural—to the non-person inscribed in the person, to the person open to what has never been before."[29]

However, *Two* is the volume in which Esposito shows his closest proximity to the French philosopher,[30] having highlighted the "unbreakable bonds that tie the semantics of the person to the machine of political theology."[31] Indeed, it is the search for a movement capable of surpassing the oppositions produced by the theological-political device that makes Deleuze one of the founding theoretical references of this work. What interests Esposito in Deleuze is once again the progression of his thought, the process that is able to deactivate the dual contraposition typical of Western metaphysics and thus the theological-political circle. The reference to immanence makes the system unassailable from the outside, leaving no space for anything external and entrusting all transformation to what Deleuze defines as "conversion" into its opposite. Deleuze, notes Esposito, is the first to make a paradigm shift "with respect to attempts to counteract the political-theological machine by attacking it head-on [. . .]. Rather than attempt, in vain, to escape from the single dimension in which we are caught, Deleuze proposes to reconvert it, by freeing the potential energy residing within it."[32]

In this way, a shift can be made from an exclusionary inclusion that underlies political theology and would find its highest celebration in the Hegelian dialectic to an inclusive relationship between immanence and transcendence.

Mortal Embrace

Politics and Negation becomes the pivoting of Esposito's thought from an immanent and affirmative tone (still in A *Philosophy for Europe* he assumes affirmation as the positive characteristic of Italian Thought) to a reading in which the same affirmation is inhabited by the negation. This divergence inevitably involves a distancing from Deleuze, which does not yet take place, however, in definitive terms. It is not a matter of illusory reversal of negation into its opposite, but "the aim is to trace out the affirmative figures that lie within negation itself, by working inside its fault lines: not from a dialectical viewpoint, expecting a positive outcome from the use of the negative, but by conceiving affirmatively of negation itself."[33] Compared to Machiavelli, Spinoza, Kant, Nietzsche, and Foucault, who constitute important antecedents of this reading, Deleuze now assumes the role of a "shifting margin"[34] thanks to the interplay between affirmation and erasure of the negative. Obviously, the reference to Deleuze even in this work remains essential, since the concept of difference elaborated by him is considered by Esposito as the first form of an affirmative negative. That is, Deleuzian difference would represent the first figure in the history of thought to positively assume the role of the negative.

The great speculative gain associated with Deleuze consists in his choice not to begin thinking from the enemy, from nothingness, from death, but from affirmation, from life, from the friend. To reverse the perspective from the negative to the positive is to resemantize all the fundamental elements of philosophical reflection. Thus desire becomes affirmative drive and not lack, the institution becomes different from law. Central to this change of pace becomes the young Deleuze's work on the institution, in which the French philosopher makes clear the "difference between institution and law: law is a limitation of actions, institution a positive model for action. Contrary to theories of law which place the positive outside the social (natural rights), and the social in the negative (contractual limitation), the theory of the institution places the negative outside the social (needs), so as to present society as essentially positive and inventive (original means of satisfaction)."[35] It is not a matter of expelling the negative, because that would sanction its reaffirmation. The negative must remain within the affirmation, so that repetition takes the place of negation. But, asks Esposito, "what are we to understand exactly by 'substitution'? That difference abolishes an existing negation? Or that difference reveals the inexistence of the negation? [. . .] At stake in this alternative is the ontological status of the negative. Does the negative exist or not?"[36]

With this question begins the divarication from Deleuze. According to Esposito, Deleuze ultimately does not dissolve the reservation between these two options. Thus, while in his early essay "Instincts and Institutions" and in the anthology on the institution (*Empiricism and Subjectivity*[37]), negation appears in its affirmative form,[38] later a Deleuze marked by Bergson will be more docile and inclined to deny its existence.[39] Negation, in the Bergsonian perspective, would not in fact have an ontological dimension but be rather a negation produced by judgment. From this moment, negation becomes in turn an affirmation. Deleuze takes the Bergsonian position, but not all the way. In the total absorption of the negative into the positive, Deleuze would have the problem of justifying the distinction between difference and affirmation. To overcome this obstacle, Deleuze turns to Plato's *Sophist* in which not only does the negative make its debut in Western philosophy for the first time but finds a declension that, rather than pitting non-being against being, seeks their form of cohabitation. With this effort to rethink the role of negation as difference, Deleuze can "escape the alternative in which western thought appears to be stuck, on the basis of which 'either there is no non-being and negation is illusory and ungrounded, or there is non-being, which puts the negative in being and grounds negation.' "[40]

Such an understanding of the negative leads to a different formulation of the synthesis, which has nothing to do with the process of the Hegelian *Aufhebung*. As Esposito points out: "This is how synthesis can be disjunctive—in the sense that it puts its terms in relation without necessarily making them identical—indeed, even by differentiating them. [. . .] The fact that this is synthesis and not analysis means that the distance does not exclude the various predicates of the thing in favor of the unity of the concept. On the contrary, each thing is defined by the infinite multiplicity of its modes."[41] Nevertheless, denying the negative has a deleterious effect on any political process. The question Esposito therefore now seeks to answer is the possibility of

> *affirming* the negative, tearing it away from its defensive semantics and reinstating its function as an internal limit, through which the community differentiates itself from itself. [. . .] Without that negative edge, which cuts across community but does not negate it, immunity would draw dangerously close to an organic totality. It would homogenize its heterogeneities and close up its wounds, which would put it at risk of imploding from excessive fullness. [. . .] if the negative were negated instead of being reformulated, it would not be abolished: it would be duplicated and reinforced.[42]

From here, the need to let "the affirmative figures of the negative—difference, determination, and opposition—to resurface. Without them, human experience loses energy and life remains flattened into its opposite."[43]

Showdown

If this is the open project with which *Politics and Negation* concludes, hoping for a "collective work" (199) that can develop the implications of a rearticulation of these two terms, it is in *Instituting Thought* that Esposito finally settles accounts with Deleuze. *Instituting Thought* is definitely the final act of a trilogy, which began with *Two*, and continued with *Politics and Negation*, and which can precisely be read as a process of gradual distancing from Deleuze. As the subtitle of *Instituting Thought*, "Three Paradigms of Political Ontology," makes explicit, the author analyzes three paradigms of political ontology: the Heideggerian one, the Deleuzian one, and the one he himself advanced: "If the Heideggerian paradigm can be called destituting, the Deleuzian, even taking its most influential political translations into account, can be called constituting."[44] To these two paradigms the author adds his own proposal of an instituting paradigm. In this process, which follows, one cannot but recognize a kind of philosophy of history, the constituent function of the paradigm identified in Deleuze which obviously does not refer in a technical sense to the legal-political plane. Rather, it refers to the ontological plane, to a form of thought

> as an eternally creative form, and also, precisely for this reason, one that is decreative of the reality just created. Just as the primacy of constitutive power—one proposed within the same ontological perspective by Antonio Negri—overwhelms constituted power, so the infinitely productive power of being resolves each "state" into its own becoming, dissolving it as such. This is the effect of the substitution of the category of production for that of praxis, transposed to an ontological level, a category still too charged with the negative to be able to merge with the plane of immanence. In the course of an extensive interpretation of *creatio ex nihilo*—taken beyond the moment of Genesis and rendered co-eternal with the world—productive creation exposes the created to an unceasingly renewed creation, which is made possible only via the abolition of what precedes.[45]

We are evidently faced with a concluding act in which a path of analysis and comparison with post-metaphysical Western thought arrives at the original proposal for a rethinking of politics in post-deconstructionist terms.

The novelty and further step forward in the thought of the negative, which in this work is welded to the idea of an affirmative biopolitics, is determined by the assumption of the negative as conflict. Which, inexorably, cannot but mean a return to the confrontation with Hegel. This confrontation follows a wholly unusual path, as is in the realm of the Italian thinker, who precisely from the tradition of Italian thought draws the sideways glance that cuts the negative into a different form. As he had already explained in *Living Thought* (2010), Machiavelli and Gramsci are the two foundational authors of a philosophical tradition that makes conflict a constitutive moment. For the Florentine, the space of the political is what unites society through its division, making a hitherto unconscious and therefore potentially destructive fracture symbolically productive. More precisely in the wake of Machiavelli, the proposal of the instituting paradigm consists in letting difference live without resulting either in a destituting ontological rupture (as happens in Heidegger) or in a neutralization of distinctions between ontology and politics, as happens in Deleuze.

It is therefore necessary to begin where *Politics and Negation* left off. Now Esposito clearly perceives the capacity of the negative to set being in motion. Thanks to the negative, all the categories of the Western metaphysical tradition can be resematized (from the subject becoming subjectification to power becoming potentiality to the institution becoming instituting). If, however, this function was already clear to Hegel, who recognizes, from the first pages of the *Preface* to the *Phenomenology*, that negation consists precisely in that movement that allows being to become, the "sideways" step that Esposito takes with respect to the Hegelian dialectic consists in replacing the liberal-bourgeois perspective with the democratic one and in escaping from the theological framework, handing over the advancement of thought to what comes from outside (an act of heterologous fertilization, to use a biological metaphor). In *Instituting Thought*, Esposito thus abandons the *Third Person* and *Bios* perspective. The judgment on Deleuze remains positive; he still represents a great thinker whose purely constituent political machine, however, is in danger of imploding on itself, since his ideal of fullness does not appear to offer a solution to the exit from neoliberal thought. The possibility of finding a way out of the crisis of politics, which we have been experiencing for more than half a century, must probe precisely the core that has always married being to politics (i.e., the political character of every event) and politics to being (the ontological configuration of political praxis). "The unresolved problem, to which neither Spinoza nor Deleuze manages to provide a convincing answer, remains that of a political ontology marked by the complete identity of the two terms—the political and being. If being is in and of itself political, and if the political is no more than the conscious assumption of the affirmative nature of being, what is the use of the comparison and conflict between different types of political organization?"[46] This problem facilitates the understanding as to why Deleuze ultimately considers it impossible to overcome capitalism: "Within Deleuze's ontological *dispositif* there are two ways in which capitalism cannot be denied: on the one hand, because negation does not exist, only affirmative difference does; on the other, because no other social formation can unleash the flows of desire and nomadic movement to the degree capitalism can."[47]

If Heidegger radicalized the negative to the point of depriving the political of all ontological value, arriving at an "impolitical" outcome, of which the entire reception along the Heideggerian line bears traces, Deleuze, on the other hand, erased it by superimposing it entirely on being and losing all contact with the category of negation. A way out, however—and this is Esposito's solution—can be found in thinking of "a productive relationship with negation that allows one to articulate being and politics in a reciprocally affirmative relation."[48]

In Deleuze, a possibility was allowed that was, however, unhinged by the choice to follow the Bergsonian path, and consigning politics to a marginal space, to "philosophical voids."[49] As Esposito so clearly writes: "Until the latter [the negation] withholds the negative inside itself in the form of difference, it is still possible to articulate a political question. When instead the tendency he inherited from Bergson, of reducing negation to a simple error of perspective within an entirely affirmative framework, prevails, the political, compressed into the self-generative process of being, loses the critical shore to push off from and is at risk of dissolving into the indeterminate."[50] That is, the problem is translated from ontological into a political effect of impossibility to act and transform. This evolution is the subject of a sharp and insightful chapter in *Instituting Thought*, in which Esposito commits an elegant patricide by giving the French philosopher the honor of arms. Through a careful genealogical reconstruction, the Italian philosopher shows the evolution of Deleuzian thought, namely how it has moved from the initial identification of an instituting force, in which there still remained margins for action, to "the incorporation of the political into the uninterrupted flow of becoming" which "entails its dissolution as an antagonistic force."[51]

To summarize, in taking leave from Deleuze, Esposito acknowledges him for having identified, albeit at an early stage of his work, the power contained in the institution. Along these lines he will continue his personal path of thought.[52]

Notes

1. As Antonelli states, in the 1980s and 1990s "la relaboración de temas y conceptos de Foucault fue acompañada, en particular en los casos de Negri y de Esposito, por la apelación a ciertos motivos deleuzianos, especialmente a su interpretación de Foucault. Dicho de otro modo, la reactivación de la biopolítica foucaulteana fue mediada por la interpretación vitalista de Deleuze" (Marcelo Antonelli, "La deriva deleuziana de Roberto Esposito," *Revista Pléyade*, no. 12 (2013): 37).

2. On this, see Dario Gentili, *Italian theory: Dall'operaismo alla biopolítica* (Bologna: Il Mulino, 2012).

3. On the persistence of Hegel's influence on Deleuze, see Henry Somers-Hall, *Hegel, Deleuze, and the Critique of Representation: Dialectics of Negation and Difference* (New York: State University of New York Press, 2012).

4. The historicist or realist immanence that Gramsci opposes in his notebooks to speculative immanence—see Antonio Gramsci, *Prison Notebook*, ed. and trans. Joseph A. Buttigieg (New York: Columbia University Press, 1996), 10, ii—is based on the inalienable presence in the dialectic of the objective dimension and historical facts. Indeed, the immanent dimension confers on dialectics the ability to know things in their reality, allowing also for a new *praxis*.

5. Gilles Deleuze, *Difference and Repetition* (1968), trans. Paul Patton (New York: Columbia University Press, 1994), 55 [henceforth DR].

6. Deleuze refers here to Gabriel Tarde, *L'opposition universelle* (Paris: Alcan, 1897), 19, who "described dialectical development in this manner: a process of repetition understood as the passage from a state of general differences to singular difference, from external differences to internal difference—in short, repetition as the differenciator of difference" (*DR*, 76). As he clarifies, in Tarde there is "a different sort of repetition: that of generation" (*DR*, 313).

7. DR, 10.

8. DR, 22.

9. Deleuze describes as follows his departure from modern tradition: "One is negative, occurring by default in the concept; the other affirmative, occurring by excess in the Idea. One is conjectural, the other categorical. One is static, the other dynamic. One is repetition in the effect, the other in the cause. One is

extensive, the other intensive. One is ordinary, the other distinctive and singular. One is horizontal, the other vertical. One is developed and explicated, the other enveloped and in need of interpretation. One is revolving, the other evolving. One involves equality, commensurability and symmetry; the other is grounded in inequality, incommensurability and dissymmetry. One is material, the other spiritual, even in nature and in the earth. One is inanimate, the other carries the secret of our deaths and our lives, of our enchainments and our liberations, the demonic and the divine. One is a 'bare' repetition, the other a covered repetition, which forms itself in covering itself, in masking and disguising itself. One concerns accuracy, the other has authenticity as its criterion" (DR, 24).

10. DR, XIX.

11. Esposito observes: "As Deleuze rightly argues, at the origin of this conceptual passage isn't the masked propensity for the dialectic (a sort of reverse Hegelianism), but rather the definitive release from its machinery: affirmation is not the synthetic result of a double negation, but instead the freeing of positive forces, which is produced by the self-suppression of the negation itself." Roberto Esposito, *Bios: Biopolitics and Philosophy* (2004), trans. Timothy Campbell (Minneapolis: University of Minnesota Press, 2008), 102.

12. Maurizio Ferraris, *Differenze: La filosofia francese dopo lo strutturalismo* (Milan: AlboVersorio, 2007), 144. See Gilles Deleuze, *Proust and Signs* (1964), trans. Richard Howard (Minnesota: University of Minnesota Press, 2000).

13. DR, 42.

14. See Roberto Ciccarelli, *Immanenza: Filosofia, diritto e politica della vita dal XIX al XX secolo* (Bologna: Il Mulino, 2008), 79. As Deleuze writes at the beginning of the chapter on *Difference in Itself*, "Indifference has two aspects: the undifferenciated abyss, the black nothingness, the indeterminate animal in which everything is dissolved—but also the white nothingness, the once more calm surface upon which float unconnected determinations like scattered members" (DR, 28).

15. Georg Wilhelm Friedrich Hegel, *Phenomenology of Spirit* (1807), trans. Terry Pinkard (Cambridge: Cambridge University Press, 2018), 29.

16. On the meaning of delirium in the structuring of subjectivity, and the controversy about it from Deleuze and Foucault, see Roberto Esposito, *A Philosophy for Europe: From the Outside*, trans. Zakiya Hanafi (Cambridge: Polity, 2018).

17. The concept of haecceity, which derives from Duns Scotus, used in this context indicates individuality, that which determines the entity and causes it to be "this thing" and not another. For Deleuze it is not an ontological determination, since he does not presuppose the distinction between essence and entity, but rather a degree of power, an intensity. With respect to Scotus' concept, Deleuze clarifies: "It is a haecceity no longer of individuation but of singularization: a life of pure immanence, neutral, beyond good and evil, for it was only the subject that incarnated it in the midst of things that made it good or bad. The life of such individuality fades away in favor of the singular

life immanent to a man who no longer has a name, though he can be mistaken for no other. A singular essence, a life . . ." Gilles Deleuze, *Pure Immanence: Essays on a Life* (1998), trans. Anne Boyman (New York: Zone Books, 2001), 29.

18. Roberto Esposito, *Two: The Machine of Political Theology and the Place of Thought* (2013), trans. Zakiya Hanafi (New York: Fordham University Press, 2005), 198.

19. Esposito, *Two*, 27.

20. Esposito, *Two*, 27. On this topic, see Giorgio Agamben, "L'immanence absolue," in Gilles Deleuze, *Une vie philosophique*, ed. Eric Alliez (Paris: Synthélabo, 1998).

21. Ciccarelli, *Immanenza*, 684.

22. See Roberto Esposito, *Termini della politica: Politica e pensiero*, vol. 2 (Milan-Udine: Mimesis, 2018), 29 [my translation].

23. Esposito, *Termini della politica*, II, 29.

24. Esposito, *Bios*, 192.

25. Esposito, *Bios*, 193.

26. Esposito, *Bios*, 194. The quote referred to Gilles Deleuze, *The Logic of Sense* (1969), trans. Mark Lester and Charles Stivale (New York: Columbia University Press, 1990), 107.

27. Esposito, *Termini della politica*, ii, 136.

28. Roberto Esposito, *Third Person: Politics of Life and Philosophy of the Impersonal* (2007), trans. Zakiya Hanafi (Cambridge: Polity, 2012), 150. Gilles Deleuze and Felix Guattari, *A Thousand Plateaus: Capitalism and Schizophrenia* (1980), trans. Brian Massumi (Minneapolis: University of Minnesota Press, 1987), 241.

29. Esposito, *Third Person*, 151. On this, see:Timothy Campbell, ""Foucault Was Not a Person": Idolatry and the Impersonal in Roberto Esposito's Third Person," http://www.biopolitica.cl/docs/Campbell_idolatry_and_the_impersonal.pdf.

30. As Antonelli summarizes: "En la producción previa a Bíos, Deleuze no era una referencia significativa en la elaboración de su pensamiento. Ello cambió a tal punto desde dicho texto que el índice de Due muestra a Deleuze como uno de los autores más mencionados. Este dato, en sí meramente cuantitativo, es acompañado por el hecho de que Esposito recurre a Deleuze en momentos ilosóicamente relevantes de sus trabajos: para elaborar una concepción airmativa de la biopolítica" (Antonelli, "La deriva deleuziana," 59).

31. Esposito, *Two*, 14.

32. Esposito, *Two*, 195.

33. Roberto Esposito, *Politics and Negation: Towards an Affirmative Philosophy* (2018), trans. Zakiya Hanafi (Cambridge: Polity, 2019), 8.

34. Esposito, *Politics and Negation*, 8.

35. Gilles Deleuze, "Instincts and Institutions" (1955), in *Desert Islands and Other Texts*, trans. David Lapoujade (Los Angeles, CA: Semiotext(e), 2004), 19.

On the topic "Institution," see *Il problema dell'istituzione: Prospettive ontologiche, antropologiche e guiridico-politiche*, special issue of *Discipline filosofiche* 29, no. 2 (2019), ed. Enrica Lisciani-Petrini and Massimo Adinolfi.

36. Esposito, *Politics and Negation*, 142.

37. Gilles Deleuze, *Empiricism and Subjectivity: An Essay on Hume's Theory of Human Nature* (1980), trans. Constantin V. Boundas (New York: Columbia University Press, 1991), 45.

38. This process is taken up and explained very clearly in *Instituting Thought*: "In his first works Deleuze proposed a more dynamic interpretation of the institution, connecting it precisely with the expression of instincts. While it does not indulge them directly, if favors their development, stimulating their growth: Deleuze adopted a thesis he derived from Hume and argued that, as opposed to the law, which is imposed from above, the institution presupposes the social utility of those it represents. This does not mean that the transition between instincts and institutions is fluid and linear. On the contrary, it passes through a bottleneck that selects for the naturalness of tendencies, subjecting it to conditions and objectives that are historically determined. In this phase, far from removing the 'negative,' Deleuze made it the necessary conduit for institutional functionality. While the law, which is expressed in obligations and prohibitions, is the negation of an affirmative behavior, the institution is the affirmation of a constraint that is functional to its realization. In sum, institutions are the negative filter that provides social demands with the necessary articulation to ensure their endurance by distancing them from their immediacy." Roberto Esposito, *Instituting Thought: Three Paradigms of Political Ontology* (2020), trans. Mark William Epstein (Cambridge: Polity, 2021), 151).

39. See Henri Bergson, *Creative Evolution*, trans. Arthur Mitchell (New York: Dover, 1998), 296.

40. Esposito, *Politics and Negation*, 145. DR, 63.

41. Esposito, *Politics and Negation*, 146.

42. Esposito, *Politics and Negation*, 198.

43. Esposito, *Politics and Negation*, 199.

44. Esposito, *Instituting Thought*, 9.

45. Esposito, *Instituting Thought*, 9. As Esposito states further: "From a theoretical point of view, Negri's impasse arises, as it did already in Deleuze, from an entirely affirmative conception of social power, which excludes the negative from the political horizon. As in the case of Marx's proletariat, the multitude is a political subject that is entirely immanent to the capitalist social order. [. . .] What is missing, within a political ontology of absolute immanence, is not the transcendence of power, but a politically articulated theory of conflict. In its absence, neither the multitude nor its imperial enemy, from which it is generated in contradictory fashion, exhibit the historical determination without which the political loses its characteristics" (Esposito, *Instituting Thought*, 112–13).

46. Esposito, *Instituting Thought*, 111.
47. Esposito, *Instituting Thought*, 10.
48. Esposito, *Instituting Thought*, 4.
49. Esposito, *Instituting Thought*, 78. On this, see Slavoj Zizek, *Organs without Bodies: On Deleuze and Consequences* (London: Routledge, 2004); and Philippe Mengue, *Gilles Deleuze ou le système du multiple* (Paris: Kimé, 1994).
50. Esposito, *Instituting Thought*, 79–80.
51. Esposito, *Instituting Thought*, 80.
52. Roberto Esposito's most recent works are devoted to the topic of institution: *Istituzione* (Bologna: Il Mulino, 2021); *Institution*, trans. Zakiya Hanafi (Cambridge: Polity, 2022); and *Vitam instituere: Genealogia dell'istituzione* (Turin: Einaudi, 2023).

Two

From Biopolitics to Common Immunity

The Role of Michel Foucault in the Philosophy of Roberto Esposito

Laura Cremonesi

To grasp the relevance of Michel Foucault's thought in the work of Roberto Esposito, a simple glance at *Bios: Biopolitca e filosofia*[1]—one of his major books—is enough: the title itself, in fact, makes it clear how it revolves around the category of biopolitics, which Foucault elaborated in the seventies. However, Foucault's presence is also clearly visible in other significant moments of Esposito's reflection: for instance, in his considerations on the role of philosophy in the crises that have recently shaken Europe, discussed in *Da fuori: Una filosofia per l'Europa*[2] but also in *Immunità comune: Biopolitica all'epoca della pandemia*,[3] which clearly shows how during the pandemic crisis, the question of biopolitics became central again.

The presence of Foucault's philosophy, however, seems to fade in the most recent research project inaugurated by Esposito, relating to the instituting thought. His latest works, *Pensiero istituente: Tre paradigmi di ontologia politica*[4] and *Vitam instituere: Genealogia dell'istituzione*[5] in fact revolve around the construction of a paradigm of instituting political ontology, alternative to two other major paradigms developed in contemporary European thought, the destituent and the constituent one. In none of these three paradigms does Foucault's philosophy seem to play a central role: the reference points for each are in fact identified by Esposito in the thought of Martin Heidegger, Gilles Deleuze, and Claude Lefort.

This chapter aims to retrace the main steps that led Esposito to dwell on Foucault's thought, in order to show which themes most attracted his attention and led him to discuss and redefine Foucauldian categories, intensifying their ability to interpret our present time and deal with the main challenges it poses to us.

As already noted, one of the moments in which Foucault's thought appears in all its relevance is when Esposito reflects on the relationship between contemporary philosophy and Europe. Indeed, in *Da fuori*, he traces some of the main steps in this relationship, beginning with the first of the great crises, the one that occurred between the two world wars.

At that time, what had brought European thought into a real impasse was the attempt, brought forward by authors such as Heidegger or Husserl, to cope with the loss of Europe's historical-political centrality, read in terms of nihilism, through a return of European thought to its origin. Although formulated in different terms, the need for a reappropriation of the origin as the only way of salvation pervades a whole side of European thought, locking it into what Esposito defines as a true "crisis *dispositif*":[6] "Since philosophy has no terrain other than Europe for its development, it can only retrace its steps, going backwards in search of something dormant that it left behind. A problem of space—the historical-political crisis of the European continent—is interpreted as a problem of time, focused in its turn on the teleological primacy of the origin. In this way a subjective philosophical option took on the appearance of a necessity, or even of a destiny. Since the road ahead appeared to be blocked by the risk of going uncontrollably adrift, nothing remained but the path leading backwards. Not imagining the possibility of projecting beyond itself and breaking free of its geopolitical orbit, European philosophy was forced to plunge further into crisis, delving deeper inside itself."[7]

If there is nothing in sight but the spread of nihilism, it will then seem necessary to go back to the Greek origin. In doing so, however, philosophy remains closed in itself and within its own boundaries, unable to break out of the historical and political horizon from which the crisis was generated. To escape the *dispositif* of the crisis, philosophy will have to assume a distance from itself: it will then be three geographic displacements that will regain European thought's full centrality and critical force. Although they are real displacements in space, they are interpreted by Esposito as "deterritorializations,"[8] which bring together a spatial dislocation and an exit from the categorical horizon of European thought, taking philosophy in a double outside and renewing in depth its theoretical tools.

The first of these displacements emerged from the need of German philosophers to leave Nazi Germany in the thirties: the Frankfurt School is thus the first to take European philosophy out of itself and its geographical and conceptual boundaries, giving it a new critical impetus. Despite the diversity of its authors, a common motif can be identified that contributes to this renewal of European thought: they all grasped the significance of exteriority and the need to keep it as such. On this philosophical side, thought accepts to approach its outside: "the unbreakable line beyond which what is foreign remains foreign and refuses to be assimilated."[9]

The relevance of outside and exteriority is also at the center of the second deterritorialization of European thought: in this case, those leaving Europe are the French philosophers who, especially in the seventies and eighties, enjoyed a very good reception in American universities. The term "French Theory"[10] can thus be understood, according to Esposito, as the phenomenon by which French philosophy of those years finds itself projected to the core of the international scene as a result of its American reception. Thanks to this displacement, the works of Michel Foucault, Gilles Deleuze, Jacques Derrida, Jean-François Lyotard, and Jean-Luc Nancy thus contribute to revitalizing European philosophy, giving it a new critical force. Although part of the same movement, this set of philosophies is traversed by several important differences, the main one being those thinkers most indebted to Heidegger's thought and who can be linked to deconstruction—such Derrida and Nancy—on the one hand and, on the other, those most rooted in Nietzsche's philosophy, such as Foucault and Deleuze.

According to Esposito, if Foucault is one of the principal figures in this deterritorialization of European thought, it is precisely because of his capacity to deal with the "outside" of thought. As he suggests, the entire philosophy of Foucault can be read, in its following phases, as a series of successive exteriorizations, from *L'histoire de la folie*,[11] which locates madness as the external boundary of reason, through the archaeological method in *L'archéologie du savoir*,[12] according to which statements (*énoncés*) are not intentionally produced from the interiority of the speaking subject but in an exteriority and dispersion, which defines the position and form of subjects entering a discursive regime. Finally, in the "genealogical" moment of his research, power relations bring into play an energetic field of forces in clash and struggle with each other, which defines a further passage to the outside, overcoming the search for a formal historical a priori that still characterized archaeology.

However, as Esposito notes, recalling some of Deleuze's insights, this is neither the last nor the most radical of the moments in which Foucault's thought moves toward the outside. Indeed, in the last phase of his work there is a kind of strange coincidence with the most outside and the closest inside: "By exteriorizing itself into the farthest form, the outside seems to end up coinciding with the innermost inside. For that matter, what is there outside the outside, if not the inside?"[13] This point of coincidence of outside and inside that marks the reflection of the last Foucault is, according to Deleuze, Life,[14] that same life that, in his well-known text on biopolitics, the last chapter of *La volonté de savoir*,[15] Foucault had designated as the element that is, at the same time, what power is exercised over and what power resists. As he writes: "Against this power that was still new in the nineteenth century, the forces that resisted relied for support on the very thing it invested, that is, on life and man as a living being."[16]

A power that characterizes our modernity by its ability to take life into account, and a life as what always opposes a resistance to it: with this link between power and life Foucault opens his reflection on biopolitics that he will develop, in addition to the already mentioned *La volonté de savoir*, in some equally well-known pages of his 1976 course at the Collège de France, *Il faut défendre la société*.

It is thus with the last passageway toward the outside that Foucault's philosophy inaugurates a "new thought on life"[17] that characterizes the biopolitical and vitalist side of French Theory, of which Deleuze's thought is also a relevant part.

According to Esposito, this new thought on life is one of the vectors that operates the transition to the third, great deterritorialization of European philosophy, operated in the early millennia by Italian philosophy. It is precisely the debate that some authors opened around the question of biopolitics that has generated great interest, internationally, for Italian thought and for its ability to redefine this Foucauldian category, making it an indispensable tool for understanding our present time. Esposito beautifully summarizes how Italian thought has drawn a new critical force precisely from this discussion: "Although its roots lie in the workerism (*operaismo*) of the Seventies, the notion of 'Italian Thought' actually arose much more recently, in tandem with the elaboration of the category of 'biopolitics.' Over a period of a decade, a few texts in particular set in motion what, especially outside Italy, took on the appearance of the new Italian thought. What connected them in a common horizon, despite a marked difference in approach, was their reference to the biopolitical paradigm. One of these texts identifies in biopower a modality of exclusionary inclusion of 'bare life' in the sovereign dispositif; another views biopolitical production as the constitutive factory of the new global order; and a third interpretation offers a genealogical reconstruction of the concept that recaptures its specifically modern character."[18]

If the debt of these three major works[19] quoted by Esposito—*Homo sacer: Il potere sovrano e la nuda vita*, by Giorgio Agamben; *Impero: Il nuovo ordine della globalizzazione*, by Michael Hardt and Toni Negri; and Esposito's *Bios*—to Foucault is obvious, it also seems clear that they all share the need to integrate and modify the category created by Foucault. The Foucauldian notion of biopolitics thus appears to Italian thinkers to be both fundamental and inadequate: fundamental for a critical understanding of current events but inadequate because of the way Foucault formulated it, leaving it excessively undefined.

In *Bios*, Esposito deals at length with precisely these two aspects of the Foucauldian category of biopolitics, shedding light on its indeterminacies and proposing possible ways of integrating it and making it in all respects an effective political category. To better grasp what Esposito identifies as the indeterminacies of Foucauldian biopolitics, it may be useful to briefly describe its main features.

As already mentioned, by the term "biopolitics" Foucault denotes the link between life and power that has characterized and still characterizes our modernity. On the side of power, it is exercised in a specific set of mechanisms that have the ability to apply to the biological life of populations. Their purpose is to ensure the management of the populations they take in charge by acting on their biological aspects, such as general health, birth or mortality rates, epidemic risks,and so on.

From this point of view, population appears as a different sphere than those over which other technologies of power were exercised. Sovereignty, for example, had a specifically territorial character: it took as its object a territory in which a group of subjects resided permanently. The lives of the subjects were not in charge of particular techniques of power but came into relation with the sovereign only in the form of a "right of life and death (*droit de vie et de mort*)."[20] Instead, disciplinary power, the other major set of power technologies studied by Foucault, does not apply to whole populations but is exercised over a multiplicity of individuals, in a confined space, in order to compose and multiply individual forces to make them available to the highest possible degree. It is a power that requires permanent surveillance of spaces and has the form of an anatomo-politics of the human body.[21]

In contrast to these two major technologies, the biopolitics of populations is exercised in an open spatiality, in which flows circulate freely: its goal is in fact the management of the circulation of the events it intends to take charge of, to make it flow along defined channels. Compared to these two other sets of technologies of power—sovereignty and disciplines—for Foucault, biopolitics represents a radical novelty, since with it life enters, for the first time in history, the sphere of attention of power: a biopower, a power over life, makes its appearance on the political horizon of our modernity. It is worth noting that, according to Foucault, a biopolitical *dispositif* can manage and secure the biological well-being of a population at a price: that of letting another population, or a part of a population itself, go to its death: "Foster life or disallow it to the point of death (*faire vivre ou rejeter dans la mort*)"[22] is for Foucault an effective description of biopolitics, which would thus always have a potential thanatopolitical reverse.

In *Bios*, Esposito thus starts from Foucault's elaboration of the category of biopolitics to highlight both its potential for a critique of actuality and some problematic points that Foucault left unresolved. First, Esposito notes that the category of biopolitics was not first elaborated by Foucault but has an interesting earlier history, which he retraces in the first chapter of the book.[23]

However, even if Foucault does not take into account other elaborations of the idea of biopolitics, he shares with them a dissatisfaction with the way modernity has thought of the relationship between politics, life, and history. According to Esposito, the purpose of the category of biopolitics is in fact to disrupt the modern discourse of sovereignty, replacing the dualities traditionally established by it, such as those between individuals and power, or right and sovereignty, with a real conflict between powers, of which right would be the historical and provisional outcome, a consolidation of the new state of forces.[24]

At the core of this conflict is life: modernity can thus be defined as the moment in which life enters the mechanisms of power and, inversely, in which power becomes an agent of life's transformation. As a consequence, biological life is withdrawn from its supposedly unalterable naturality and is traversed and modified by the techniques of power and knowledge and relocated in human historicity. A power, then, the modern one, aimed at the empowerment of its object: as already in *Surveiller et punir*, the purpose of disciplinary technologies was that of the multiplication and empowerment of the forces of individual bodies, so biopolitical practices are aimed at increasing, securing, and protecting life, understood as the common biological substratum of the populations they take charge of. In this, biopower is deeply different from sovereign power, which, of life and its enhancement, takes charge only in the residual form of "letting live (*laisser vivre*)."[25]

As Esposito notes, this empowerment of life implies two key elements: the participation of individuals in their own subjectification and the establishment of conditions of freedom for their action. In fact, in the same years in which he elaborates the category of biopolitics, Foucault carries on a reflection on the modes of subjectification of individuals and the relations that, historically, they have entertained with techniques of subjectivation, rooted in a specific interaction between obedience and obligations of interior truth.[26] The specificity of these forms of subjectivation is in the chiasmatic figure[27] that is put in place between subjection to relations of power and subjectivation, understood as the active participation of individuals in their own subjective constitution, where the former cannot take place unless the latter is also assured, at least to some extent. Similarly, the empowerment of life cannot be given unless subjects are assured a field of action in which they can act freely, a field produced and regulated by biopolitical techniques themselves.

As many critics have pointed out, these two elements that emerge at this stage of Foucauldian reflection can be thought of as starting points for practices of resistance: the active role of individuals in their subjection, which takes place through practices and techniques adopted by them, can be reversed into different forms of subjectivation, starting from different techniques. The empowerment of life in a space of freedom can become a power of life capable of overcoming power and changing its forms and conditions.

As Esposito notes, however, although it has been given credit for "breaking apart the modern discourse of sovereignty,"[28] Foucault's category of biopolitics leaves a number of interpretive alternatives open, without definitively leaning toward any of them and risking leading to an impasse. One element that is not entirely clear in this Foucauldian description of the three major technologies of power is that of their mutual relationship: is it a chronological succession or a coexistence? Indeed, Foucault seems uncertain about the answer to be given, hesitating between two alternatives. In certain passages, he presents them as successive stages, in which the advent of one technology would render the previous one obsolete, causing it to exit history or remain only in a residual form. In other texts, he seems instead to describe a kind of summation, in which each new technology would be added to the others, creating increasingly complex *dispositives*. In the latter case, in our present time we would simultaneously have an anatomo-politics of the human body and a biopolitics of populations, while the sovereign power's right of death would insert itself into this double *dispositif*, configuring its necessary thanatopolitical reversal vis-à-vis other populations, those whose lives it cannot or will not secure.

According to Esposito, more than the possible coexistence of disciplines and biopolitics, the key point to clarify is that of the relationship between sovereignty and biopolitics. If, in fact, biopolitics and sovereignty both characterize our present time and sovereignty has not taken its leave of history, how do the power to enhance life and the right of death articulate each other? Should biopolitics be understood as a phase of a sovereign power that still characterizes our modernity? This hypothesis would make thanatopolitics and the power of death the paradigm of our modernity. If, on the contrary, biopolitics has completely replaced the structures of sovereignty, it can be thought that sovereign power, with its right of death exercised over entire populations, is only a residue of the past, reoccurring once with Nazi thanatopolitics but destined never to be repeated. Current biopolitics would then have only the affirmative form of the free unfolding of the power of life.

As Esposito clearly underlines, Foucault's thought does not offer the tools to reach a full understanding of the overlap between sovereign power's right of death and biopolitics' empowerment of life: this is because in Foucault they are thought as external and alternative powers that can apply to life. Instead, the category that allows thinking the power that negates life and the power that enhances life not as alternatives but as inseparable aspects of a same figure—the negative protection of life—is that of immunization: this notion designates the power to preserve life by partially negating it and reducing its expansive power.

In our modernity, this immunological protection of life takes the form of political and institutional categories that give life an artificial order, limiting its expansive and dissolutive power and negating its being in common. Sovereignty is, therefore, neither a political configuration subsequent to biopolitics nor a spectral and sinister residue of the past but is "the most powerful response to the modern problem of the self-preservation of life."[29]

The moment of its greatest thanatopolitical intensity—that of Nazi "applied biology"[30]—renders visible what categories of the biopolitical *dispositif* need an urgent work of conceptual reconfiguration to subtract them from all possible autoimmune outcomes and open them to a new and original philosophy of *bios*. Body, birth, and life: several authors of the twentieth century, whom Esposito discusses in the last chapter of the book, contribute to operating a reversal of these three crucial categories in a direction that is no longer immunitary but goes toward "a more originary and intense sense of *communitas*";[31] thanks to them, it is therefore possible to trace the "initial features of a biopolitics that is finally affirmative. No longer over life but of life, one that doesn't superimpose already constituted (and by now destitute) categories of modern politics on life, but rather inscribes the innovative power of a life rethought in all its complexity and articulation in the same politics."[32]

If Foucault therefore provides a solid reference for Esposito's reflection on biopolitics, it should be noted that it is not to his philosophy that the conclusion of the book recurs: in order to formulate his original view of an affirmative biopolitics, Esposito turns to other contemporary authors. In Esposito's formulation of biopolitics, Foucault's thought must at some point make room for other philosophers to complete it and allow it to solve some of the uncertainties and indecisions that Foucault leaves open. In particular, the work of Gilles Deleuze enables Esposito to emphasize that "vitalism" can be foreseen in Foucault's pages on biopolitics and in his reference to life's ability to resist, which Foucault himself does not fully develop.

Deeply reformulated within the Italian debate—of which *Bios* is a key part—the category of biopolitics becomes a fundamental tool for thinking the crises that are currently traversing Europe. As Esposito wrote in 2016, in his introduction to *From the Outside*, it is necessary to acknowledge the inadequacy of the traditional political philosophical lexicon, which is no longer able to fully understand our present time, and to move toward new categories, such as the interconnected categories of biopolitics and thanatopolitics, which are more apt to grasp the reality of what was happening—and is still happening—on the borders of Europe and to give birth to an effective political action: "No wonder, then, that the most fitting analytical toolkit for interpreting the European situation comes precisely from the creative work spaces opened up by philosophical research. I am referring to the biopolitical paradigm developed over the past twenty years in France and Italy and spreading from there throughout the world, among the guardians of the old philosophical-political lexicon and their skepticism. Because, without sufficient warning, what was experienced for a long time as a simple economic crisis—one that soon implicated the European Union's political institutions—turned out to be a much more dramatic, biopolitical crisis."[33]

It is the category of biopolitics that makes it possible to interpret migratory crises and the ongoing humanitarian emergency that has placed, "perhaps for the first time since World War II [. . .] politics in direct contact with the biological lives of millions of human beings in flight from their homelands, devastated by war and hunger. Without exaggerating the importance of the ultimate question regarding their fate, they can be kept alive or left to die,"[34] according to that thanatopolitical alternative that Foucault had shown to be the main feature of biopolitics.

Only a few years later, the category of biopolitics returns again powerfully to the scene of philosophical-political debate about the other great crisis that shook not only Europe but also the whole world: the health emergency caused by the pandemic. In the context of Italian philosophy, in fact, a very wide discussion opens up about the ability of this category to understand the pandemic crisis and the health measures put in place by European governments.[35] Esposito offers a very significant contribution to this discussion with the publication of the book *Immunità comune*, which strongly emphasizes the relevance of the category of biopolitics for grasping the health crisis and for thinking the most suitable measures to cope with it. What is politically and socially important to think about and achieve is in fact a "common immunity," a new figure that Esposito's book aims to introduce.

To do so, however, it is necessary to acknowledge the biopolitical character of the crisis and the thanatopolitical risk—the vital risk that entire populations face—it may imply and that must be prevented. As Esposito writes in *Immunità comune*, with the pandemic crisis, "events have substantiated and even surpassed Foucault's insights with disconcerting punctuality."[36]

Just think of the three main responses to the pandemic envisioned and implemented by governments: natural herd immunity, social distancing, generalized vaccination of populations. In Esposito's view, each of these can be read in a biopolitical key: the first, herd immunity, by letting the weakest groups of a population die, would have a distinctly thanatopolitical character; the second, protection by distancing, is instead configured as a negative biopolitics. Only the third, vaccination extended to the entire world community, can have the features of an affirmative biopolitics.

It is the latter option that needs to be explored, because it alone prefigures the possibility of a common immunity. This requires a rethinking of all three categories at play in the pandemic crisis: not only biopolitics but also community and immunity.[37] Indeed, new studies have made it possible to rethink the way the immune system functions, abandoning the defensive images of war against a foreign element, and instead depicting immunity as a filter that allows interaction with the outside: "This was a profound change in the biological immune paradigm, a change that has been reinforced over recent decades. Far from being a discriminatory barrier against the external environment, the immune system is now seen as that which, under certain conditions, facilitates a relationship with the outside."[38] This shift then allows a change in the image of the relationship between community and immunity: they are no longer one the reverse of the other, but they can form a common figure: a co-immunity, or a common immunity, "meant to protect human beings—not some from others but some with and for others."[39]

In *Immunità comune*, Esposito highlights a new aspect of why, in his view, the Foucauldian category of biopolitics is insufficient and Foucault's thought needs to be integrated: it is unable to think institutions and a relationship between biopolitics and institution. Esposito writes:

> One almost gets the impression that Foucault's discourse, in default of answers to its own questions, at a certain point folds in on itself. Here again, one of the reasons for this hermeneutic block could be that the concept of institution was not adequately developed. Although Foucault paid constant attention to it, his efforts were directed to bringing out its repressive side more than its potentially innovative aspects. From this perspective, too, the pandemic has given the theory a push forward, by shining a spotlight on the irreplaceable role of institutions and the need to transform them. What emerges from this is the necessity to rebuild a relationship

between biopolitics and institutionalism that has thus far been impeded by an inadequate interpretation of both.[40]

In this short passage, Esposito most effectively describes the reasons for the absence of Foucault's thought from the last of the research projects he opened: that of Instituting Thought. In the years between *Da fuori* and *Immunità comune*, Esposito's research has in fact focused on the elaboration of a new paradigm of political ontology, defined by Esposito as "instituting."

Among the authors whom, according to Esposito, it is possible to refer in order to think the instituting paradigm, the name of Foucault does not figure: it is more to the research of Maurice Merleau-Ponty, Claude Lefort, or the early Deleuze that it is useful to turn in order to draw tools for defining a possible innovative role of institutions with respect to the political and the social.

In *Pensiero istituente*,[41] a book in which the instituting paradigm is defined in its radical differences from the other two, the constituent and the destituent, the description offered by Esposito of the contemporary political-philosophical horizon is still divided, as in *Da fuori*, by the main fracture that marked French Theory, separating it into a side more rooted in Heidegger's thought and another centered on Nietzsche's philosophy. This same division is now reflected in the two paradigms of political ontology criticized by Esposito and is projected from French Theory to Italian Thought as well: destituent thought in fact unites philosophers such as Nancy, Derrida, and, in Italy, Agamben in the same paradigm, while constituent political philosophy originates from Deleuze's political ontology and in Negri's political reflection.

If Foucault does not appear in any of these three paradigms, it is precisely because of his insufficient elaboration of the concept of institution. As it is clear from reading his texts on prisons or hospitals, for Foucault institutions are always traversed by relations of power, which tend to have a particular intensity in them. Esposito writes in *Istituzione*: "Foucault tended to characterize all institutions as oppressive. For him, taken together, they constitute a solid block destined to confine life within guarded and rigidly divided spaces, compressing natural instincts and tendencies."[42]

For this reason, according to Esposito, Foucault's thought needs once again to be integrated: indeed, it leaves open the task of thinking a relationship between the category of biopolitics and institutions, a task that the pandemic crisis has made particularly urgent. Is this, however, Esposito's last word on Foucault? Does the opening of the instituting project truly imply a definitive dismissal of Foucault's thought?

Some pages of *Immunità comune* seem to open a window onto a different scenario. Indeed, Esposito notes how a certain way of reflecting on institutions can be found in Foucault's work itself.[43] In the passages of *Naissance de la biopolitique*[44] on German ordo-liberalism, Foucault seems to recognize a positive role for institution: "This guarantees that power is limited, but it also protects the possibility to resist it."[45]

Foucault would thus think of the possibility of institutional bodies capable of a regulatory intervention in economic processes. This is, according to Esposito, a short but important suggestion: "The insight, albeit left undeveloped and dormant, that an affirmative biopolitics must pass by way of a new discourse on instituent power."[46] The task of current political philosophy will then be to start from here to think in a new way the relationship between biopolitics and institutions.

From *Bios* to the more recent project on Instituting Thought, the relevance of Foucault's reflection in the philosophy of Esposito thus appears evident and constant. Although he does not figure among contemporary authors who have contributed to the three main paradigms of political ontology, his category of biopolitics never loses its philosophical-political prominence: central to the revitalization of European philosophy and the transition from French Theory to Italian Thought, relevant in understanding more recent political and social crises, such as migration and pandemics, it continues to play a central role even in the project of the Instituting Thought, which, as Esposito notes, cannot avoid "reconstructing the broken link between life and institutions,"[47] taking root in that "new thought on life" inaugurated by Deleuze and Foucault: "only in this way" Esposito concludes, can "biopolitics and institutions find the affirmative drive that gives a political value to our lives."[48]

Notes

1. Roberto Esposito, *Bios: Biopolitica e filosofia* (Turin: Einaudi, 2004); *Bios: Biopolitics and Philosophy*, trans. Timothy Campbell (Minneapolis: University of Minnesota Press, 2008).

2. Roberto Esposito, *Da fuori: Una filosofia per l'Europa* (Turin: Einaudi, 2016); *A Philosophy for Europe: From the Outside*, trans. Zakiya Hanafi (Cambridge: Polity, 2018).

3. Roberto Esposito, *Immunità comune: Biopolitica all'epoca della pandemia* (Turin: Einaudi, 2022); *Common Immunity: Biopolitics in the Age of the Pandemic*, trans. Zakiya Hanafi (Cambridge: Polity, 2023).

4. Roberto Esposito, *Pensiero istituente: Tre paradigmi di ontologia politica* (Turin: Einaudi, 2020); *Instituting Thought: Three Paradigms of Political Ontology*, trans. Mark William Epstein (Cambridge: Polity, 2021).

5. Roberto Esposito, *Vitam instituere: Genealogia dell'istituzione* (Turin: Einaudi, 2023).

6. "The Crisis *Dispostif*" is the title of the first chapter of *From the Outside* (17–47). "Dispositif" is a translation of Foucault's French term *dispositif*. On Foucault's *dispositif*, see Gilles Deleuze, *Qu'est-ce qu'un dispositif?*, in *Michel Foucault philosophe: Rencontre international, Paris 9, 10, 11 janvier 1988* (Paris: Seuil, 1989), 184–95.

7. Esposito, *From the Outside*, 23.

8. Esposito, *From the Outside*, 8. "Deterritorialization" is a notion elaborated by Gilles Deleuze and Felix Guattari in the seventies. See, for instance Gilles Deleuze and Felix Guattari, *Mille Plateaux: Capitalisme et schizophrénie* (Paris: Éditions de Minuit, 1980); *A Thousand Plateaus: Capitalism and Schizophrenia*, trans. Brian Massumi (Minneapolis: University of Minnesota Press, 1987).

9. Esposito, *From the Outside*, 65.

10. Esposito quotes François Cusset, *French Theory: Foucault, Derrida, Deleuze, et Cie et les mutations de la vie intellectuelle aux États-Unis* (Paris: La Découverte, 2003); *French Theory: How Foucault, Derrida, Deleuze, and Co. Transformed the Intellectual Life of the United States*, trans. Jeff Fort (Minneapolis: University of Minnesota Press, 2008).

11. Michel Foucault, *L'histoire de la folie à l'âge classique* (Paris: Gallimard, 1972); *History of Madness*, trans. Jean Murphy and Jonathan Khalfa (London: Routledge, 2006).

12. Michel Foucault, *L'archéologie du savoir* (Paris: Gallimard, 1969); *The Archaeology of Knowledge*, trans. Alan M. Sheridan Smith (New York: Pantheon Books, 1971).

13. Esposito, *From the Outside*, 140. See Gilles Deleuze, *Foucault* (Paris: Les Éditions de Minuit, 1986); *Foucault*, trans. Sean Hand (London: Continuum, 1986).

14. "Is not the force that comes from outside a certain idea of Life, a certain vitalism, in which Foucault's thought culminates?" (Gilles Deleuze, *Foucault*, 77). Quoted by Esposito in *From the Outside*, 140.

15. Michel Foucault, *La volonté de savoir: Histoire de la sexualité 1* (Paris: Gallimard, 1976); *The Will to Knowledge: History of Sexuality 1*, trans. Robert Hurley (London: Penguin Books, 1990). The chapter on biopolitics is "Right of Death and Power over Life," 133–59.

16. Foucault, *Will to Knowledge*, 144.

17. Esposito, *From the Outside*, 147.

18. Esposito, *From the Outside*, 143.

19. Giorgio Agamben, *Homo sacer: Il potere sovrano e la nuda vita* (Turin: Einaudi, 1995); *Homo Sacer: Sovereign Power and Bare Life*, trans. Daniel Heller-Roazen (Stanford, CA: Stanford University Press, 1998). Micheal Hardt, Antonio Negri, *Impero* (Milan: Rizzoli, 2003); *Empire* (Cambridge, MA: Harvard University Press, 2000). Esposito, *Bios: Biopolitics and Philosophy*.

20. Foucault, *Will to Knowledge*, 136.

21. Michel Foucault, *Surveiller et punir: Naissance de la prison* (Gallimard: Paris 1975); *Discipline and Punish: The Birth of the Prison*, trans. Alan Sheridan (New York: Pantheon Books, 1977).

22. Foucault, *Will to Knowledge*, 138.

23. Esposito, *Bios*, chapter "The Enigma of Biopolitics," 13–44.

24. Michel Foucault, *Il faut défendre la société: Cours au Collège de France 1976* (Paris: Seuil/Gallimard, 1997); *"Society Must Be Defended": Lectures at the Collège de France, 1975–1976*, trans. David Macey (London: Palgrave, 2003).

25. Foucault, *Will to Knowledge*, 136.

26. See Michel Foucault, *Sécurité, territoire, population: Cours au Collège de France 1977–1978* (Paris: Seuil/Gallimard, 2004); *Security, Territory, and Population: Lectures at the College de France, 1977–1978*, trans. Graham Burchell (London: Palgrave, 2009). On the link between subjectivation and subjugation, see Laura Cremonesi et al., *Foucault and the Making of Subjects* (London: Rowman & Littlefield, 2016).

27. On the chiasmatic form of subjectivation in Foucault, see Judith Revel, *Between Politics and Ethics: The Question of Subjectivation*, in Cremonesi et al., *Foucault and the Making of Subjects*, 163–73.

28. Esposito, *Bios*, 30.

29. Esposito, *Bios*, 57.

30. Esposito, *Bios*, 112.

31. Esposito, *Bios*, 157.

32. Esposito, *Bios*, 157.

33. Esposito, *From the Outside*, 2.

34. Esposito, *From the Outside*, 3.

35. An overview on this debate is in Simona Forti, *Totalitarianism: A Borderline Idea in Political Philosophy* (Stanford, CA: Stanford University Press, 2023). On Italian discussion on biopolitics and pandemic, see the issue of *Micromega*, no. 8 (2020), *Biopolitica: Inganno o chiave di volta?*, and in particular these articles: Paolo Flores D'Arcais, "L'inganno della biopolitica," 4–33; Esposito, "Immunitas: Oltre le feconde contraddizioni di Foucault," 35–47; Jean-Luc Nancy, "La sindrome biopolitica," 56–61; and Carlo Galli, "Il doppio volto della biopolitica," 94–105.

36. Esposito, *Common Immunity*, 8.

37. The categories of "community" and "immunity" are a relevant part of Esposito's philosophy; see Roberto Esposito, *Commnuitas: Origine e destino della*

comunità (Turin: Einaudi, 1998); *Communitas: The Origin and Destiny of Community*, trans. Timothy Campbell (Stanford, CA: Stanford University Press, 2009); and *Immunitas: Protezione e negazione della vita* (Turin: Einaudi, 2002); *Immunitas: The Protection and Negation of Life*, trans. Zakiya Hanafi (Cambridge: Polity, 2011).

38. Esposito, *Common Immunity*, 184.
39. Esposito, *Common Immunity*, 156.
40. Esposito, *Common Immunity*, 9.
41. Esposito, *Instituting Thought*. On the Instituting Paradigm, see also Roberto Esposito: *Almanacco di Filosofia e politica*, vol. 2, *Istituzione: Filosofia, politica, storia* (Macerata, Italy: Quodlibet, 2020); *Istituzione* (Bologna: Il Mulino, 2021); *Institution*, trans. Zakiya Hanafi (Cambridge: Polity, 2022); and *Vitam instituere*.
42. Esposito, *Institution*, 11.
43. On the question of institutions and Instituting Thought in Foucault, see Rita Fulco, "Crítica y productividad de las instituciones: El quiasmo entre Roberto Esposito y Michel Foucault," *Dorsal: Revista de estudios foucaultianos*, no. 14 (2023): 132–39.
44. Michel Foucault, *Naissance de la biopolitique: Cours au Collège de France (1978–1979)* (Paris: Seuil/Gallimard, 2004); *The Birth of Biopolitics: Lectures at the Collège de France, 1978–1979*, trans. Graham Burchell (London: Palgrave, 2008).
45. Esposito, *Common Immunity*, 116.
46. Esposito, *Common Immunity*, 117.
47. Esposito, *Common Immunity*, 118.
48. Esposito, *Common Immunity*, 118.

Three

Conflict and Institution
Roberto Esposito and Claude Lefort

Mattia Di Pierro

In the following pages, I will try to follow the traces of Claude Lefort's thought in Roberto Esposito's work. I will start with the most recent writings, by focusing on the 2020 study *Instituting Thought*, and then go backward, looking at some earlier studies. However, I do not intend to make an exhaustive list of the works and pages where Lefort is cited. I will rather select a few points that seem particularly significant to the reconstruction of Lefort's influence on Esposito's thought. Through this brief and synthetic history, my aim is to better understand the meaning of this relationship. In particular, I will try show how we can recognize and follow a consistent *thread* in Esposito's work through his references to Lefort.

As is well known, in his later books the Neapolitan thinker devoted much space to Lefort's thought.[1] In them, Esposito approached the topic of "institution" shaping what he called an "instituting thought." In this way, his work practiced a kind of internal turn, going in a direction that was not in perfect continuity with his previous work.[2]

However, one cannot interpret this attention toward the French philosopher exclusively within the boundaries of this recent "turn." One can find references to Lefort's work in much earlier works, scattered at several points in Esposito's theoretical journey. Esposito was among the first to bring this author to Italy: he read with interest Lefort's work on Machiavelli and discussed his reading of Hannah Arendt's texts as early as the beginning of the 1990s. Beyond these historical elements, however, I would like to ask whether these references can point to the problematic core in Esposito's thought that has somehow "exploded" into a clearer form only in recent years. Perhaps this problematic core, in contact with a profoundly changed political landscape that has acted as a reactant, has thus taken shape in the idea of an ontology of the institution.

1.

Let us therefore start from the end. In his latest book, *Vitam instituere*, Esposito sets out to conclude the research begun three years earlier with *Instituting Thought* and deepened with the short volume *Istituzione* published in 2021.[3] Tracing the occurrences throughout history of the Latin locution that gives the work its title, he looks at the modern philosophical tradition by choosing a precise point of view: that of the instituting thought.[4] From this perspective a sui generis genealogy emerges that, starting with Niccolò Machiavelli, reaches Spinoza and then Hegel. On the one hand, working within the classical canon, the author intends to give historical depth and a certain prestige to the instituting thought. On the other, he wants to show the retroactive productivity of this theory in rethinking the canon or proposing a new one. Moreover, the problem that moves Esposito's research still seems to be the search for a productive philosophy for the Left—or the progressive political area—and for Europe.[5]

The starting point of the genealogy is the relationship between law and nature as it emerges in ancient Roman law. Nevertheless, according to Esposito, Machiavelli inaugurates modern thinking on institutions.[6] Its novelty is in the politicization of Roman legal categories, in the incorporation of life into the formalism of *Ius*. In this framework, the Florentine argues for the primacy of the instituting over the instituted moment and by placing conflict at the basis of order. Breaking with the long tradition of *concordia ordinum* and humanism, the Florentine Secretary thinks that order and conflict are not two opposite dimensions. On the contrary, they are always intertwined. Good institutions, the stability of governments, and the freedom and strength of states do not come from concord, from the ability of rulers to put an end to conflict. They are rather the result of conflict between "the humors" always present in every community, in every city: between the great and the plebs. According to Machiavelli, the institution is an ongoing result and a process. It is what, by keeping conflict open, leads to good laws and the health of the state. This new approach makes the Florentine Secretary an indispensable point of reference for instituting thought.

The intertwining between form and life that Spinoza assumes is the reason for his inclusion in this genealogy.[7] In his thought, matter and form, life and institutions, immediacy and mediation are involved in a single instituting movement.[8] According to Esposito, this is evident first and foremost in his idea that each person's right coincides with the power of which he/she is capable. Consequently, Spinoza does not see the institution as something distant from the lives of citizens but as something closely related, according to the most radical meaning of *institutio vitae*.

In this framework, Hegel's importance lies first of all in his detachment from Hobbes, Rousseau, and Kant, that is, in the shift of political reflection from the philosophical to the ontological level. The Stuttgart philosopher, Esposito says, thinks of society and institutions as in a continuous relationship with the "living spirit." In this sense he takes a step beyond Machiavelli and Spinoza. If for the latter human life appeared immersed in the natural dimension, according to Hegel life and institutions are included in the unique dialectic of the Spirit.[9] In this context, nature is not a status but a process, as the political state is a prerequisite and a result, mediated by civil society.[10]

Looking at the twentieth century, Esposito first denounces a common rejection of institutional logic. From Sartre to Foucault to contemporary neo-anarchism, for more than a century, philosophy seems to have taken refuge in a dichotomous conception that contrasts the emancipatory dynamic of movements with the repressive fixity of the institution. However, Esposito argues that this schematic bipolarity sacrifices the creative potential of the instituting process by neglecting the inextricable intertwining of instituting and instituted, conflict and law, event and form that Machiavelli, Spinoza, and Hegel already highlighted. Ultimately, it could be said that, if considered from this perspective, contemporary thought has a deficit in politics. It is incapable of thinking politically.

Esposito's idea, already expounded in the book *Istituzione*, is then to look for a way out of this weakness, finding allies in authors and traditions that do not oppose instituting and instituted, event and form. He offers three alternatives: the Italian legal tradition (Santi Romano), German anthropology (Arnold Gehlen), and French phenomenology, represented by Maurice Merleau-Ponty and his student Claude Lefort.[11] Esposito's final reflections focus on the work of Lefort, analyzing the relationships he establishes among imagination, conflict, and order. According to Esposito, Lefort's thought is particularly important: in it, as in no other case, the instituting dynamic becomes the heart of political and theoretical praxis.

To fully understand this central role entrusted to the French philosopher, it is necessary to take a step back and turn toward the essay *Instituting Thought* published in Italian in 2020. As I stated earlier, this work marked a kind of course correction in Esposito's path. It opened a broad new field of research around the theme of institution and a new political ontology.[12] Such ontology emerges from a tension with some authors who have been part of Esposito's usual references for years. However, this cannot overshadow the fact that, as I want to emphasize, this new ontology itself recovers some themes that have always been part of his work.

Instituting Thought thus describes a political ontology based on the concept of institution that gives the book its title. In particular, the last chapter presents institution as a way out of the difficulties peculiar to two other traditions of thought that are so important as to be hegemonic in contemporary theoretical-political thought.

2.

However, before I begin the analysis it is worth specifying, as the author himself does in the first lines, that by the term "political ontology" he does not refer to "the area of being that concerns politics, but rather to the essential relationship that conjoins being and politics."[13] With this expression he indicates both the political character of ontology and the relationship that political praxis necessarily has with the conception of being, that is, of space, time, society, and humanity. From the very first pages, Esposito warns the reader: he deploys a thought that rejects easy dichotomies—in this case that between thought and reality, between theory and politics—in order to unearth the intertwining between the various components of the real and the thought that thinks about it.

In *Instituting Thought*, the analysis focuses on the twentieth and twenty-first centuries. Esposito's intention here is not to reread the tradition or create an alternative canon. Rather, he stresses the necessity to intervene in the contemporary debate by outlining the hegemonic theories and highlighting their inadequacy.

The "destituent" paradigm is the first to be discussed. It relates to politics only negatively, through the deactivation of action and power. Martin Heidegger is the most significant representative of such current. According to Esposito, a *dispositif* works within the German philosopher's thought by always and increasingly contrasting the political and the impolitical dimensions. As the author himself states, "The specificity of the Heideggerian conception of the political resides precisely in its antinomical relationship with the impolitical dimension,"[14] which constitutes the presupposition of the political and at the same time something subtracted from it. In this framework, the political becomes meaningful only against the background of an impoliticality that constitutes its condition even without ever coinciding with it.[15] Furthermore, after the 1930s, the two terms become increasingly divorced and the impolitical, from being a foundation for the political, becomes an explicit negation of it. When the political comes to coincide with the generalized dominance of technology, the impolitical becomes the necessary critical device that can be made explicit only negatively.[16] That is, it can only be negation, deactivation, dismissal of the political. The impossibility of origin declared by Heidegger, the inescapable corruption of every action, of every work that follows, leaves as the only possibility the withdrawal from all politics. If time coincides with the victory of technique, all that remains to be done is to not participate in this time. There is only one choice: let what is be—as the term *Gelassenheit* indicates.[17]

With the end of the *polis*, and therefore of any possible politicization of the *Da* ("there"), the political completely transfers into the horizon of the negative. If power, in all its possible configurations, has been definitively consigned to technical machination, freedom can no longer be understood as a subjective option but as the allowing of everything, devastation included, to be.[18]

This destituent relationship with the political sphere is not confined to Heidegger's work. On the contrary, it has characterized a substantial part of contemporary philosophy. Moreover, "a quasi-transcendental presupposition of the entire Western conception of the political is that it has a negative foundation."[19] It is precisely the belief in the dissolving outcome of the possible loss of this negative foundation that links the reflections of Hannah Arendt and Carl Schmitt. Simone Weil also clearly fits into this destituent paradigm. The concept of de-creation she uses to point at transcending pure force toward the "force that is not of this earth" precisely expresses a negative relation to politics and action. Jean-Luc Nancy—an important author in Esposito's work—also argues for the impossibility of a political understanding of community by explicitly referring to Heidegger.[20]

Giorgio Agamben, however, is the author who, from within this paradigm, has perhaps most influenced contemporary debate.[21] He criticizes constituent power because of its being inseparable from the constituted power and for its intimate bond with the category of sovereignty. According to Agamben, the only way to escape this framework, as criticized in *Homo Sacer*, is an ontological shift in favor of a "destituent power." This must succeed in rendering human action inoperative without annihilating it. As Agamben states, "Living in the form of the 'as not' means rendering all juridical and social ownership destitute, without this deposition founding a new identity."[22]

Constituent power characterizes the second paradigm questioned by Esposito, and the point of reference is, in this case, Gilles Deleuze.[23] The analysis begins questioning the politicity of Deleuze's thought in which Esposito distinguishes two different ontologies.[24] The first, as developed in *Difference and Repetition* and *Logic of Sense*, expresses the gap between generative process and immaterial effects.[25] The productive becoming of molecular multiplicities defines the second one.[26] The different relation to the negative marks the difference between these two ontologies. The first one admits a "negative fold" within it and therefore, while not directly political, allows for a thematization of the political. The second, by fully adhering to the plane of immanence, eventually loses its relation to the negative and thus to the political. In short, as long as Deleuze thinks negation as difference, it remains possible to articulate a political question. But when he begins to think Being as directly political and reduces negation to a simple error of perspective in an integrally affirmative level, then politics, crushed on the affirmative being, becomes useless and resolves itself into pure becoming. Esposito argues: "While in Heidegger's case a productive relationship between being and politics was impeded by the negative principle that both of them presupposed, in Deleuze's case the political seems to be inhibited by an excess of affirmation that shades its contours, making it indistinguishable from the ontological horizon in which it is inscribed. In this fashion the deactivation theorized by Heidegger is reversed into a constitutive moment that is equally devoid of a grip on reality, because it is completely immanent in its objective development."[27]

In other terms, with the help of Bergson and Spinoza, Deleuze removes the negative from Being by asserting that it is difference itself. He thus succeeds in delineating the same totally affirmative ontology that both Hegel and Heidegger missed. In this way, however, politics becomes confused with an immanent, affirmative ontological plane and loses meaning in its autonomy. It becomes lost in Being. Esposito detects Deleuze's mistake: his thought is no longer capable of a contact with politics and resolves itself into an assumption and justification of existing reality. Therefore, as the Italian philosopher argues, Deleuze fails in his critique of capitalism, whose deep logic he seems rather to justify. The only politics Deleuze conceives "does not pass through conflict with, or resistance to, power, but rather through its reintegration into the flow of desire."[28]

If everything escapes and gets deterritorialized in Deleuze's univocal ontology, there are no forces that can reciprocally oppose one another. There is nothing but a single plane of immanence, or a body without organs, "as biological as it is collective and political." Nothing but the body without organs itself, in its opposition to "all strata of organization, the organism's organization as well as power organizations," can be political.[29]

According to Esposito, Antonio Negri is the one who, more than anyone else, tried to give political content to Deleuze's philosophy. His theory of constituent power is in fact a political translation of the French philosopher's ontology made possible by the use of the Marxian category of "living labor."[30] For Negri, ontological creation, that is social production, is conditioned only by its internal development and requires no institutional mediation. His ontology of the absolute immanence of the social reduces all institutional forms to oppression. Once more, the negative is expelled from the political horizon and politics, dissolved in the affirmation of the social, disappeared.[31]

The first two chapters of *Instituting Thought* and some articles that appeared shortly before the book not only propose an interpretation of the works of Heidegger and Deleuze, they also feature a harsh critique to contemporary critical philosophy and theory. For Esposito, these ontologies, which have occupied the critical field in recent decades, fail to think politics in its autonomy and, at the same time, in its entanglement with the real. They expelled it from their horizon by relegating it into negation or diluting it into complete affirmation. His analysis also highlights that at the heart of these problems lies the inability to think the negative adequately, a central theme in Esposito's work as a whole. By highlighting these inadequacies, the Italian thinker intends to disengage himself from these perspectives and outline an alternative, an escape route from destituent power and constituent thought capable of truly thinking Being and politics together, capable of thinking negative.

3.

In a 1980 article in the journal *Kontinent Skandinavia*, Claude Lefort notes the Left's inability to think in political terms.[32] Even though "socialists are determined advocates of state intervention in every domain of social life in order to diminish or suppress the inequalities that arise in the context of civil society, to attenuate the effects of the appropriation of wealth by a minority or to make it impossible,"[33] they fail to grasp the political dimension of the social. An article Lefort published a few years earlier in the first issue of the journal *Libre* clarifies this position. It is titled *Maintenant* (Nowadays) and considers the French debate in political and social theories of the past sixteen years—eight years before and eight years after the watershed date of 1968.[34] The eight years prior to 1968 are described as marked by a renewed scientific spirit, which, thanks to structuralism, linguistics, and the rational analysis of power networks, had an impact on humanities. According to Lefort, all these theories, even in their heterogeneity, share the same fascination for a formalism under which they hide the "horizon of reality," any difference between the object and knowledge. They suppress any difference between knowable object and the knowing subject, eliminating the discourse on interpretation, the other of the symbolic.

At first glance, Lefort continues, the eight years after 1968 seem to inaugurate an entirely different discourse that questions every concept of science, the very idea of theory, and every scientific method for analyzing the social. But at a closer look it becomes clear that, despite its innovative aspect, this discourse does nothing but bring modern objectivism to a different level. In fact, even this new discourse reduces knowledge to the known object and power to a matter of strength. It, too, crushes every element on a plane of perfect immanence by failing to grasp the symbolic dimension of the social, to grasp the dimension of the political. The critical references here are the theories of desire in Wilhelm Reich and Herbert Marcuse, and above all, the works of Gilles Deleuze and Michel Foucault.[35]

Lefort's critique of the debates of his time is similar to that put forth by Esposito in *Instituting Thought*. Admittedly, the closeness appears clearest with regard to Deleuze's critique of constituent power and immanence. Both critiques seem driven by the same issues: the crushing of social and political reality on a plane of complete immanence and a bipolar conception that sharply divides event and form, instituting and instituted, where the latter term indicates only the negation of the former. It is only repression. For both authors, at the bottom of these problems lies a deeper question: the place and the role of the negative. A negative element declined in different ways: as alterity, as the vacuum on which the foundation of modern society and community rests, as the division that cuts every social identity and produces conflict, as the unattainability of unity, of the totality of the social, as impolitical dimension.

Esposito fully understands Lefort's position as moving into a particular terrain, indicting both the social sciences and the political philosophy of the time. The French thinker criticizes any objective analysis of the social that looked at this as from the outside and any analysis that identifies in a single element—economy, ideology, or religion—the cause of a given conformation of the social, the solution of the enigma that lies at the heart of the social itself. On the contrary, for Lefort, one must understand the social in its totality, as a web of meaning and *praxis*, as "experience." That of ontology, Esposito argues, is the proper terrain of this kind of reflection.[36]

The relations among the political, the economic, and the juridical, between public and private, or between legality and legitimacy, while they are important, remain opaque so long as they stay outside a fundamental question that concerns the symbolic framework they are situated in. Whoever practices or thinks about the political presupposes a particular relationship with her or his "being" in time and space, in nature and history, in life and the world.[37]

In other words, according to Lefort, social sciences, political sciences, but also philosophical theories, by leading everything back to immanence, remain blind to the ontological web from which they emerge and onto which they are grafted. This "structure" is what he refers to as "symbolic." Indeed, he thinks one should always understand the social as a "symbolic institution," that is, as an inextricable web of social praxis and meanings. In this sense, there is no reality behind social meanings: the social is the real. In this theorical framework, the social appears as the continuous questioning of itself around its own identity and the legitimacy of power as a symbolic place. However, this means that the social can never coincide with itself. There is always an irremediable and an unattainable division running through it.[38] In turn, this division is not traceable to a "factual division," a division perhaps economic and objective, measurable with the tools of the social sciences. It is rather an elusive division that translates the impossible coincidence between thought and Being, the necessity of mediation.[39]

As Esposito rightly points out, from this point of view, politics and Being do not coincide. The very fabric of Being is political, that is, it is traversed by an insurmountable division. Lefort's thought thus situates itself precisely on the line that divides the perspectives of Heidegger and Deleuze.

Lefort's perspective, like theirs, exhibits the deeply rooted traits of ontology. The triangular relationship among being, difference, and the political plays out in his ontology too. But his interpretation of difference modifies the relationship between ontology and the political, preventing both a radical divergence and a complete superposition. There is neither Heidegger's irreducible distance nor Deleuze's absolute superposition between the political and ontology—one instead finds a conflictual tension that simultaneously connects and distances them. This involves giving up both Heidegger's destitution and Deleuze's constitution in favor of something we can certainly define as "instituting thought.[40]

4.

Beneath Lefort's ontology Esposito rightly discerns the important presence of the phenomenology of Maurice Merleau-Ponty, who was a mentor and a friend of Lefort. Beginning with *Phenomenology of Perception*, Merleau-Ponty built his rejection of any overlooking thought (*pensée de surplomb*), of any sharp division between subject and object, between thought and being. Through the concepts of "reversibility," "flesh," and "chiasm" he intended to name the irresolvable entanglement between subject and objects, between Being and the experience of Being. Within this framework, the concept of *institution* draws Esposito's attention.[41]

With this word Merleau-Ponty translated the term *Stiftung* used by Husserl to think permanence and change together. He had thus sought to grasp how each new event, each new meaning, was at once the resumption, rearticulation, and change of previous elements, which in this dynamic, however, do not remain the same as themselves but change by transforming the very general structure on which they act. In this dynamic, Esposito explains, the negative is not expelled but rather "becomes the filter through which each human experience can identify itself only by distancing itself from itself and by exposing itself to its own otherness."[42]

Lefort fully grasps the importance of this concept and advocates a radical politicization of it: he thinks the social on the model of *institution*. As noted by Esposito, this concept is a central tool of Lefort's philosophy. For him, society institutes itself from an inappropriable origin, from a lack of foundation that expresses the need to know itself through a movement of continuous externalization and return to itself. This is a succession of contingent and precarious refoundation, a continuous instituting movement in which unity and separation coexist. In other words, according to Lefort an internal division affects every society, implying a necessary relation to otherness. And the political is nothing but the explanation, the interpretation, that a society gives itself of its own division. This, ultimately, is the meaning of the idea of "institution of the social." Esposito therefore affirms: "That society can relate to itself only by distancing itself from itself, testing its own exteriority, means that the institution does not have the shape either of a decision—much less an ex nihilo one, as occurs with constituent power—or of a self-institution. What decides it is neither a presupposed subject nor itself, its own self-productive power."[43]

In this framework, politics establishes the social not directly but through a passage throughout alterity, through the mediation of the negative. In short, to relate to itself, society must separate from itself and then return to itself. It must continually relate to its own division in order to find unity.[44]

This is exactly the point that interests Esposito. In the concept of the "institution of the social" and in Merleau-Ponty's phenomenology behind it, he can recognize a new and more productive conception of the negative that allows one freedom from the difficulties of destituent power and constituent power. Here the negative "unlike any dialectical dispositif, is not a moment of the process destined to be overcome by a subsequent affirmation, but its dark side—the difference that prevents the real from closing on itself, with exclusionary effects on to what is not."[45] The negative is neither rejected nor absorbed but is conceived as the very engine of the dynamics of the social, of political ontology.

5.

Before concluding, it is time to ask ourselves how much Esposito's attention to Lefort's work and to the topic of the institution represents a turning point in his work or, better, whether it lies in substantial continuity with his theoretical path.

Turning again to Machiavelli can offer an answer. The final pages of the last chapter of *Instituting Thought* feature Lefort's interpretation of the works of the Florentine author—that is, the point where his political ontology emerges most clearly. In the "theory of humors" presented in the *Discourses over the First Deca of Titus Livy*, the Parisian philosopher reads the ideal representation of the division that separates and relates the social to itself. In contrast, in the chapters of *The Prince* devoted to the virtues that the sovereign must possess, he can read the importance of representation and the imaginary for a modern politics lacking a stable foundation. Thus, through Machiavelli, Lefort can clearly expose the dynamics of the political (*le politique*), so the conflict develops between the two *umori* and toward the symbolic place of power (the prince) creating institutions.[46]

The Florentine Secretary is certainly one of those authors at the core of Esposito's reflection. Since the 1980s, he has devoted many pages of commentary to Machiavelli's thought.[47] In his readings, he has always highlighted the relationship between conflict and order as well as the novelty of Machiavelli's conception of politics without foundation. Against this background, it is interesting to note how the interpretation set forth in *Instituting Thought* differs from that proposed a decade earlier in *Living Thought*.[48]

In this book, Esposito seeks to trace the distinctiveness and the characteristics of an Italian philosophy. The latter, the author argues, is marked by the attention to the productivity of conflict, contact with praxis, and the theme of life. Machiavelli naturally plays a prominent role in this line of thought. He is almost a founder. His thinking, characterized by continuous contact with changing times, politics, and attention to the productivity of conflict is the clearest example of Italian thought. Moreover, the Florentine Secretary is the model to which several other authors, interested in grasping what unites the thought and the movement of life, of politics, turned over the centuries, making Italian thought even more recognizable.

However, in this context Esposito's interpretation highlights a prevalence of event over form, of change over preservation, of conflict over order that is missing in *Instituting Thought*. He reads the theory of humors set forth in the ninth chapter of *The Prince* and the celebration of conflict carried out in the *Discourses* from a perspective that gives primacy to the constituent moment over the constituted.[49] While the dimension of order by no means disappears from Esposito's perspective, his reflection becomes a search for a conscious affirmation of its inevitable implication with negation.[50] This prevalence of the event—or life—is not accidental but is the common thread that runs through and unifies all Italian philosophy that, not by chance, also includes the theories of Antonio Negri and Giorgio Agamben.

Beneath this shift in perspective, however, it is easy to grasp the continuity that guides Esposito's thinking and that led him to *Instituting Thought*, surpassing the views embraced in *Living Thought*: the relationship between affirmation and negation. Indeed, this theme obsessively returns in all of his books. So much so that one could read his work as a continuous attempt to think the negative out of the dichotomy and of the exclusions of the theological-political, beyond pure negation. It is the search for a kind of productivity of the negative. After all, is this theme not running through his conception of community expressed in *Communitas*? In this book, the Italian philosopher describes the modern community as built around a void, a lack of foundation, the impossibility of completely identifying with itself. It is in continuous tension between the *munus* and the *cum*.[51] From this point of view, the concept of institution is the final landing place on this path, the concept through which it is possible to conceive a thought of affirmation that does not disqualify but assumes negation, the empty, the impolitical dimension at the core of society, the lack of foundation.

This same need had also driven Esposito's search for an affirmative biopolitics. It involves the elaboration of a thought of life that does not deny the latter as pure negativity, nor as full immanent affirmation.

Esposito is still searching in this challenging field of research, as the title and the analysis of his latest book demonstrate.[52]

Notes

1. I refer in particular to Roberto Esposito, *Vitam instituire: Genealogia dell'istituzione* (Turin: Einaudi, 2023); *Instituting Thought: Three Paradigms of Political Ontology*, trans. Mark William Epstein (Cambridge: Polity, 2021); *Istituzione* (Bologna: Il Mulino, 2021).

2. See Costanza Serratore, ed., *Para una filosofía de la institución: El giro institucionalista del Italian Thought* (Buenos Aires: Rededitorial, 2022).

3. The content of the latest study was anticipated in a series of lectures given in autumn and winter 2022 at the Scuola Normale Superiore in Pisa and now in *Vitam Instituere*.

4. See Esposito, *Instituting Thought*.

5. This problem already moved Roberto Esposito's research in *A Philosophy for Europe: From the Outside*, trans. Zakiya Hanafi (Cambridge: Polity, 2018).

6. Esposito, *Vitam instituere*, 31–58.

7. Esposito, *Vitam instituere*, 59–86.

8. Esposito, *Vitam instituere*, 63.

9. Esposito, *Vitam instituere*, 91.

10. Esposito, *Vitam instituere*, 99.

11. See Esposito, *Vitam instituere*, 134–37 and 137–41. Esposito also places Cornelius Castoriadis alongside Lefort. He too, in fact, conceives of the social as an institution. Esposito's interest is mainly in his conception of the imaginary. See Cornelius Castoriadis, *The Imaginary Institution of Society: Creativity and Autonomy in the Social-Historical World*, trans. Kathleen Blamey (Cambridge: Polity, 1997).

12. Esposito had inaugurated this new site in the essay *Pensiero istituente*, which appeared the year before in the *Almanacco di Filosofia e Politica I*. See Roberto Esposito, "Pensiero istituente: Tre paradigmi di ontologia politica," in Mattia Di Pierro and Francesco Marchesi, eds., *Crisi dell'immanenza: Almanacco di filosofia e politica 1* (Macerata, Italy: Quodlibet, 2019), 23–39.

13. Esposito, *Instituting Thought*, 2.

14. Esposito, *Instituting Thought*, 18.

15. Esposito, *Instituting Thought*, 18.

16. Esposito, *Instituting Thought*, 45.

17. Esposito, *Instituting Thought*, 63.

18. Esposito, *Instituting Thought*, 63.

19. Esposito, *Instituting Thought*, 20.

20. See Esposito, *Instituting Thought*, 45–6. Jean-Luc Nancy's thought is one of the main references in Esposito's work. Consider, in particular, Roberto

Esposito, *Communitas: The Origin and Destiny of Community*, trans. Timothy Campbell (Stanford, CA: Stanford University Press, 2010). About Nancy see Jean-Luc Nancy, *The Inoperative Community*, trans. Peter Connor et al. (Minneapolis: University of Minnesota Press, 1991).

21. See Esposito, *Instituting Thought*, 67–68. See Giorgio Agamben, *Homo Sacer: Sovereign Power and Bare Life*, trans. Daniel Heller-Roazen (Stanford, CA: Stanford University Press, 1998); *The Use of Bodies*, trans. Adam Kotsko (Stanford, CA: Stanford University Press, 2015).

22. Agamben, "Epilogue: Toward a Theory of Destituent Potential," in *The Use of Bodies*, 274. Quoted in Esposito, *Instituting Thought*, 68.

23. Consider the pages devoted to it in Roberto Esposito, *Politics and Negation: Toward an Affirmative Philosophy*, trans. Zakiya Hanafi (Cambridge: Polity, 2019); and *A Philosophy for Europe: From the Outside*, the use of its works in *Terms of Politics* or in works on biopolitics.

24. Esposito follows Slavoj Žižek's reading of Deleuze. See Slavoj Žižek, *Organs without Bodies: On Deleuze and Consequences* (London: Routledge, 2004).

25. See Gilles Deleuze, *Difference and Repetition*, trans. Paul Patton (New York: Columbia University Press, 1994); *The Logic of Sense*, trans. Mark Lester and Charles Stivale (New York: Columbia University Press, 1990).

26. See Gilles Deleuze and Félix Guattari, *Anti-Oedipus: Capitalism and Schizophrenia*, trans. Robert Hurley, Mark Seem, and Helen R. Lane (Minneapolis: University of Minnesota Press, 1983).

27. Esposito, *Instituting Thought*, 80.

28. Esposito, *Instituting Thought*, 143.

29. Esposito, *Instituting Thought*, 144.

30. Esposito, *Instituting Thought*, 112.

31. Esposito, *Instituting Thought*, 113. Here Esposito asserts, "What is missing, within a political ontology of absolute immanence, is not the transcendence of power, but a politically articulated theory of conflict. In its absence, neither the multitude nor its imperial enemy, from which it is generated in contradictory fashion, exhibit the historical determination without which the political loses its characteristics."

32. Lefort asserts, "Why, I asked, was the Left reluctant to employ the concept of totalitarianism? At first I replied: because it had been invented by the Right. That is true. But, I went on to ask, why did it allow itself to be outstripped by its adversaries? I would now dare to say: because this concept is political and the Left does not think in political terms." Claude Lefort, *The Political Forms of Modern Society, Bureaucracy, Democracy, Totalitarianism*, ed. John B. Thompson (Cambridge, MA: MIT, 1986), 277. This same sentence is quoted by Esposito, *Instituting Thought*, 201.

33. Now in Lefort, *Political Forms of Modern Society*, 277–78.

34. The article is now in Claude Lefort, *Le temps présent: Écrits 1945–2005* (Paris: Belin, 2007), 275–300.

35. On this topic, I would like to refer to Mattia Di Pierro, *Claude Lefort's Political Philosophy* (Cham, UK: Palgrave, 2023) and "Archaeology or interpretation: Michel Foucault and Claude Lefort," *Constellations* 29, no. 4 (December 2022): 434–46.

36. Esposito, *Instituting Thought*, 146–47.

37. Esposito, *Instituting Thought*, 147.

38. See Claude Lefort, *Political Forms of Modern Society; Democracy and Political Theory*, trans. David Macey (Cambridge: Polity, 1988); and *Les formes de l'histoire* (Paris: Gallimard, 2000).

39. Esposito highlights the anthropological studies that help Lefort think about the division and institution of the social and the antinomian relationship between socialization and division. It is precisely through anthropology that Lefort is able to think of stagnation as a form of historicity. See Esposito, *Instituting Thought*, 170–77; and Lefort, *Les formes de l'histoire*. Among Lefort's references are Gregory Bateson and Margaret Mead, *Balinese Character: A Photographic Analysis* (New York: Academy of Sciences, 1942); and Edward Evans-Pritchard, *The Nuer: A Description of the Modes of Livelihood and Political Institutions of a Nilotic People* (Oxford: Clarendon, 1968). On this topic, see also François Hartog, *Regimes of Historicity: Presentism and Experiences of Time*, trans. Saskia Brown (New York: Columbia University Press, 2016); and Marshall Sahlins, *Island of History* (Chicago, IL: University of Chicago Press, 1985).

40. Esposito, *Instituting Thought*, 149.

41. Esposito, *Instituting Thought*, 150–54. The close relationship between Lefort's philosophy and that of Merleau-Ponty has been emphasized by critics and highlighted more productively in some more recent studies. See Gilles Labelle, "Maurice Merleau-Ponty et la genèse de la philosophie politique de Claude Lefort," *Politique et Sociétés* 22, no. 3 (2003): 9–44; Bernard Flynn, "Lefort in the Wake of Merleau-Ponty," *Chiasmi International*, no. 10 (2008): 251–62; and Nicolas Poirier, *Introduction à Claude Lefort* (Paris: La Découverte, 2020) or—I dare say—my own Mattia Di Pierro, *L'esperienza del mondo: Claude Lefort and the Phenomenology of the Political* (Pisa: ETS, 2020).

42. Esposito, *Instituting Thought*, 154.

43. Esposito, *Instituting Thought*, 158. This, I would add, is where the reflections of Claude Lefort and Cornelius Castoriadis separate and where Castoriadis's concept of institution appears problematic. On this theme, see Nicolas Poirier, "Wild Being, between Ontology and Politics: Merleau-Ponty, Lefort, Castoriadis," *International Journal of Social Imaginaries*, no. 1 (May 2022): 84–106.

44. Esposito, *Instituting Thought*, 166–67.

45. Esposito, *Instituting Thought*, 182.

46. See Claude Lefort, *Machiavelli in the Making*, trans. Michael B. Smith (Evanston, IL: Northwestern University Press, 2012).

47. See, for example, Roberto Esposito, *Ordine e conflitto: Machiavelli e la letteratura politica del Rinascimento italiano* (Naples: Liguori, 1984).

48. Roberto Esposito, *Living Thought: The Origins and Actuality of Italian Philosophy*, trans. Zakiya Hanafi (Stanford, CA: Stanford University Press, 2012). On *Italian Theory*, see at least Dario Gentili, *Italian Theory: Dall'operaismo alla biopolitica* (Bologna: Il Mulino, 2012); Enrica Lisciani-Petrini and Giusi Strummiello, eds., *Effetto Italian Thought* (Macerata, Italy: Quodlibet, 2017); and Dario Gentili and Elettra Stimilli, eds., *Italian Critical Thought: Genealogies and Categories* (Lanham, MD: Rowman & Littlefield, 2018).

49. Esposito, *Living Thought*, 57. A reading similar to that of Miguel Vatter, *Between Form and Event: Machiavelli's Theory of Political Freedom* (New York: Fordham University Press, 2014).

50. As is evident from his output as a whole, Esposito never succumbs to defining a clear-cut primacy of power or the constituent moment. Even in his desire to find an affirmative way of philosophy, the Italian philosopher never pushes toward pure affirmativity. While this is already evident in works such as *Communitas*, it is certainly even clearer in the recent *Politics and Negation*, in which the attempt to seek a way to think politics beyond the contrastive pair of affirmation and negation is explicit.

51. See Esposito, *Communitas*.

52. See Esposito, *Vitam instituere*.

Four

Polis and *Polemos*
Esposito between Hannah Arendt and Simone Weil

Rita Fulco

Mankind's being-in-the-world, its communal existence: Hannah Arendt and Simone Weil contemplated this subject in particular, from different angles and perspectives, during one of the darkest periods of European history. The reciprocal implication of the thought of two of the greatest philosophers of the twentieth century, despite their undoubted differences, is the focus of Roberto Esposito's attention. Is such attention just the result of a fortuitous intersection, or does it have deeper roots than might appear?

In fact, in Categories of the Impolitical,[1] the pages that Esposito devoted to Simone Weil opened up new perspectives, above all that of the "impolitical" thinker, which had a significant impact on Weilian studies. Meanwhile, Arendt is undeniably present in Esposito's reflections and her philosophy is not infrequently used to weave together some important conceptual constellations. However, neither Weil nor Arendt could be considered among Esposito's key authors, unlike Spinoza, Nietzsche, Heidegger, Foucault, Deleuze, and even Machiavelli and Schmitt. It is therefore particularly significant that Esposito, almost twenty years after the first edition of the book that he dedicated to them in 1996,[2] felt the need to come up with a new introduction for the reprint in 2014,[3] in which he tries to sum up his relationship with Arendt and Weil. This shows, in my opinion, that this dialogue "in the margins" with Weil and Arendt is a milestone in the progression of Esposito's philosophy. We can better understand the reason for his interest if we interpret these "margins" not as synonymous with a "marginal place," that is, secondary, but rather as a *threshold* where *inside* and *outside* come into contact, yield to each other and implicate each other.

The margin concept that Esposito decides to explore together with Arendt and Weil is the one contained in the title of the book dedicated to them: *origin* and, in particular, the *origin of the political*, in regard to which Esposito follows the different paths proposed by the two thinkers.

The fundamental questions posed by Weil and Arendt, which Esposito echoes, are persistent: Does totalitarianism have a tradition, or is it born of destruction? How deep are its roots? The challenge is to understand what scope there is to create, though the categories of Western philosophy—democracy, law, order, conflict—a communal being-in-the-world that is not oppressive.

Philosophy according to Esposito: Genealogy and Actuality

On the occasion of Jean-Luc Nancy's death, Roberto Esposito, "responding" to the questions posed by Nancy in *The End of Philosophy and the Task of Thinking*,[4] takes up a theme dear to both of them, namely that of the essence and role of philosophy. This offers him the opportunity to revisit some fundamental moments of Western philosophy and the development of his own thought. For the purpose of a genealogical investigation into Esposito's philosophy, I believe it is interesting to analyze his arguments in brief. In fact, such an investigation is important for better understanding his relationship with Hannah Arendt and Simone Weil, two philosophers who were already present in his early works.

The concepts first called into question in Esposito's analysis of the essence of philosophy are those of "difference" and "repetition." The latter are closely related to concepts of "origin" and "actuality," which, as we shall see, are influenced by his reading of Arendt and Weil: "Philosophical reflection is marked by the continual repetition of the same questions which, depending on the context in which they are formulated, receive different answers each time. This philosophically pregnant relationship between repetition and difference refers to the relationship between origin and actuality. That something is repeated in different situations and at different times proves the impossibility of breaking the thread that links the present to its origin. Far from contradicting or opposing each other, origin and actuality belong to each other, illuminating each other."[5]

This is the position that Heidegger articulates in *What Is Philosophy?* concerning Greek philosophy.[6] Esposito agrees that questioning the meaning of philosophy involves a two-way path, from origin to actuality and vice versa. Indeed, it is true that without questioning the origin, actuality fails to find its deepest meaning, but it is equally true that without constant attention to its current legacy, the origin remains beyond grasp: "The constitutive place of philosophy is situated precisely in the chiasma delineated at the intersection of these two trajectories—at the point of tension between origin and actuality."[7]

Therefore, philosophy and history are not contingently, but essentially entwined. This means that in one and the same moment we must be aware of both the continuity and the differences that separate us from the origin. The historicity proper to philosophy is not a mere chronological succession. Rather, it is a succession of meanings; hence, it is transformation and differentiation but it is also a fracture, as it inaugurates a very complex relationship between ancient and contemporary times: "Contemporaneity should be understood, according to its literal meaning, as the coexistence and friction of heterogeneous times within the same time."[8]

A first response that emerges from this—Heideggerian—way of thinking about the essence of philosophy emphasizes the importance of temporality, and in particular of the relationship between the present and the past, which philosophy must assume responsibility for: "A philosopher—this is a first answer to the question of what philosophy is—is the one who inhabits the interstice between different and even opposing temporalities, experiencing the antinomic impact that arises from the co-presence of the archaic and the present. Philosophy is the ability to sustain this friction, giving voice to the dilemmas it entails."[9]

Esposito, however, is equally aware of the other answer to the question of the essence of philosophy, namely that of Deleuze and Guattari.[10] Without denying the question of the necessary relationship between philosophy and history, they bring into play another element, namely spatiality. The origin of thought cannot be thought of merely chronologically, without analyzing its relationship with space: "To the point that even the so-called national philosophies—German, French,

Italian—should be understood not in their identity, but in their mutual contamination. What matters, with respect to the question of what philosophy is, is not its territorial rooting, but, on the contrary, the antinomic tension between border and trespassing."[11]

In this tension philosophy's most proper activity is the formation and invention of concepts. While acknowledging his proximity to the position of Deleuze and Guattari, Esposito nonetheless maintains their answers are insufficient. Equally insufficient remains for him the answer provided by deconstruction, despite recognizing the innovative charge that Derrida has imprinted on it.[12]

According to Esposito, philosophy today needs reconstruction as well as deconstruction. It needs, therefore, to move away from a "reactive" and "negative" paradigm that has characterized much of Western thought. The latter—as one might say in the wake of Nietzsche—has operated in a "resentful" manner, precisely because it was captured by the "machine of the negative": "What does it mean that modern thought has predominantly thought in the negative form; and indeed that it has been so caught up in the machine of the negative as not to recognize it as such? It means that philosophical reflection, instead of affirmatively stating its concepts, has inferred them from the negation of their opposite."[13] A method that, for example, paradigmatically operates in the philosophico-political categories of Carl Schmitt, who assumes the category of "enemy"—and not that of "friend"—as the cornerstone of his idea of politics. Schmitt ontologizes the category of enmity and, consequently, his idea of politics assumes an "inimical" overtone. In reality, however, as Esposito underlines, this is typical of the entire twentieth-century philosophy. In fact, the semantic shift from the logical plane of "not" to the ontological plane of "nothing," to the practical plane of annihilation, overwhelmingly characterizes the twentieth-century conceptual lexicon.

Esposito therefore believes that the most urgent task of thought today is to rearticulate "affirmation" and "negation," working toward a reconversion of the negative within the context of an affirmative philosophy. However, he is also convinced that such a rearticulation should not "eliminate" the negative, since such an operation would keep philosophy within the paradigm of the negative. It is not surprising, then, that his path ends with Kant, or rather with Foucault's reading of Kant. In fact, Foucault confronts the present with the past and takes up the questions that the relationship between the present and the past poses for thought: "Thinking of the present as a philosophical problem does not mean immersing oneself integrally in it, adhering to its outermost surface. It means, on the contrary, confronting what is eternal in it. Once again, the relationship between origin and actuality, from which we started, returns."[14] It is important not to superimpose the "present" with the "actual" on a conceptual level. If one were to limit oneself to speaking of the "present," one would lose the very sense that Foucault—and Esposito with him—attributes to his way of thinking, which is always directed to the "here and now" as the source of thought: "While the present, the pure present, is what we are and, for this very reason, we are no longer, the present is what we are *not*, but we are becoming, the otherness that disturbs us and urges us, the possible becoming-other than us-being ourselves."[15]

The Origin: Philosophy and the Political

Starting from this general premise on the idea and tasks of philosophy, I would like to show that the thought of Hannah Arendt and Simone Weil does *not* have marginal importance in Roberto Esposito's philosophy, although it does not take center stage like that of Deleuze, Foucault and Machiavelli.[16] Arendt and Weil have been present since his earliest studies, and he dedicated a monograph to them both, *The Origin of the Political: Hannah Arendt or Simone Weil?*[17]—an interest that seems in line with Esposito's focus on actuality, given that, during one of the darkest periods of European history, Hannah Arendt and Simone Weil, from different angles and perspectives, reflected on mankind's being-in-the-world.

The concept that Esposito decides to explore together with Arendt and Weil is the one contained in the title of this important book: "origin" and, in particular, the "origin of the political," in regard to which Esposito follows different paths proposed by the two thinkers:

> *The Origin of the Political* analyzes various aspects of their relation that are attributable in particular to their tension between origin and history, between the originary war (that is the Trojan War) and the constitution of the political city; or, in the words of Arendt and Weil, to the tension between *polemos* and *polis*. How does origin relate to what follows?

Does it do so from outside or from inside, as a beginning or its opposite, as a genetic moment or as a point of contrast? Is War part of a politics that always implies an agonistic dimension, or the negative it leaves in its wake?[18]

Why, ultimately, is it so important for Weil and Arendt to question the origin of the political? Their reflection is always provoked by actuality; therefore, their questioning of the origin makes sense in relation to their understanding of their own present. For Weil and Arendt, the present was that of totalitarianism, a specter that even today, unfortunately, continues to circulate in Europe and throughout the world, albeit in different forms. Biopolitics at work in national socialism has today assumed less explicitly violent forms, but it can always change again into *thanatopolitics*: Esposito draws attention to this risk, scrutinizing its transformations.

This issue recurs almost obsessively in Arendt and Weil, both explicitly and between the lines of their works, throughout their lives. The challenge is to understand what scope there is to create, though the categories of Western philosophy, a communal being-in-the-world that is not oppressive.

At the origin of Western history, both Weil and Arendt, however, identify a war, the Trojan War—hence the importance of the *Iliad* in the reflections of both thinkers—which also marks the beginning of Western politics; war that does not end with an armistice but with the total destruction of the city: "Politics in this sense, is born at the heart of a *polemos* whose outcome is the destruction of a *polis*. It is upon this constitutive antinomy that the two authors measure themselves, fully aware of what it means not only in relation to the reconstruction of the initial event itself, but also in relation to the interpretation of everything that follows."[19] The specter of this beginning of history, coinciding with destruction, will always haunt the history and politics of the West, forcing us to question the role that this beginning has had in forming the conceptual constellations that underlie them: "It is this bond between origin and politics—the political destiny of the origin but also the constitutive originarity of politics—that captures the attention of both thinkers, who had already made the *polis* the primary concern of their reflexion. [. . .] The question to be resolved is, precisely, that of relationship between origin—a specific originarity—and what originates from it."[20]

Although Arendt and Weil identify the causes of oppression from different theoretical and political standpoints, both lucidly and extensively analyze the oppressive nature of power. Esposito manages to highlight the most original features and most enlightening insights of their philosophy and, above all, to emphasize the peculiarity of their conclusions: "Arendt reads the phenomenon of totalitarianism in terms of absolute exceptionality [. . .]. Totalitarianism [. . .] is the product of different subjective choices taken at specific points that, from that very point, are consequently rendered inevitable by subsuming the overall context in which they were articulated."[21] Therefore, Arendt emphasizes the substantial extraneousness of totalitarianism in relation to the previous forms that oppression assumed in the West. It is an event that is not due to an original predisposition of Western political categories but to the convergence of individual wills, which warped these categories in an unprecedented, unpredictable way. Weil takes a diametrically opposed position: it is true that totalitarianism is a new phenomenon in its twentieth-century form, yet it is *internal* to the logic of Western politics. If we dig genealogically into the tangle of European history, we can trace some totalitarian aspects not only in modern history but also in ancient history. Taking an approach that may seem paradoxical, Weil identifies some totalitarian characters in French imperialism and, above all, in Roman imperialism, as Esposito rightly notes: "They can be extended to the point of constituting a line of continuity that concurs ultimately with the dominant line of Western history, and, what is more important, with its constitutively politic dimension."[22]

As Weil asserts in her analyses of the *Iliad* and Thucydides's works, force is the basis of human life. However, Esposito highlights that, for Weil, such force has an *internal* limit. It is like the waves of the sea, which must necessarily descend having reached a certain height. Nazi fascism, similarly, at its apogee had to yield to the force of the allies. According to Weil, however, grasping this limit is a "counter-natural" possibility, because the law of nature is that of the supremacy of the strongest, as emerges in the Thucydides's dialogue between Meli and Athenians. Justice, therefore, is possible only if human beings correspond to a reality that goes beyond the law of nature. Consequently, spiritual education in politics is necessary.[23]

Similarly, according to Hannah Arendt, force and violence dominate human relationships. However, for her the most powerful barrier to force is neither internal nor counternatural. The limit is putting force into shape, as law does. It is no coincidence that Arendt considers ancient Rome to be the bearer of civilization precisely because of the law. For her, justice is a just law that must be supervised. The *polis* should be the place where justice and law coincide. Therefore, her idea of justice is immanent and positive. In this respect, Arendt is distant from Weil, who criticizes both the law and ancient Rome.[24]

The way to find a *pharmacon* within the Political but against the violence of the Political appears to be precluded in Weil's thought. However, and this is particularly the case in her later years, Weil's philosophy can be read as an attempt to rethink institutions in relation to life. As she wrote in 1943: "Above those institutions which are concerned with protecting rights and persons and democratic freedoms, others must be invented for the purpose of exposing and abolishing everything in contemporary life which buries the soul under injustice, lies, and ugliness. They must be invented, for they are unknown, and it is impossible to doubt that they are indispensable."[25]

In fact, political *institutions* are not empty vessels, mechanisms that work regardless of the people who rule them; rather, they are places in which wills, hopes, needs, and plans are addressed and take shape on the basis of some shared value: "The first objective of forms of political institutions is to allow the head of government and the people to express their feelings. They are analogous to love letters, exchanges of rings, and other tokens between lovers. [. . .] Political institutions essentially constitute a symbolic language."[26]

From this point of view, we can trace the affinity between Weil's search for a new relationship between institutions and the daily life of those who are governed and Esposito's recent thought, which emphasizes the importance of the relationship between institutions and life.

In his latest essay on the instituting thought, Esposito aptly emphasized that the creativity of the institutions must effectively respond to the need to institute life: life and institutions cannot be two diverging or even opposite dimensions.[27] The inseparable bond between *polis* and *bios*, between politics and life, already masterfully explored by Esposito since the early 2000s, has come back with a vengeance in the philosophical and political debate given that the pandemic has once again posed the question of "immunity."[28] Taking inspiration from Foucault's latest works, Esposito finds that the role of contemporary philosophy is to integrate the biopolitical with the instituting paradigm. A process within which the instituting thought should, on its part, try to overcome the juxtaposition between life and institution, which is most obvious in the biopolitical paradigm. Both the deadly, static view of the institutions and the view of life as impossible to institute should be overcome.

It is from such a perspective that Simone Weil's hope that the symbolic language of the institutions can "translate" the needs and wishes of the people who help maintain and innovate them and who, therefore, pin their hopes on them can be understood. The legislative and judicial apparatuses reflect the values of a specific community. Laws then play a preferential role in building and maintaining the institutions. However surprising—in light of her radical criticism of the law—Simone Weil claims that the only ways we can save ourselves from the arbitrariness of personal perspectives driven by the most diverse interests are precisely the laws and, consequently, the morality of magistrates and rulers, who must issue, interpret and apply them.

It is no surprise that Weil, especially in the final years of her life, focused on the need for "spiritual education" for individual citizens and, above all, for all those responsible for governance. For Weil, the central question, in the absence of the intrinsic "goodness" of the Political, is *metanoia*:[29] it is not an action that can be solely ascribed to the religious horizon.[30] Rather, it is the *conversio* of the mind: changing the mind because, though it seemed infallible, it has failed, transforming power that should have been at the service of life into a terrible instrument of death. To avoid this deviation, we must be able to clearly comprehend it in order to recognize and prevent it, and to do so, *metanoia* is essential. It is from this perspective that we should read the profound pages that Roberto Esposito devotes to the concept of *hero*, which Weil develops, taking her cue from Plato, by establishing an interesting dialectic between the two gods that embody this figure: "Eros battles Ares without utilizing arms, prescinded from force. But he does *battle with* him and does so *forcefully* with a strength that is not only equal but also superior to that of Ares. In the end, this allows Eros to grasp Ares *in the palm of his hand*. Despite its contrary inspiration, Love too fights. It wages war even against the god of war. It opposes war, but with a peace that resembles war, except for the fact that is not a simple war but its contrary: a war of war, *on* war."[31]

Esposito finds the connection between *love* and *nous*—evident in the *metanoia* that Weil hopes for, so that there is a connection between the ability to love and the ability to think and therefore the ability to think of a struggle in the name of Eros, rather than Ares—in Arendt's last work, the unfinished *The Life of the Mind*.[32] The "hero of thought," or "heroic thought"[33] in this connection acquires those warlike traits that keep him standing in the conflict, ready to make up his mind at any moment, judging the justness of a cause, without giving up the fight: "*He is no longer obliged to flee from conflict, because in the final analysis He coincides with it, for conflict is his origin and destiny to the extent that only in battle can He finally 'remain,' having found rest and truce in the 'immobility' of the movement [. . .]. He*—the thought—no longer limits itself to battle. He is by now, like the "first war," the battle to which we are eternally entrusted."[34]

Thought, therefore, is the margin in which Weil and Arendt—joined by Esposito—contend with the origin of history and the origin of the political, entrusting it with the task of conducting a fair fight. This is certainly why Esposito is convinced that the reflection that both philosophers dedicate to thought is of central importance: "If I had written this book today, I would have paused longer on the meaning that both thinkers attribute to the dimension of thought."[35] Even if it is an activity of the mind, apparently specially focused on interiority, it can acquire a communal and political dimension, since it is closely linked to the faculty of *judgment*. Judgment, as Arendt argues in several works, is the most political of the human faculties: "Judgement is the most political faculty not only because it is the means by which we decide on an action, between what is right and wrong, or between the just and the unjust, but also because [. . .] it explicates itself while sharing out something for everyone."[36]

Therefore, we return to mankind's being-in-the-world, its communal existence, which ultimately constitutes the origin and goal of Esposito's reflections on Weil and Arendt. Far from being a deviation, it falls firmly within the progression of Esposito's philosophy. It constitutes almost a sign indicating a direction that has always remained constant, despite a few "hairpin turns." As Simone Weil put it, "thinking is a heroic act": then as now, as always, it is impossible to make political decisions geared toward justice if we do not start with a *rigorous*—and thus heroic—thought exercise.

Impolitical and/but Instituting Thought?

In *Categories of the Impolitical*, published in Italy in 1988, the pages that Esposito devoted to Simone Weil opened up new perspectives. Above all, his view of Weil as "impolitical" thinker, had a significant impact on Weilian studies. The fact that Esposito placed Hannah Arendt among the impolitical thinkers has raised some issues. Esposito, aware that readers might be struck by such an image, explains in what terms Arendt can be considered an impolitical thinker:

> If I ascribe Arendt an impolitical stance—only problematically and partially, on the basis of her final writings—it is not because she adopts an external point of view from which to observe the political. Arendt always remains rigorously internal to politics, with the possible exception of the line of flight that her final work opens to the "in-between" time of thought. If Arendt is an impolitical thinker, it is because she gradually constricts the available space in which the political can be positively identified: the result is that any understanding of the political as something plural is fundamentally unrepresentable (as a plurality or as natality, considering that the origin, for Arendt, is always plural).[37]

I believe that the fact that Arendt and Weil are placed among the impolitical thinkers helps us clarify what Esposito means by "impolitical": certainly, neither an anti-politics nor an a-political attitude. Such terms are indeed formed starting from what they deny, namely politics. For this reason, they inevitably remain intertwined with politics. Esposito thinks that the impolitical—and therefore the thought of those who fall within its perimeter—is characterized by the rejection of the tendency to conciliation and by the rejection of the theological-political principle of vertical representation. Worldly power fails to represent a higher instance; in other words, there is no power that can embody the Good. On the one hand, this attests to the unfounded character of the Political; on the other, it lends radical critical power to the impolitical thought. This critique provokes a profound rethinking of politics itself. Perhaps there can be no "just" government. However, we need to think of institutions that tend to be more and more just. It is important to be aware that the conflict between the forces that inhabit the institutions is unavoidable. These opposing forces must be neither denied nor neutralized but governed. Therefore, the political realism and the ability to see great politics should be an inseparable. This synthetic definition of the impolitical is in line with the choice to place Weil in this horizon. With regard to Arendt, Esposito is interested in the way she thinks of "plurality" and political community, without any reference to a higher, theological instance. Arendt radically affirms the autonomy of the political: indeed, she excludes the economic sphere and basic needs from the definition of politics. Arendt focuses on the analysis of "horizontal" conflict and on the rethinking of the "instituting" moment of politics, which Esposito takes up in his most recent works. However, we must point out that Esposito dedicated an essay to the relationship between *polis* and community in Arendt. In this essay he questions the Arendtian overlap between the "public dimension" and being-in-common—especially in *The Human Condition*. Esposito's complex interpretation of *communitas* cannot be identified with the life in the *polis*, as described by Arendt.[38]

Esposito wonders whether Hannah Arendt is a thinker of community or intersubjectivity. In order to answer this question, he clarifies what the "community" means for him. Is community synonymous with *polis*? If it were, Arendt would be a thinker of the community. For Arendt, the *polis* is a plural space of mutual belonging, in which human beings act. In *The Human Condition*,[39] she states that the public dimension and being in common are synonymous. Unfortunately, I cannot dwell here on her notion of subjectivity. Anyway, I want to emphasize that, for Esposito, community does not coincide with such plural space. The *communitas* is not the *polis* nor the *res publica*. Arendt speaks of a world of things, which exists in-between those who have it in common; this world unites and separates them. Thus, there are multiple subjects that relate to each other. It is a form of intersubjectivity that is based on mutual recognition. For Esposito, on the contrary, in the *communitas* the relationship between subjects is broken: the *munus* of the *communitas* indicates a loss, a lack, a debt, an obligation, a gift, which one is obliged to give. Therefore, the subject is expropriated, exposed to its own other. Community is not relationship nor communication. Esposito affirms that human beings have in common "the impossibility of 'making' the community that they have always been."[40]

Esposito points out that some Arendtian notions are close to his thought, such as that of *limit*, linked to finitude, which emerges in her works on Augustine and Kant.[41] However, in his opinion, these intuitions remain in the background compared to the conception of the *polis*, in which the intersubjective relationship dominates.

Yet, in his volume on the concept of *Institution*, Esposito decides to return to Arendt's thought in a more articulate and detailed manner. Arendt's political philosophy is part and parcel of the "instituting paradigm" that Esposito does not find developed, for example, by Michel

Foucault. However, the problematic point of Arendt's thought consists precisely of her inability to elaborate on biopolitics in an affirmative sense, since she considers only its thanatological aspects

> To begin with, one must acknowledge that the twentieth century's most powerful instituting thought is that of Arendt. Her entire work revolves around the attempt to construct political institutions capable /of resisting the impact of time, outside of the sovereign regime accepted as the unchallenged presupposition by the overwhelming majority of the thinkers of modern political thought. It is precisely on this basis that one can judge both the originality of her perspective in relation to the surrounding philosophical perspectives and the divergence of her thought from the semantics of biopolitics, which she assumes, but merely negatively, considering its risks, rather than opportunities.[42]

Esposito emphasizes Arendt's distance from the Hobbesian conception of order, from any monistic register and from contractualist theories. In contrast, he underlines the proximity of Arendt's theses to Montesquieu and the theory of the separation of powers; a theory that will be taken up by American federalism. On Arendt's account, the multiplicity of institutions protects against the concentration and accumulation of power. According to Esposito, Arendt's originality lies not so much in her analysis of institutional mechanisms as in the importance she attributed to the instituting principle itself: "If American federalism has resisted growing depoliticization longer than European countries, it is because the founding fathers placed the principle of legitimacy in the act of foundation itself, thereby preserving the connection between permanence and change to which the intrinsic meaning of institutions refers."[43]

The fact that contemporary politics is the victim of continuous relapses into the sovereign paradigm is due to the continuous oscillation between "instituting" and "instituted," where the instituting pole seems to prevail: "For Arendt, politics coincides with the creation of the *novum* to the point that in the continuous proliferation of beginnings it loses any form of stability. None of the characteristics she bestows upon political action—plurality, irreversibility, novelty—can ensure its permanence in time."[44]

In Esposito's view, Arendt's radicalization of the instituting logic entails the identification of political action with the genetic moment, misplacing the second meaning of the Greek term *archein*. The latter could also mean "to command," but Arendt considers only the "initiating": human beings, due to their always being "born," are, first and foremost, "initiators" originating history and politics. Thus, Arendt is far from a "biologistic" concept of birth, which would, in any case, be stretched toward death. Rather, it is about an "act of radical renewal which escapes the natural cycle and brings about the experience that is symbolic in nature. [. . .] Thence a contrast in principle between institution and biological life."[45]

In opposition to Foucault, politics for Arendt is an action unconditioned by the needs of life. These must be kept out of its horizon, or else the political space would result weakened, as happened, for example, in the French Revolution. The self-destructive drift of the French Revolution did not take place during the American Revolution, precisely because the latter was not subdued by natural needs and thus remained within an institutional dialectic. Nonetheless, the French Revolution seems to have marked a moment of irreconcilable fracture between biological life and instituting praxis: "At the origin of this separation we find the Christian notion of the sanctity of life, which became the supreme good to which all others must be sacrificed."[46] A primacy reinforced by the sanctity of life professed in Christianity, culminating in the process of socialization of late modernity, where individual life is thought of as closely linked to the development of the human species: "It was then that all human activities, previously distinct from one another, were mobilized in defence of this single living process, resulting in depoliticization which affected the whole of the society [. . .]. From then on, biological life became the unstoppable surge that engulfs the political action."[47]

It is not a coincidence that the question of the relationship between biological life and institutions constitutes one of the most important themes of Esposito's most recent reflection whose development we cannot follow at this point. I was interested in emphasizing the decisive role that Arendt's reflection had in relation to some of the theoretical presuppositions of Esposito's thought.

With regard to Simone Weil, the question is more articulated. Esposito affirms that Simone Weil can illuminate our time, but only by contrast—starting from what we have lost sight of. Esposito refers, in particular, to the fact that for Simone Weil human existence has a root in the supernatural; for her, there is a relationship between reality and transcendence, between politics and spirituality. This relationship is difficult to recognize in our current situation, in which politics is secularized, that is, removed from faith as well as from thought. Simone Weil criticized this politics, which is reduced to pure technical-economic administration. In any case, Esposito indicates a way to understand the Weilian link between politics, rights and spirituality:

Her thesis is that if one departs from the demand for rights—as the post war culture of the left had done—one remains within the vocabulary of bargaining, effective only if backed by the force capable of imposing it. If instead one inverts the perspective, departing from duties toward any human being, one enters a different horizon governed by the Justice itself. Only then, according to Weil can a new moral civilization arise, giving primacy to the needs of human beings. Needs of the body—food, warmth, sleep, hygiene, clean air. And the needs of the soul—truth, freedom, intimacy, as well as grounding in spaces and settings necessary for life.[48]

As previously stated, Simone Weil's thought is still necessary if we want to rethink the relationship between life and institutions, since it offers a reading of the Law that renews its possibilities from within. Not incidentally, Esposito believes that in some of Weil's London writings there are ideas from which it is still possible today to learn new ways of doing politics and new way of starting again, not from the camp of the victors, but from that of the vanquished: "The defeat, notwithstanding all the tragedies it brings, has a constitutive force which the victory lacks at times. This is why the institutions to come have to be thought from the defeat before it has become a victory. Starting from the new source of legitimacy which cannot but be a renewed idea of justice."[49]

Trying to summarize, Esposito's relationship with Arendt and Weil seems to be fundamental, but also slightly asymmetrical. Hannah Arendt deals in a philosophically systematic way with some of the issues that are most important to Esposito, particularly as regards the political. Weil—partly due to her untimely death—addresses the question of institutions, but always starting from some contingencies and within occasional writings. Her systematic writings concern the relationship with Marxism. Her last unfinished work, *Enracinement*, is placed on a threshold between politics and spirituality; this threshold is not easy to cross for a critic of political theology such as Esposito.

However, having taken note of this difference, I think I can say that Esposito's thought as a whole is indebted to the two philosophers. It would have been profoundly different, without their categories. In addition, it is important to underline that the studies on Weil and Arendt are indebted to the analysis that Esposito has dedicated to them.

I believe Esposito himself acknowledges his debt in the new preface to *The Origin of the Political* in 2014. After talking about the importance of the concept of the *impersonal* and its link with that of the impolitical, Esposito adds:

> With this final reference, which touches upon questions of theology and politics—and indeed upon the very functioning of the theological-political apparatus—I come to my most recent work which traces the discontinuous line connecting the notions of "the impolitical" and "the impersonal." The following pages, which were written almost twenty years ago regarding the relation between two of the most radical thinkers of the twentieth century, place these notions into tension with each other, while in the process bearing witness to the centrality of Hannah Arendt and Simone Weil's thought for my own.[50]

In conclusion, it seems important to me to take up a central point. That is, the relationship between war and politics. We have shown how Esposito addresses the fundamental relationship between politics and war, from which politics seems to originate. He has done so, in particular, by focusing on Weil and Arendt's interpretation of the Trojan War. According to their analyses, Esposito sheds light on the deep roots of totalitarianism and thanatopolitics. The question that still resonates today is: to what extent does the Trojan War—that "original war" symbolic of all war—constitute the demonstration of an ineradicable violence of the Political? For Hannah Arendt, the political is not irredeemably violent, while for Weil force is what dominates politics. The two philosophers, however, agree on one diriment point: thought is the only remedy to combat violence; the only way to be-in-the-world without force and violence having supremacy. A thesis with which Esposito fully agrees. For this reason, too, I believe that the arguments carried out in this contribution can demonstrate that the comparison with Weil and Arendt constitutes not a deviation, but rather a decisive stage in Esposito's thought, even of the last instituting phase.

Notes

1. Roberto Esposito, *Categories of the Impolitical* (New York: Fordham University Press, 2015).

2. Roberto Esposito, *L'origine della politica: Hannah Arendt o Simone Weil* (Rome: Donzelli, 2014).

3. Roberto Esposito, *The Origin of the Political: Hannah Arendt or Simone Weil?*, trans. Vincenzo Binetti and Gareth Williams (New York: Fordham University Press, 2017).

4. Jean-Luc Nancy, "The End of Philosophy and the Task of Thinking," *Philosophy World Democracy*, July 29, 2021, https://www.philosophy-world-democracy.org/other-beginning/the-end-of-philosophy.

5. Roberto Esposito, "What Is Philosophy?—Tribute to Jean-Luc Nancy," *Philosophy World Democracy*, September 14, 2021, https://www.philosophy-world-democracy.org/other-beginning/what-is-philosophy. The fundamental theoretical cores of the essay had been discussed and published in Italian in Roberto Esposito, "Che cos'è la filosofia?," in *Termini della politica: Politica e pensiero*, vol. 2 (Milan: Mimesis, 2018), 175–87. On the role of Esposito's philosophy within the broader horizon of Italian thought, see Dario Gentili and Elettra Stimilli, eds., *Differenze italiane: Politica e filosofia: Mappe e sconfinamenti* (Rome: Deriveapprodi, 2015); Enrica Lisciani Petrini and Giusi Strummiello, eds., *Effetto Italian Thought* (Macerata, Italy: Quodlibet, 2017); Corrado Claverini, *La tradizione filosofica italiana: Quattro paradigmi interpretativi* (Macerata, Italy: Quodlibet, 2021).

6. See Martin Heidegger, *What Is Philosophy?*, trans. Jean T. Wilde and William Kluback (New Haven, CT: College and University Press, 1958).

7. Esposito, "What Is Philosophy?."

8. Esposito, "What Is Philosophy?."

9. Esposito, "What Is Philosophy?."

10. Gilles Deleuze and Felix Guattari, *What Is Philosophy?*, trans. Hugh Tomlinson and Graham Burchell (New York: Columbia University Press, 1996).

11. Esposito, "What Is Philosophy?."

12. An interesting reading of the relationship between deconstruction, philosophy and politics in Derrida is that of Caterina Resta. In particular, see Caterina Resta, *L'evento dell'altro: Etica e politica in Jacques Derrida* (Turin: Bollati Boringhieri, 2003); Caterina Resta, *La passione dell'impossibile: Saggi su Jacques Derrida* (Genova: il melangolo, 2016); Caterina Resta, "Bio-thanato-politica: Una questione di vita e di morte," in Elettra Stimilli, ed., *Decostruzione o biopolitica?* (Macerata, Italy: Quodlibet, 2017), 39–54.

13. Esposito, "What Is Philosophy?."

14. Esposito, "What Is Philosophy?." I reflected on the relationship between Esposito and Foucault in Rita Fulco, "Crítica y productividad de las instituciones: El quiasmo entre Roberto Esposito y Michel Foucault," *Dorsal: Revista de estudios foucaultianos*, no. 14 (2023): 123–39.

15. Esposito, "What Is Philosophy?."

16. Regarding Machiavelli, it is remarkable that Roberto Esposito was one of the first to emphasize Simone Weil's admiration for Machiavelli's realism. On this issue and on the relationship between Weil's thought and Machiavelli's,

I focused in Rita Fulco, "Pensare l'evento nella congiuntura: Simone Weil e Machiavelli," in Rita Fulco and Andrea Moresco, eds., *Sull'evento: Filosofia, storia, biopolitica: Almanacco di Filosofia e Politica* 4 (Macerata, Italy: Quodlibet, 2022), 313–22.

17. Esposito, *Origin of the Political*.
18. Esposito, *Origin of the Political*, X.
19. Esposito, *Origin of the Political*, 13.
20. Esposito, *Origin of the Political*, 13.
21. Esposito, *Origin of the Political*, 4–5.
22. Esposito, *Origin of the Political*, 5.
23. On the relationships between politics, justice and vulnerability, see Rita Fulco, *Soggettività e potere: Ontologia della vulnerabilità in Simone Weil* (Macerata, Italy: Quodlibet, 2020); Caterina Resta, "Vulnerable Existences," in Silvia Benso, ed., *Rethinking Life: Italian Philosophy in Precarious Times* (New York: SUNY, 2022), 133–44.
24. For an excellent overview on Arendt's thought, see Simona Forti, *Hannah Arendt tra filosofia e politica* (Milan: Mondadori, 2006).
25. Simone Weil, "Human Personality," in *Simone Weil, An Anthology*, ed. Sian Miles, trans. Richard Rees (London: Penguin, 2005), 98.
26. Simone Weil, "The Legitimacy of the Provisional Government," trans. Peter Winch, *Philosophical Investigations* 10, no. 2 (April 1987): 87–88. On this question, in particular the relationship between legality and legitimacy within the Weilian project of a new constitution for post-war France, I have reflected in Rita Fulco, "'Seul ce qui est juste est légitime': Limite du politique et obligation de justice," in Robert Chenavier and Thomas Pavel, eds., *Simone Weil, réception et transposition* (Paris: Classiques Garnier, 2019), 307–20.
27. I'm referring to the volumes Roberto Esposito, *Instituting Thought: Three Paradigms of Political Ontology*, trans. Mark William Epstein (Cambridge: Polity, 2021), but also to the six volumes of *Almanacco di Filosofia e politica* (Macerata, Italy: Quodlibet, 2019–24) of which Esposito is the editor in chief and whose reflections are focused, in particular, on the subject of institutions. I have discussed on the *institutional turn* of Roberto Esposito more thoroughly in Rita Fulco, "A Political Ontology for Europe: Roberto Esposito's Instituent Paradigm," *Continental Philosophy Review*, no. 54 (2021): 367–86, Open Access: <https://doi.org/10.1007/s11007-021-09542-z>.
28. See Roberto Esposito, *Bios: Biopolitics and Philosophy*, trans. Timothy Campbell (Minneapolis: University of Minnesota Press, 2008); Roberto Esposito, *Immunitas: The Protection and Negation of Life*, trans. Zakiya Hanafi (Cambridge: Polity, 2011). With regard to the thought of Roberto Esposito, see Inna Viriasova and Antonio Calcagno, eds., *Roberto Esposito: Biopolitics and Philosophy* (New York: SUNY, 2018); and Tilottama Rajan and Antonio Calcagno, eds., *Roberto Esposito: New Directions in Biophilosophy* (Edinburgh: Edinburgh University Press, 2021); but also Antonio Calcagno, ed., *Contemporary Italian Political Philosophy* (Albany: State University of New York Press, 2015); Timothy Campbell, "Bios,

Immunity, Life: The thought of Roberto Esposito," in Esposito, *Bios: Biopolitics and Philosophy*, 7–42.

29. *Metanoia* (Ancient Greek: μετάνοια). It's meaning is "changing one's mind." The theological meaning is "conversion."

30. On this issue, see Rita Fulco, "Le rapport entre politique et religions," *Cahiers Simone Weil*, no. 3 (2017): 325–43.

31. Esposito, *Origin of the Political*, 69.

32. Hannah Arendt, *Life of the Mind*, vols. 1–2 (San Diego, CA: Harcourt Brace Jovanovich, 1978).

33. These are Esposito's expressions: "It will not be surprising, then, if, in the end—in the final metaphor to which Arendt seems to almost entrust her own legacy—the hero of thought, heroic thought, assumes the very same 'bellicose' traits that Weil bequeathed to us throughout the course of her life's work" (Esposito, *Origin of the Political*, 77).

34. Esposito, *Origin of the Political*, 78.

35. Esposito, *Origin of the Political*, XI.

36. Esposito, *Origin of the Political*, XII.

37. Esposito, *Categories of the Impolitical*, 8.

38. Roberto Esposito, "Polis o communitas?," in *Termini della politica: I: Comunità, Immunità, biopolitica* (Milan: Mimesis), 65–76. On the Esposito's concept of "community," see Roberto Esposito, *Communitas: The Origin and Destiny of Community* (Stanford, CA: Stanford University Press, 2010).

39. Hannah Arendt, *The Human Condition* (Chicago, IL: University of Chicago Press, 2018).

40. Esposito, "Polis o communitas?," 69.

41. On these issues, see, Esposito, *Origin of the Political*, 14–16; and Hannah Arendt, *Love and Saint Augustine* (Chicago, IL: University of Chicago Press, 1996).

42. Roberto Esposito, *Institution*, trans. Zakiya Hanafi (Cambridge: Polity, 2022), 81.

43. Esposito, *Institution*, 82.

44. Esposito, *Institution*, 82.

45. Esposito, *Institution*, 83.

46. Esposito, *Institution*, 83–84.

47. Esposito, *Institution*, 84.

48. Roberto Esposito, preface to Rita Fulco and Tommaso Greco, eds., *L'Europa di Simone Weil: Filosofia e nuove istituzioni* (Macerata, Italy: Quodlibet, 2018), 8–9. On the question of Law in Simone Weil, Esposito had already reflected in *Categories of the Impolitical*, 145–55.

49. Esposito, *Prefazione*, 8.

50. Esposito, preface, *Origin of the Political*, xv. About the concept of "impersonal" between Esposito and Weil, see Antonio Calcagno, "Repositioning Simone Weil and Roberto Esposito: Life, the Impersonal and the Renunciant Obligation of the Good," in Tilottama and Calcagno, eds., *Roberto Esposito: New Directions in Biophilosophy*, 193–207.

Five

The Political in Roberto Esposito and Carl Schmitt

Francesco Marchesi

Roberto Esposito's conception of politics is the conception of politics of Carl Schmitt. Politics, or better "the political," is for both these authors the conflict, or the "Two," that dwells in every concrete political order. Esposito inherited this claim, during the seventies and the early eighties, from the Italian, workerist and left-wing interpretation of the Schmittian work, made up especially by Mario Tronti. However, starting from this assumption that remains the same throughout his philosophical trajectory, Esposito derives contrastive implications in different periods of his production: the antifoundational theory of democracy and community in the impolitical years, the rejection of any kind of political form in the biopolitics period, and the (also Machiavellian in Esposito's view) identification between order and conflict in his works on Machiavelli and in his recent institutional turn. This chapter does not try to account the role of Carl Schmitt during the whole intellectual biography of Roberto Esposito; instead it tries to show how two specific Schmittian theses about politics, the role of decision and the figure of enmity, profoundly shape the philosophical reflection of Esposito. They are, in other words, the origin and the theoretical foundation of Esposito's philosophy.

It has been a steady practice to describe Carl Schmitt as an ambivalent, if unambiguous thinker.[1] This persists despite the role of Schmitt's theses in fulfilling fundamental needs within contemporary political thought: among others, the break with a strong origin, the discovery of an empty structure at the heart of politics, and a rereading of European modernity in light of these philosophical points.

> Schmitt's greatness lies in his genealogy, i.e., in his idea that in order to understand politics, it is necessary to understand the concrete origin of a concrete structure of power and knowledge. And this origin must be not be understood as a stable origin, but rather an energy, an imbalance, a conflict within every order, which relativizes it but also keeps it alive; concreteness, in Schmitt, always comes with nihilism. The theoretical discovery of the "origin of politics" thus has as a counterpart a practice that can be revolutionary (activating a new origin in the conflict: revolutions, constituent power) but also a "politics of origin," i.e., the extra-legal, decisionist defense of an existing political order, through reference to its originary legitimacy as a stabilizing factor against internal enemies (and therefore, a stabilization through exclusion).

Here the ambivalence of a mediation emerges in order to grow over time into a rigid alternative and a relation of mutual exclusion. It is the systemic impossibility, so to speak, of Schmitt's thought to articulate form and energy, order and conflict, thereby producing interpretive oscillations between a conflictualist and empty result and a homogenizing, excluding, and full anchorage. This can be defined, preliminarily and thus summarily, as a manifestation of Schmitt's Hegelianism,[2] whose substitution with Marx as a reference for a theory of conflict can perhaps illuminate some of the widespread approaches in contemporary thought.[3] We will try to show this by first focusing on the production of this elementary alternative through a process of disarticulating form and energy, in order to then analyze the first conceptual effects on the Schmittian doctrine of political conflict.

Form or Energy

Consider the following references in which Roberto Esposito tries to define what is politics:

The antipolitical cannot be the same thing as the impolitical because it already the same thing as the political. It descends from the political, and it reproposes the political in the very act of negating it. The antipolitical is not something contrary to the political, but simply its mirror image: a manner of doing politics that consists in setting itself against politics. That is, it works by putting to use the same enmity that characterizes the political in its essential form.[4]

From that came cities—the political life that opened the horizon of history, although without ever cutting the thread that binds it to its biological roots. However different the regime of nomos may be from that of bios, it has never separated from it. If anything, their relationship has become tighter and tighter, to the point that it is impossible today to talk about "politics" without mentioning life. Institutions are at the center of this shift. They are the bridge by means of which law and politics shape societies, differentiating and uniting them.[5]

These quotations represent only a sketch of Esposito's notion of politics, but we can note from them two specific observations. First, that they cover the entire intellectual biography, or a large part of it, from the eighties to today, and, second, that they show a concept of the political that remains, in its central conceptual framework, the same. The concept of political is essentially enmity as a tool of building a, necessarily empty, political form (sovereignty, immunity, institution). As we will see, this is an interpretation—among others—of the concept of the political of Carl Schmitt. Now let's see what are the main characteristics of this model.

In order to think politics in its specificity (namely, outside of a direct relation with the normativity immanent to the economic and the social), then it is necessary to construct conditions marked by the character of undecidability—this assumption seems to be the foundation of a large part of recent political philosophy. However, undecidability, informality, and disorder are ideas of a primary structure, whose prerogatives are influential for what is found above them. In Schmitt, the awareness of the essential nature of what does not have the usual form of essence and foundation finds one of its primary points of reference. One of his best-known passages deals with the spirit of exception: "Contrary to the imprecise terminology that is found in popular literature, a borderline concept is not a vague concept, but one pertaining to the outermost sphere. This definition of sovereignty must therefore be associated with a borderline case and not with routine."[6] The systemic character of the exception as the basis of a politics that is taken here, typically, as decision, is not external to the strategic results that are to be obtained. In short, it is not simply one methodological aspect among others. The two-way link between the specificity-limit of the situation of exception and its generality has the following function: "The assertion that the exception is truly appropriate for the juristic definition of sovereignty has a systematic, legal-logical foundation. [. . .] Because a general norm [. . .] can never encompass a total exception, the decision that a real exception exists cannot therefore be entirely derived from this norm."[7]

In this way, the conceptual knot in this opening passage of Schmitt's discourse links two different moments of the argument: the methodological presupposition of the plural and differentiated nature of the primary elements of politics, which the juridical tradition would to some extent try to relativize and place at the margins, and the epistemological thesis of the central and systemic location of these differently fundamental structures. The blurring of the exception not so much into the rule,[8] but into the normality of its epistemic constitution, concerns precisely these aspects. These aspects preside over the accomplishment of a double theoretical and political result. Offering this image as the origin of politics, at least as a limit-possibility, first allows the relevance of the current system to be bracketed for the purposes of the decision, in this way opening the path to the emptying of the foundations of politics as such. Strictly speaking, however, rather than blurring, we can note in this renewed schema the disarticulation between a personal instance carried out on a level of undecidability and a normative background, or, we will see elsewhere, an energetic and conflictual background that is no longer capable of affected the former.

> A jurisprudence concerned with ordinary day-to-day questions has practically no interest in the concept of sovereignty. [. . .] Such a jurisprudence confronts the extreme case disconcertingly, for not every extraordinary measure, not every police emergency measure or emergency decree, is necessarily an exception. What characterizes an exception is principally unlimited authority, which means the suspension of the entire existing order. [. . .] The existence of the state is undoubted proof of its superiority over the validity of the legal norm. The decision frees itself from all normative times and becomes in the true sense absolute.[9]

Separation and distinction, but not without reason or rule. The triangulation between exception, sovereignty, and order is inherent in a peculiar and circumscribed structure of politics, capable of replacing the harmonious or conciliatory convergence between form and energy. In other words, exception is not chaos, or merely disorder, but a presence that lacks real articulation with anything else. From this demarcation, this present draws the possibility of a politics, or for the moment and provisionally, a decision: "The exception remains, nevertheless, accessible to jurisprudence because both elements, the norm as well as the decision, remain within the framework of the juristic."[10]

The proper place of sovereignty, its chosen ground, is therefore in this context political creation, whose essential condition is given by the fluidity and uniformity of the background on which it is crafted. If full and empty take on a borderline indistinct aspect, it is precisely for this reason: both describe a primarily undifferentiated field, within which the instance of decision can freely move, without faults or points of friction. Thus "the two elements of the concept legal order are then dissolved into independent notions and thereby testify to their conceptual independence."[11] In this delimited sense, full and empty come to correspond to one another. In one case form and energy open a distance between them that cannot be bridged by politics and law—and on the contrary, the action of the former is rigorously permitted by such an assumption—while the other option is that of superimposing them up to an identity. This is a theoretical move that now knows its specific nature—but that will be typical of multiple twentieth-century philosophico-political experiences—effectively revoking the possibility of an encounter or clash between politics and what is not political, whether it be economic determinism or whatever form of social production. There is no real divergence between separation and superimposition from this perspective, but instead a common theoretical project, poles of an apparent dialectic that constantly rotates on itself: "There exists no norm that is applicable to chaos. For a legal order to make sense, a normal situation must exist [. . .] The exception reveals most clearly the essence of the state's authority. The decision parts here from the legal norm, and (to formulate it paradoxically) authority proves that to produce law it need not be based on law."[12] What emerges clearly in this passage is the schema of juridical filling as essentially subsequent to the action of politics. Order is established in absence, and only the presence that follows it is susceptible to ordering, just as the exception is the condition of order. Law is thus applicable after the state and within it, but not prior to or outside of the normal situation. The juridical context favors the assumption of such a thesis—of a rigorously modern structure, as opposed to a juridical institutionalism in which the autonomization of the parts from the whole actually recalls a premodern, pluralistic framework—and the theoretical weight of this thesis was perhaps most clearly visible when it was, at times in an improvised way, generalized outside the context of an election. Indeed, there is no doubt that such a thesis is endowed with a rigor close to the obviousness within the juridical framework, but if the laws of economics and society replace the laws of right, to what extent is it still possible to hold to the discourse? The flat uniformity of politics can only be the result of a structure for which "the rule proves nothing; the exception proves everything: It confirms not only the rule but also its existence."[13]

However, it is not here a question of the correct functioning of the theory as much as the observation of the theoretical effects of an argument. At this point, we can indeed recognize the conceptual crux of starting a theory of political conflict with definite characteristics, to which we will return. For the moment, it is necessary to observe how on this ground we can identify, as we anticipated above, a certain Hegelianism in Schmitt. Rather than a stretched notion of the dialectic—which for Schmitt focuses only on the constant restlessness of the negative, but can be led back to a positivity or overcome—or in the different relation established between mediation, negation, and totality (which is also influential on the strictly political side of both authors), Schmitt's Hegelianism can be seen in the lack of a scanning between levels and stages that ends up assuming the form of a sphere that lacks autonomy, albeit relative autonomy. Whereas the Hegelian conjunction of spheres tends to give rise to a spiritual totality, which therefore removes the difference between the parts, making them uniform to manifestations of a homogenous principle (*pars totalis*), Schmitt's emptying and superimposition never produces relations between different elements, whose connection must precisely be established, measured, or even contested.[14] That effect of uniformity and pure immanentization that gives rise to a unified and flat plan, lacking faults and distinctions, thus operates in this way on the level of politics. This is so whether it is empty or full. In this sense—perhaps more than in the directions frequently taken up by interpreters in terms of the affinity and difference between the two—Schmitt's totality appears as a whole, if not exactly through in a Hegelian way, finally analogous although obtained with other means.[15]

In this framework, the clearest and most obvious articulation would seem to concern Schmitt's doctrine of enmity and the conflict connected to it as the nucleus of the political. However, the configuration that this conflict assumes in Schmitt's text gradually and not without gaps seems to converge, and to some extent derive, from this primitive schema of understanding the internal politics of the exception.

The Symmetry of Conflict

In Schmitt's thought at the origin there is thus a constitutive instability, a primary energy that is systematically the source and the failure of politics. This is a politics whose autonomy paradoxically emerges in the double crisis of state and society: a state that is no longer the exclusive domain of politics, and a society no longer capable of organizing its own internal life. This is an autonomy of politics that, again, has the task of managing the void through the most radical form of decision. Such a practice is then paradoxical because it is deeply connected to a lack of foundation and balance, but it is equally "foundationalist" in its unfolding as a decisionism that transforms the conflict into exclusion. This is a case of Schmittian ambivalence and oscillation, between the lack of foundation and the "politics of origin" in the autonomy of politics, as well as between politics itself and social determinisms. When super-, or at the limit, extralegal legitimacy sets for itself the goal of stabilization and legitimation of both the political and economic spheres, there is a further occurrence of the relation between separation and superposition that we have already identified. Lacking classical mediation in either the rationalist or dialectical manner, but also through distribution, opposition, and articulation, this connection never becomes a true relation between differences. For the autonomy of politics, it generates what has been called the "politics of origin," that is, a paradoxical attempt to resort to the origin itself in a framework that has been characterized as unfounded, absolutely lacking a stable beginning, while in the elaboration of the autonomy of the political, it will run into another impasse.

The lack of relation, the oscillation between identity and distinction of elements—this is a philosophical principle that seems to return: "The equation state = politics becomes erroneous and deceptive at exactly the moment when state and society penetrate each other. What had been up to that point affairs of the state become thereby social matters, and, vice versa, what had been purely social matters become affairs of the state [. . .] In such a state, therefore, everything is at least potentially political, and in referring to the state it is no longer possible to assert for it a specifically political characteristic."[16]

In the search for the specificity of the "political" and the claim of its autonomy from the other, that is, the assumption that the specificity of its domain cannot derive from the outside, one of the most typically Schmittian arguments is given by the opening of politics beyond the state. An immediate consequence of Schmitt's logic is the mutual penetration between society and politics, of which the latter represents the occurrence of a particular intensity in its relations. His reasoning is here focused on polemicizing with positions that postulate a rigid continuity between society, economics, and politics, effectively canceling its own domain, as well as in the attempt to claim a certain political realism. What stands out less apparently is instead his superimposition of politics and society that derives from these distinctions, or rather the effective subsumption of society by politics that owes much to his perspective and the historical moment. Once again, however, these theses, the full and empty homogenization, are made under certain conditions with general philosophical assumptions, and not without the collaboration of Schmitt himself, and they have configured an overall modality of the understanding of politics within a flat and fluid terrain on which it encounters no restraints.

> The specific political distinction to which political actions and motives can be reduced is that between friend [*Freund*] and enemy [*Feind*]. This provides a definition in the sense of a criterion and not as an exhaustive definition or one indicative substantial content. [. . .] In any event it is independent [. . .] in that it can neither be based on any one antithesis or any combination of other antitheses, nor can it be traced to these.[17]

Enmity is therefore the definition of the imbalance, at once productive and lacking stable form, which characterizes the political if isolated from further instances. From this perspective, the presence of the successive distinctions, both relative to the frame of reference (politics rather than morality or aesthetics), as well as in the elements of the relation, seem aimed at preventing the reactivation of a balance and homogeneity, whether internal or deriving from the outside: "The distinction of friend and enemy denotes the utmost degree of intensity of a union or separation, of an association or dissociation."[18] In Schmittian thought we have no denotation, objectivity, exclusively intensity, obtained not only by means of the regressive movement of his particular phenomenology (or as we have said, genealogy). And above all, this is the result of the subtraction of the figures of the private enemy, of economic competition, against which the reproposal of a harmony appears possible on the surface.

A constitutive and exhausted imbalance that Schmitt summarizes in two fundamental characteristics of the relation: first in the polemical nature of properly political terms, the qualification of which simultaneously denotes their concreteness and thus the materiality and generality of the references. Second, Schmitt emphasizes the connection with the possibility of a struggle, according to the model of civil war, about which it will be necessary to return. Struggle is again understood in the service of disharmony, whose battle is "to the death,"[19] with a radical existential significance. In this way, an origin in the proper sense is configured, albeit one with a peculiar structure: "War is neither the aim nor the purpose nor even the very content of politics [but is] an ever present presupposition as real possibility."[20] In what direction does this instability lead? What movement does it produce? Among the many criticisms addressed to this definition of the political, from irrationalist activism and vice versa, the ontologization of conflict, the discussion of the specific structure that Schmitt assigns to politics, the particular form in which the relation presents itself, has assumed less centrality. This is a relation that at first glance is profoundly asymmetrical. Indeed, what greater difference can be given than that between friend and enemy? The connection of enmity, including Schmitt's clarifications against objections, shows itself as a radical interference, which is programmatically aimed at giving an account of the always conjunctural nature of politics and the provisional character of its acquisitions. This is a dichotomy now qualified not by ambivalence, such as that between fullness and the void, but that to which emptying itself seems to give a direction that cannot bend toward asymmetry.

Yet the radicality of Schmitt's description of political conflict as its original background appears to overturn its own profile as soon as we look to its connection with the specific position in which it is placed, on the one hand, and to the outcomes that it produces, on the other. The process of emptying from, and of the possible superposition to, every circumscribed field, implies an anonymity of the factors of discord, an indistinction between the poles of antagonism that renders the presupposition of asymmetry an attribution of right rather than what is done. Friend and enemy, in their respective and reversible positions, then appear as aspects of a relation destined by paradox—this time not sought after—to a stabilization of instability.[21] By claiming and attempting to account for the conjunctural status of every given political, there is a continuous center of gravity found below the phenomena to which they can be brought back, which interprets every conflict as always equal to itself. This is an origin whose form presents itself as symmetrical in this way, through the attribution of the same role to every social, economic, or moral actor who from time to time comes to fulfill the role of the pole of enmity: "The political can derive its energy from the most varied human endeavors, from the religious, economic, moral, and other antitheses. It does not describe its own substance, but only has the intensity of an association or dissociation of human beings whose motives can be religious, national (in the ethnic or cultural sense), economic, or of any other kind and can effect at different times different coalitions and separations."[22] Outcomes, productive capacities, are thus limited to repetition: a single symmetrical notion of political conflict that structures the origin of every phenomenon that can qualify as such. This repetition is nondifferential and therefore precisely of the same, insofar as it is marked by the social, economic, or moral anonymity of its factors, from whose exit, however, what would be obtained is not so much a submission of the political to external conditioning as the encounter and interference with diversified fields with respect to which a relation is defined. This is a conflict that, in the last instance, cannot be resolved due to the formation of a stasis that does not attribute divergent tasks and purposes to the parties involved. It is an abstraction relocated to the empty origin, which is aimed at accounting for a claimed concreteness of politics: lacking mediation, consigned to the splitting and fusing, but never open to articulation.

The identification between politics and (civil) war is consubstantial with this logic, which Schmitt will consolidate and transform in the postwar period. This is a conflict conceived according to a rigid military model:

1. The intrinsic nature of the political assumes a binary schema at its origin. Every phenomenology is traced to

this schema by starting from the elements that emerge. It is a prototype that displays asymmetry while assuming the guise of perfect symmetry by means of a process of emptying and superposition.

2. This model is configured as struggle, investing with itself the paradigm of civil war and in the last instance always reproducing the same figure of struggle, in a way that is consistent with the military matrix. There is no outcome here because of the genealogical framework that is sketched, and its search for concreteness changes into abstraction.

3. Every possible objectivity with regard to politics, understood as a mirroring between energy and order, is therefore subject to final judgment. This is an epistemological background which, in the history of interpretations, has not struggled to translate itself into a vindication of the perspective, reproducing this thesis on the cognitive terrain.

4. If there is thus a truth of politics, it is that of not being susceptible to a knowledge that is not conjunctural. But this is a conjuncture that, we will see, finally presents itself as subtracted from history rather than as a factor of radical historicization. In this way specific time (*il puntuale*) is opposed to the eternal, not the sequence or the process.

5. Finally, a political that is structured but alien to any form of closure, constitutively open but only to repetition. A rupture with the essence that, even in the search for origins which Schmitt carries out, does not justify the possibility. In short, far from irrationality, it is a choice for immanence.

The lack of a landing place for politics through this hollow form now seems to have Schmitt draw close to a number of Nietzschean positions, particularly regarding the centrality of negation. However, it is worth noting how, in the first place, for Nietzsche the negative is the place of the subsumption of this flat, irreducible contrast—in other words, that there is exactly a negation of this perspective. For Schmitt, instead, negation is always of order, the constitutive impossibility of a protection from its bottomless origin. In the same way, the coincidence of the genealogical perspective was authoritatively emphasized in the figure of *Enstehung*, or emergency, which however presents a divergence concerning the end between the two others: for Nietzsche, the liberation of contrast and power, whereas for Schmitt, the search for the origin of form, to the point of being configured as *arché*.

This distinction cannot be underestimated: to the Nietzschean liberation of form, Schmitt opposes contingency, which is however rooted in something like an originary form of the particular structure. It is this structure, as we have seen, that probably generates effects of proximity and distance at the same time, for different reasons, between Hegel and Nietzsche: with respect to the sphere as *pars totalis* in the former and the liberation of the will in the latter, Schmitt places, as a halfway point, the specific model of political enmity. This is a flat relation between anonymous parts, such as the identical nuclei of dialectical and expressive totality, and a permanent relation between forces that does not produce development, such as the counterpoised will to power.

The effect is a stasis on the smooth plane of symmetrical conflict, of the manifestations of totality and the dispersion of forces.[23]

Notes

1. See Giuseppe Duso, *La logica del potere* (Rome: Laterza, 1999).

2. See Jean-François Kervegan, *Que faire de Carl Schmitt* (Paris: Gallimard, 2011).

3. See, among others, Mario Tronti, "Marx e Schmitt: Un problema storico-teorico," in *La politica oltre lo Stato*, ed. Giuseppe Duso (Venezia: Arsenale, 1981), 25–40. For a balance sheet, see Mattia Di Pierro, "Mario Tronti lettore di Carl Schmitt. Da Marx alla teologia politica," *Storia del pensiero politico* no. 2 (2017): 261–80. There is curiously no reference to the "Italian' interpretation of Schmitt, even in passing, in Matthew G. Specter, "What's 'Left' in Schmitt? From Aversion to Appropriation in Contemporary Political Theory," in *The Oxford Handbook of Carl Schmitt*, ed. Jens Meierhenrich and Oliver Simons (Oxford: Oxford University Press, 2016), 426–54. This interpretation in many ways anticipates the problems Specter highlights in the readings of Schmitt by Habermas, Mouffe, Kalyvas, Balakrishnan, and Werner Müller.

4. Roberto Esposito, *Categories of the Impolitical* (New York: Fordham University Press, 2015), XV.

5. Roberto Esposito, *Institution* (Cambridge: Polity, 2022), 2.

6. Carl Schmitt, *Political Theology* (Chicago, IL: University of Chicago Press, 2006), 5.

7. Schmitt, *Political Theology*, 5–6.

8. See Giorgio Agamben, *Homo Sacer* (Stanford, CA: Stanford University Press, 1998).
9. Schmitt, *Political Theology*, 12.
10. Schmitt, *Political Theology*, 12–13.
11. Schmitt, *Political Theology*, 12.
12. Schmitt, *Political Theology*, 13.
13. Schmitt, *Political Theology*, 15.
14. See Kervegan, *Que faire de Carl Schmitt?*
15. See Geminello Preterossi, *Political Theology and Law* (London: Routledge, 2023); John P. McCormick, *Carl Schmitt's Critique of Liberalism: Against Politics as Technology* (Cambridge: Cambridge University Press, 1997). Jurgen Habermas has not fully appreciated how for Schmitt, political homogeneity can be given not only as a "full" totality in an ethnic or nationalistic sense but also as an emptying with respect to the materialist distinction between social groups. This anti-Schmittian preoccupation, however it is unilaterally grasped, has contributed to the pluralization and emptying of sovereignty through which Habermas has proposed a competitive stagnation, to which, as we will see, Schmitt's reasoning can also lead. See Jurgen Habermas, *Between Facts and Norms: Contributions to a Discourse Theory of Law and Democracy* (Cambridge: MIT, 1998).
16. Carl Schmitt, *The Concept of the Political* (Chicago, IL: Chicago University Press, 2007), 22.
17. Schmitt, *Concept of the Political*, 26.
18. Schmitt, *Concept of the Political*, 26.
19. Schmitt, *Concept of the Political*, 71.
20. Schmitt, *Concept of the Political*, 34.
21. "*Stasis* means in the first place quiescence, tranquility, standpoint, status [. . .]. But *stasis* also means, in the second place, (political) unrest, movement, uproar and civil war." Carl Schmitt, *Political Theology II* (New York: Polity, 2008), 123.
22. Schmitt, *Concept of the Political*, 38.
23. And thus, an identity between competitive plurality (enmity) and homogenous totality (empty decision) that remains misunderstood for those who have attempted a progressive appropriation of Schmitt in the name of an abstract agonistic pluralism, as an alternative to conflict. See Chantal Mouffe, *Carl Schmitt and the Paradox of Liberal Democracy*, in *The Challenge of Carl Schmitt*, ed. Chantal Mouffe (London: Verso, 1999), 38–53; *The Return of the Political* (London Verso, 1993); and *On the Political* (New York: Routledge, 2005). See also Gopal Balakrishnan, *The Enemy: An Intellectual Portrait of Carl Schmitt* (London: Verso, 2000); and Andreas Kalyvas, *Democracy and the Politics of the Extraordinary: Max Weber, Carl Schmitt, and Hannah Arendt* (Cambridge: Cambridge University Press, 2009). Jan-Werner Müller rightly compares these options to the aporias of Tronti's interpretation in Jan-Werner Müller, *A Dangerous Mind: Carl Schmitt in Post-War European Thought* (New Haven, CT: Yale University Press, 2003).

Part Two

Political Ontology and Community

Six

On Bodies

Perspectives of a Dialogue between Esposito and Nancy

Daniela Calabrò

> Technique has now taken up residence in our very limbs.
> —R. Esposito, *Immunitas*

> Between me and me [. . .] there is an incision's opening, and the irreconcilability of a compromised immune system.
> —J.-L. Nancy, *Corpus*

Ecotechnics of Bodies

To what extent today, in the era of biotechnology and therapeutic eugenics, artificial insemination and end of life, is it urgently necessary to think, or rather rethink, our relationship with the body, and thus with life? Why can life no longer be conceived according to the classical view that understood it—through the body—as a stand-alone living organism? Or rather, why couldn't it be understood as a biochemically and biologically structured "form" of the world, certainly subject to mutation, but always teleologically organized? The answer to these questions emerges from the events characterizing the new modernity, namely, the one in which, as Agamben described it, a "new use of bodies, of technique, of landscape" takes place.[1] In other words, the concept of form-of-life, which replaces the foundational recourse to a subjectivity, takes shape. Moreover, this is how the whole reflection on the categories of person, body, mind, thing, and human life is rethought. The *punctum dolens* of the Heideggerian view that identified man as the closer being to God than the animal, for he was the "world-forming" on a kind of scale that relegated the animal to being defined as "world-poor" and the stone as "worldless," is understood precisely from this renewed conception of corporeality.

Stone, animal, man: all are bodies; they are bodies within which sense abides, without privilege of any kind, insofar as each of those bodies is inhabited by, or simply "is" sense, which is precisely a gap, a distance, a cut, a postponement or deferral, a composition or a decomposition, and a partition, to borrow Jean-Luc Nancy's cherished lexicon.[2] The nonequivalence of bodies no longer pertains to a matrix defined by the ability to "*form the world*," but far more classically to an *ethos* to be inhabited, in a constitutively singular/plural way.[3] Thinking of such "nonequivalence" as an unquenchable resource of the "form of the world," of its meaning, and of its possibility of existing is what a reflection on the body allows us to do.

In fact, against this background stands out a theoretical horizon that is as timely as ever, namely, that relating to the practices of *grafts* or *intrusions* of bodies into other bodies; in short, to transplants and explants. Indeed, the biomedical approach delivers us a body always *bound* to other bodies, both organic and inorganic, in a sort of latent promiscuity, of permutation and exchange between vital and nonvital, between Self and other. However, let us take a step back. To Nietzsche we owe the most impressive acrobatic leap in the history of philosophical thought, as Esposito rightly observes:

> His radical deconstruction of the categories of modern thought coincided with a thought on and of the body (in the sense that the body thinks because it, too, is animate) that was destined to inaugurate a new language. To the question of whether philosophy has not been more than an incessant "misunderstanding of the body," Zarathustra responds that "there is more reason in your body than in your best wisdom."

Contrary to thinkers that Nietzsche defines as disparagers of the body, he rereads the whole history of Europe along "the guiding thread of the body." [. . .] The politics of bodies, on bodies, in bodies is the only kind that exists—not in opposition to the "spirit," but in a weave that integrates the body into the *bios* as an integral form of life.[4]

Starting from here, the theme of life, of *bios*, assumes a decisive importance in the philosophical culture of the entire twentieth century. In addition, today more than ever—namely, ever since biology appeared on the scene of history—it has become more and more the object of extensive and meticulous knowledge, so much so that its preservation—and indeed its unlimited promotion—has become utmost. First and foremost, this has led to increasingly careful, and almost invasive, legislation. An example of this is the so-called population health policy, which has become more and more capable of penetrating into the infinitesimal aspects of the biological-bodily dimension of people's lives, in an often-conflicting relationship between the natural and the artificial, from medical therapies to nutrition and fertilization. A typical aspect of this modernity goes under the now well-known name of biopolitics.[5]

All this profoundly affects philosophical, artistic-literary, political-legal, and medical-scientific reflection. What has been brought into play is the identity paradigm of the subject, and along with it, the entire relationship with the world. Consequently, the dimension of the human and the "vital" in general has been entirely deconstructed. Hence the need to thoroughly rethink today the "biotechnological" construction of the living being, in order to be able to understand its mighty change of sense.

Reducing the concept of the body to a single level of the subject, as well as linking the natural and the artificial, the real and the virtual, the organic and the inorganic, is what allows us to think of the body as a constant fluctuation between inside and outside and to its immunization and simultaneous contamination.[6] In addition, this helps us understand the body itself as the very unfolding of the skin, viscera, limbs, and senses, all in an ecotechnical profusion of bodies.[7] Today we are also dealing with hybridizations of the self and therapeutic cloning: accelerations of existence in an impalpable grain that deconstructs and exceeds all "architectures of the living." These transformations, which can be defined as radical without fear of exaggeration, thus require philosophy to question and investigate them, both in relation to the associated change of whole categorical apparatuses (from the scientific to the artistic field) and to their consequences at a more broadly ethical and even political level (i.e., in relation to what is still to be understood by "man" and "world").[8]

If we consider the change to the concept of the body in the twentieth century, we cannot but bring to the fore a new concept of life and explore its entire semantic field, from the purely philosophical to the aesthetic, political, economic, medical, and psychoanalytic spheres. What emerges then are the concepts of "ontology of the living," of "bios and biopolitics," of "person and human life," of "everyday life"[9]—concepts that represent the most problematic governmental faults nowadays, because they are directly implicated or co-implicated in the very structure of the living matter.

Therefore, one needs to understand life in its different architectures or "different guises," for it is precisely in the continuous deferral (whether hereditary or abrupt) that each body (whether living or nonliving) frees itself from any preconceived purpose, resists any synthesis, multiplies in irreducible plurality, and destabilizes the temporal-historical continuum, thus disentangling itself from that notion of indefectibly serial time that rests silently on the identity or permanence of the Self; this means thinking the living in its most abysmal *déshérence*. Starting from this backlash in the origin that is precisely the absence of inheritance, the long-distance dialogue between Esposito and Nancy, between *Immunitas* and *The Intruder*, is played out. This chapter is based on all this, aiming to understand how it is no longer man who is projected into the world today, but it is the world to be introjected and implanted in man: as Esposito wrote in *Immunitas*, "Technique has now taken up residence in our very limbs."[10] Such a statement recalls the pages of Nancy's Intruder: "Between me and me [. . .] there is an incision's opening, and the irreconcilability of a compromised immune system."[11] The identity subject discovers itself as hopelessly partitioned (Nancy) and lying on the outside (Esposito), in a space that is our unique possible community.

Immune Bodies?

Nowadays, as we have seen, the body, in its infinite—thus no longer defined and finite—semantic and speculative extension, poses a problem.

Indeed, if biology was once a purely observational and strictly experimental science, today it founds a real engineering of the living being that changes more and more our relationship with our body and with that of others. Roberto Esposito and Jean-Luc Nancy give voice to the ethical-political-philosophical questions revolving around contemporary bodily dynamics: technical and cybernetic existence, artificial or virtual existence, and the ecotechnics of bodies.

Esposito starts from the biopolitical register. As the Italian philosopher wrote in the introductory pages of *Immunitas: The Protection and Negation of Life*, "The body is the most immediate terrain of the relation between politics and life, because only in the body does life seem protected from what threatens to harm it and from its own tendency to go beyond itself, to become other than itself. It is as if life, to preserve itself as such, must be compressed and kept within the confines of the body."[12] All this—as Esposito explained further on—is not because the body, both singular and collective, is not always exposed to involution and dissolution processes, but because it is precisely there, in the body, that the defense mechanisms intended for its protection are activated. The whole metaphor of the "body politic" in the early modern age—from Hobbes onward—is connected to this mechanism, a framework that is reversed when the prevailing relationships between politics and life are reversed: "The threshold of transformation from the paradigm of sovereignty to that of biopolitics is to be located in the time when power was no longer the subject of inclusion (as well as of exclusion) of life but instead, life—its reproductive protection—became the ultimate criterion for legitimizing power."[13] Life establishes itself, sets off the mechanism of protection by itself and, in this, creates a real immunity paradigm. But here, the whole internal contradiction of the immune paradigm emerges, which Esposito unhinges and highlights:

> The immune system is actually described as a military device, defending and attacking everything not recognized as belonging to it, and which must therefore be fended off and destroyed. The most striking feature is the way a biological function is extended to a general view of reality dominated by a need for violent defense in the face of anything judged to be foreign. [. . .] the relation between "I" and "other" [. . .] is represented in terms of a destruction that ultimately tends to involve both the contrasting terms.[14]

This is a real "self-dissolution impulse" that, in the medical field, is reflected in autoimmune diseases, "in which the warring potential of the immune system is so great that at a certain point it turns against itself as a real and symbolic catastrophe leading to the implosion of the entire organism."[15] The medical metaphor adopted by Esposito highlights all the disturbing features of the ambiguity within which life unfolds. The immunity paradigm as a whole is not something that acts against something but is rather what reacts to it, in the sense of a counterforce, a backlash, an instance of closure, of blocking; even by reproducing the evil from which one must protect oneself in a controlled way (as vaccines do)—in short, protection and negation of life according to a strategy that is meant not to be that of direct contrast but of avoidance and neutralization. Following Esposito's words once again, "Evil must be thwarted, but not by keeping it at a distance from one's borders; rather, it is included inside them. [. . .] The body defeats a poison not by expelling it outside the organism, but by making it somehow part of the body. [. . .] Of course, this homeopathic protection practice—which excludes by including and affirms by negating—does not consume itself without leaving traces on the constitution of its object."[16] At this point, the path indicated by Esposito is clear: it is a matter of accessing an affirmative biopolitics. The example to which he resorts is that provided by the biological event of birth, where pregnancy exerts a kind of protection of life precisely through that immunity mechanism that should make it impossible, given the different DNAs of both father and mother. Indeed, the child conceived by fertilization, in its intrauterine life, is protected, incorporated, nourished *in its diversity and because of its diversity*, precisely because of its being "other." In short, precisely that "otherness," that diversity that implements and indeed triggers in the mother's organism a complex immunity process, protects the fetus and guarantees its future life at the same time. In this example, according to Esposito, we can trace the paradigmatic movements of a strategy in which we do not purely and simply immunize ourselves from the other, but on the contrary, we protect it by welcoming it—and thus welcoming "life in its different guises." However, in this way, what takes shape is a different philosophy of immunity, as can be seen in a recent work by Esposito titled *Immunità comune: Biopolitica all'epoca della pandemia* (Common Immunity: Biopolitics in the Age of the Pandemic)[17]—in which the Italian philosopher writes that it is a matter of "radically rethinking the constitutive link between immunity and community on the basis of this realization, by building a single common immunity, a co-immunity meant to protect human beings—not some from others but some with and for others: "From there on, a protectionism of the whole becomes the directive of immunitary reason." If this were possible, humanity would become a political concept, not an abstract ideal but a global immune design—something like a "co-immunism" to come."[18]

This is what the recent pandemic, with all the immense power of contagion and death, has taught us. "Today more than ever, in full biopolitical regime, politics has to deal with the protection and development of life. Not only for individual populations, but for humankind as a whole. When community and immunity find an extreme tangency line, the life of each one is protected only by that of all. Never more than today, in the throes of a biopolitical regime, has politics been concerned with the protection and development of life—not just of individual populations but of the human species as a whole. When community and immunity rediscover a shared boundary, the life of each is protected only by the life of all."[19] Therefore, for the first time in history, when the entire world community has required to be safeguarded, immunity seems to have lost its restrictive connotations to require a new interpretation from a biological, philosophical, and political point of view. After the COVID-19 pandemic, the functioning of the immune paradigm has been shaped according to a new interpretation mode. However, if we go back to *Immunitas*, we can understand how much Esposito's lessons, several years before the 2020 pandemic, already in unsuspected times had so much to teach us. The successful exchange with authors such as Alfred Tauber[20] and Donna Haraway[21] led the Italian philosopher to a conception of individual identity and bodily subjectivity completely opposed to the closed and monolithic one of the Western tradition. Certainly, there is no doubt that this has also been inevitable given the developments in genetic technology and bionics that have strongly contributed to changing our usual notion of the body. As Esposito writes,

> Rather than an immutable and definitive given, the body is understood as a functioning construct that is open to continuous exchange with its surrounding environment. Moreover—this is the argument (a problematic one, to be sure) put forward in the concluding section of this work—the immune system may very well be the driving force behind this exchange. Immune tolerance, understood as a product

of immunity rather than as an unraveling or a deficiency of the system, is one of its first expressions. The figure of the implant, whether an artificial prosthesis or a natural implant like fertilized eggs in the mother's womb, provides the most striking case in point. The fact that the genetic heterogeneity of the fetus rather than its genetic similarity is what encourages the mother's immune system to accept it means that the immune system cannot be reduced to the simple function of rejecting all things foreign. If anything, the immune system must be interpreted as an internal resonance chamber, like the diaphragm through which difference, as such, engages and traverses us. As we were saying: once its negative power has been removed, the immune is not the enemy of the common, but rather something more complex that implicates and stimulates the common. The full significance of this necessity, but also its possibility, still eludes us.[22]

The concept of the body, unavoidably present, appears again in Esposito's reflection. It is impossible to do without it, as it is in the body—as a body—that life is given, and the whole resulting immunity consequence with it.

Phenomenological Grafts: Merleau-Ponty, Nancy, Esposito

Esposito's and Nancy's main objective is to deepen the speculative value and semantic extension of the notion of corporeity in a continuous and close dialogue with ancient and modern tradition, in order to highlight the urgency of a thought of the body in our contemporary times. The latter is increasingly projected toward a conception of it that unhinges the notion of *bìos* on the one hand, and that of *person* on the other.

In the direction taken by Nancy, the sense of the body opens up to its own dissent and exposes itself to a new apex of thought. Here, the concept of decomposition of the body goes hand in hand with that of identity disintegration, in which vital and nonvital, organic and inorganic interplay with each other in a kind of latent promiscuity: "I am first the guest of this other: world, body, language."[23] Being the guest of the other is the very experience of bodily existence, as Nancy writes in one of his most complex and important works, *The Restlessness of the Negative*, the text dedicated to Hegel. Here Nancy rethinks the servant-master/ego-other relationship not to enclose it within a dialectic of the negative but to open that relationship up to the restlessness, the shifting movement that the other represents in the singular constitution of each self. From the deconstruction of the paradigm of the subject—posed by Nancy's critique of the Cartesian *ego cogito*—to the analyses carried out on the other as the inoperative outside that stands out over the sense of the inside, we are led to the place where precisely the inside/outside of existence unfolds and is exposed, namely the body. Therefore, it is no coincidence that the French philosopher addresses the question of the other by going through a somewhat involutional path, in which the other presents itself under the guise of an outside that is my body itself, and yet is simultaneously the inside from which I cannot distance or detach myself. Thus, it is a matter of thinking of the body as a constant fluctuation between inside and outside—as mentioned earlier—thinking of its immunization and, at the same time, of its contamination. In other words, it is necessary to think of a new way of experiencing and conceiving the body that can no longer be linked to the classical conception that intended it as a living organism in its own right; rather, it is a matter of conceiving it in relation to other bodies, whether organic or not. According to Nancy,

> Every thing outside all the others, every thing according to the stretching that spaces them and without which there would be just one indistinct thing gathered into the point at which it would annul itself, a thing unthinged, a de-realized res, a perfect, syncopated subject turned back in on itself without its having ever reached itself, an extinct, noiseless trinket, a one annihilated without its being dead: every thing, then, touching every part of every other thing, touching me in the same way, piece by piece, here and there, always, from time to time, exposing the infinity of our relations. Things: the first stone that's thrown, a sheet of paper, galaxies, the wind, my television screen, a quark, my big toe, a trapped nerve, prostheses, organs planted or grafted beneath my skin, placed or exposed inside, all things exposing themselves and exposing us, between them and between us, between them and us, together and singularly.[24]

Dissent of the body, therefore, understands this genitive in a twofold sense: both objective, meaning that it falls on the body (and this is the dissent launched by Nancy)—and subjective, produced by the body itself, meaning a body that is expressed in the plurality which erases, strikes out the sense, that is, the firm meaning that the philosophical/political/religious tradition has always assigned to it. Dissent of the body because the very body disrupts all defined meaning and endlessly opens itself to the other from itself, to the intruder who goes through it in the guise of a disease or a new donated heart that, like the legendary Trojan horse, brings with it a deceptive new beginning. A symptomatic body always turned to or turned toward, in a kind of dispossession that continually exceeds its subjectivist and objectivist instances.

Nevertheless, in one of the working notes attached to *The Visible and the Invisible*, Maurice Merleau-Ponty's last work, we can read that we must think of the "flesh of the world—distinct from my flesh: the double inscription outside and inside."[25] It is a significant invite that Merleau-Ponty leaves to future generations, a warning for reflection. Indeed, in my opinion, it is from this outcome that—albeit tacitly—Nancy starts over. Certainly, all this is in order to overcome the phenomenological impasse of the proper body and to try to supplant that concept of flesh anchored still too much in the Christian tradition.[26]

To Touch the World

However, what does it mean to think of "the double inscription outside and inside"? Moreover, why does the body attest itself as the privileged place of this experience? As Merleau-Ponty writes, "The body catches itself from the outside, [. . .] it tries to touch itself while being touched, and initiates 'a kind of reflection' which is sufficient to distinguish it from objects, of which I can indeed say that they 'touch' my body, but only when it is inert, and therefore without ever catching it unawares in its exploratory function."[27] While the body is what is always by my side, it is also what, at the same time, is by the side of others, exposing itself and myself. That is to say, the body turns out to be the place of tangibility between me and myself, as well as between the other and me. In this sense, we can say that it is the vector of our being-in-the-world. However, at this point of tangibility that is the body, what is revealed is not a total adherence to (me or the other from me) but rather a space of absence, a principle of incompleteness—as Blanchot would put it. In fact, if we analyze the very famous example of the two hands touching each other (first dealt with by Husserl and later taken up and reworked by Merleau-Ponty), we can see that in the movement of reflection—which is the active/passive transition of their mutual touching—what remains is an unquenchable gap, a space of absence, a persistent otherness. As if to say that in the self of the body dwells the other from/of the body. Therefore, a kind of essential ambiguity of the flesh texture is revealed; it is precisely this emptiness, this absence, this passivity of the other and from the other that impedes the identification with the perfectly integral and fulfilled *wholly-Full*. If, on the one hand, this line of thought is aimed at overcoming the Cartesian dichotomous instance between res cogitans and res extensa, on the other, it turns out to be as very timely, since it already alludes to the practices of grafts or intrusions of bodies from bodies, thus penetrating the meshes of philosophical culture throughout the post–World War II period up to the most recent debates in the ethical, scientific, religious and biotechnological spheres. Thus, it can be clearly understood why Nancy himself embarked—starting from the phenomenological antecedents—on a non-secondary path in the exploration of the concept of the body.

The Flesh of the World

On this path, we find Roberto Esposito's reflections in some extraordinary pages of *Immunitas*, in which he points out how the line of the body—as understood by Husserl and the early Merleau-Ponty—gains a specific significance with the concept of "flesh." The Italian philosopher writes,

> We have to go back to the phenomenological horizon that constitutes its premise and conceptual framework: to be specific, to the theme of carne (flesh), specifically in the version provided by Husserl and later by Merleau-Ponty. For both, albeit stressing different aspects, the semantics of the flesh (German *Leib*, French *chair*) do not coincide with those of the body (German *Körper*, French *corps*) to which it is nevertheless linked by a close relation of implication. Whether involving a singular experience or potentially plural one—such as what Merleau-Ponty referred to with the terms "flesh of the world" or "flesh of history"—the process of mutual incorporation of two members of the same body or between several different bodies can never be fully achieved because it is interrupted by an original difference which the author calls "carnal difference" [*difference charnelle*].[28]

In this carnal difference lies the impossibility of ultimate reversibility between the toucher and the one touched, and makes the chiasma between touching hand and touched hand always suspended, with the consequence that there can be no identification between body and flesh. As Esposito continues,

> There is something about the flesh, like a hiatus or an original break, that resists incorporation, reversing it into the opposing movement of disincorporation. But, as we were saying, this stubborn resistance of the flesh to being made body cannot come about without aporetic consequences. [. . .] What finally comes into view is the possibility of bringing to the surface that "primal flesh" no philosophy has yet been able to name, except by negatively deducing it from the element that negated it. [. . .] there will emerge the silhouette of a flesh that rebels against the One, always already divided, polarized into the Two of the chiasm.[29]

Therefore, as Esposito wonders, "How are we to understand 'primordial'? [. . .] as an ontological alternative that opposes the hegemony of the body from the outside—or the void inside which inhabits it and exposes it to its otherness? [. . .] is there another flesh beyond the body, or is this not the locus of its constitutive non-belonging—the differential limit that separates it from itself by opening it up to its outside?"[30] By these words, it seems that Esposito definitively silences the category of body, for it is unsuitable to respond to a globalized and interconnected, fluid and even cyborg world. The notion of flesh seems to be the most suitable one to correspond theoretically to living institutions: "To fully grasp the meaning of the flesh requires that we be capable of simultaneously conceiving the outside and the inside of the body: one in the other and one for the other."[31] If the flesh is what everts the inverted, then it makes the individual body no longer proper, but improper. In conclusion, "The flesh is neither another body nor the body's other: it is simply the way of being in common of that which seeks to be immune."[32]

Inappropriate Body

As previously expressed, if the path chosen by Nancy leads to a tacit dialogue with Husserl and Merleau-Ponty's phenomenology, this is because the French philosopher wants to go beyond the concept of flesh that is so closely linked to the Christian tradition.[33] Indeed, Nancy deconstructs the spiritualistic and metaphysical residue found within the concept of flesh through the notion of exposition. Hence, the deconstruction of the concept of "proper body" (*Leib*)—still surreptitiously understood as a *positum*—is what Nancy strives for as well. In *Corpus*, in fact, the body, far from being understood as "proper," becomes the place par excellence of the "improper" or rather, of the "inappropriate." The body, therefore, can no longer be understood as positum, but rather as *ex-peau-situm*, that is, as skin that has always already been exposed to the world. In this sense, he writes that the "Body is certitude shattered and blown to bits." The body, our body is "a monster that can't be swallowed."[34]

Ex-peau-sition as skin that lies outside, a covering, precisely an exposition. Exposing one's own body to oneself and to the other. Nancy dismantles any idea of exposition understood as full manifestation, elimination of concealment, readiness for grasping and knowing. The movement of the *ex* inseparably links the outside to the excess, to an excess that cannot be absorbed nor blocked. To come out of oneself does not mean unveiling oneself, making oneself fully transparent, but rather means surrendering to existence, to differing from oneself and thus to the relationship with the other in which we meet or touch each other only without being able to grasp, enclose ourselves in a stable and unified entity. This nonadherence to oneself, this impossibility of presence, which gives way to the ever-new act of presentation, to the event, is what Nancy calls "finiteness." The *ex-peau-sition* as nudity shows the excess of the finite: its being endless, unfulfilled, or that "absence of finality" that all totalitarianisms, all identitarianisms, and basically all "-isms" want to fill with all their might. The dimension of nudity is that of the intrusion/exposition of the body as such: the being of the body, as a body, exposes itself. Moreover, this exposition of one body to another, this mutual displacement or arrangement of bodies constitutes their sense relationship: the incorporeal element of meaning expressed by language. Therefore, the ontology of bodies is consequently an ontology of the incorporeal as well. That is always, at the same time, an ontology of bodies and an ontology of sense (of being) as an incorporeal element, as a space within which bodies are displaced. Nevertheless, here, according to Nancy, there is no idea of space per se, because it is the body that, as such, spaces existence. As the French philosopher writes, "Bodies aren't some kind of fullness or filled space [. . .]: they are open space. [. . .]

The body-place isn't full or empty, since it doesn't have an outside or an inside, any more than it has parts, a totality, functions, or finality. It's acephalic and aphallic in every sense, as it were."[35] No body proper: no inside, no interiority; *se toucher-toi*, "to self-touch you" instead of *se toucher-soi*, "to touch oneself." The body is an objection to the Self, an objection to the appropriation of the body, which is still "a monster that can't be swallowed" "There is not 'the' body, there is not 'the' touch, there is not 'the' *res extensa*. There is that there is: creation of the world, *technē* of bodies, weighing without limits of sense, topographical corpus, geography of multiplied ectopias and no utopia."[36]

This is what thought must strive for, what it cannot constitutively escape: the exposure of the Self to the other than itself; it can only think of itself as the blade of a knife that tears the skin and lays it bare, and literally opens it up. In this very opening lies the inside/outside of our existence. Secretless: such is exposure, such is nakedness.

As Nancy explains, there is ultimately a "corpus of tact," which is precisely a syncopated corpus, interrupted and mixed with other bodies. Con-tact between bodies, *partes extra partes*, con-tact with the body that is obstructed and obstructs itself with its own proximity. An irreducible gap between body and Self, which implodes the idea of "touching" and leads us immediately to a promiscuity of contacts, of bodies, of body-to-body. Mixing, contagion, contact of bodies, spacing; body becoming space within another body by duplicating it, multiplying it; therefore, giving rise to hybridizations of the Self, therapeutic cloning, implantation, transplantation, explantation. In one word, to the ecotechnics of the body.

Thus, according to Nancy, "openings for blood are identical to those of sense." The pages of *Corpus* we have followed so far exemplarily introduce us to those of *The Intruder*, namely, where the French philosopher has totally laid bare his own experience of "bodily partition": his cardiac transplantation, that is, the radical exposure of his own integrity carved out by the intrusion of the other (the heart of the other).

Immune, Intruding, Common Bodies

It is clear that, as Esposito points out in a passage dedicated to Nancy,

> What penetrates the body of the person who receives a transplant, even before the tubes, pliers and probes traverse it, is not even simply its outside. It is the acute point of intersection

between several forms of estrangement that oppose and impose upon each other, each challenged, replicated, and, finally, overwhelmed by the other. The first is the estrangement of our immune system from the transplanted organ. The second, with an equal force of collision, is the estrangement of the immune system of the transplanted organ that strikes against our own. The shared line between the recipient body and the donor heart coincides with the frontline in the clash between these two opposing immune systems: one committed with all its power to rejecting the other while simultaneously not allowing itself to be rejected. For this reason, the resistance on the part of the person receiving the transplant must be redoubled: against the protection system of the other and his or her own; against the maelstrom of estrangement and the impossible demand for appropriation. For this reason, even to distinguish between "self" and "non-self" is no longer admissible, since it is not simply the improper that is the intruder, but the proper as well, inasmuch as it is estranged.[37]

In this sense, then, Nancy's peremptory statement "Thus, then, in all these accumulated and opposing ways, my self becomes my intruder"[38] represents the figure and scope of his thought. The *ex-peau-sition* is the place where both the dissent of the "body proper" of the phenomenological matrix and the displacement of the ontological dimension of the *being-with* take place. The transplanted heart makes space for itself and, by spacing out the receiving body, partitions it indefinitely: there it is in con-tact; but in this con-tact it expropriates it, exposes it, exports it. The new heart is an outside that brings outside, supplants the stillness of the Self, struggles to death to implant itself in the recognition of the gift. As Nancy writes:

> Not because they opened me up, gaping, to change the heart. But because this gaping cannot be sealed back up. [. . .] I am closed open. Through the opening passes a ceaseless flux of strangeness [. . .] I certainly feel it, and it's much stronger than a sensation: never has the strangeness of my own identity, which for me has always been nonetheless so vivid, touched me with such acuity. "I" clearly became the formal index of an unverifiable and impalpable change. Between me and me,

there had always been some space-time: but now there is an incision's opening, and the irreconcilability of a compromised immune system.[39]

Therefore, the body turns out to be constitutively atomized, parceled out and reconstituted, reimplanted on any pieces of skeleton remaining, in a view entirely aimed at a performing existence. Profusions of nature and proliferations of technique: this is how all things stand together; this is how they all simultaneously touch and mutually expose each other, in an impalpable grain that unravels and exceeds the identity image of an immovable Ego. The dissent of the body thus represents our existential condition, which is infinitely finite because it has already always been exposed, lying on its very limit. In this plane of existence, we can discover the singular multiplicity of life, whether natural or artificial, actual or virtual, the plural horizon of Nature within which more or less complex constructions of bodies, existences, and wills unfold—eccentrically. What has been said so far shows how Nancy, in turn, in the framework of that French deconstructionism of which he is (as well-known) one of the greatest exponents along with Derrida, has deconstructed the occlusive gesture of the West, the founding gesture of all metaphysics and all transcendence; he has managed to deconstruct that gesture by literally staging existence, its body, its outside, its excription, its disclosure. In a time when we are exposed to contagion with others, with all others, on the wave of globalization, a thought of the "exposed body," a reflection such as the one Nancy invites us to make on the *ex-peau-sition*, on the fact that we are all exposed and crossed by others, starting from the skin itself, I think is as important and urgent as ever. The extent to which these reflections can have an impact in terms of political thought today as well (of course, in the high and philosophical sense of the term, namely, in the sense of a thought that deals with thinking about the world and what form of it we wish to have) is quite evident. In strong agreement with Nancy, Esposito points out, "Never before have we had such an accurate perception of this community of bodies—the endless contagion that combines, overlaps, soaks, coagulates, blends, and clones them. Its openings in the flesh and transfusions of blood are identical to those in meaning: every definition of the healthy and the sick, the normal and the pathological, immunity and community, vacillates."[40] If the proper mode of our "being body" consists in being absolutely and necessarily *improper*, then this very impropriety is what constitutes itself as "biologically valid." In this sense, the technique employed on our bodies represents the *vital* and no longer *natural* passage for the conquest or prolongation of existence. We have definitely become part of a different regime of meaning. As Esposito rightly notes in his dialogue with Nancy, "This happens when the body loses absolute ownership of itself through the mode of the technological prosthesis. Only then does a fragment of the body of others, or a non-bodily thing, turn the human body into a space that cannot be fully appropriated, because it is beyond, or before, the dichotomies between subject and object, internal and external, thought and living body."[41] All this, adds Esposito—who quotes Nancy here—happens "in the philosophical story of his own heart transplant" where the French philosopher expresses himself in these words: "My heart became my stranger: strange precisely because it was inside. The strangeness could only come from outside because it surged up first on the inside [. . .] The intrusion of a body foreign to thought. This blank will stay with me like thought itself and its contrary, at one and the same time."[42] Inside and outside, internal and external, forward and backward, the magma of existence is concentrated in the body. Artificial, technical, cybernetic existence, implanted in the very flesh of man, and "this is not a symbolic surrogate or even a functional extension of a natural limb, but rather, the real presence in the body of something that is not body."[43] This is a body that carries within itself another body, an outside brought inside. Here Esposito's analyses converge and turn out to be in consonance with Nancy's, although the focus on the biopolitical and immune side is at its highest in Esposito. We conclude by letting Esposito have the last word in this long-distance dialogue with Nancy:

> [There is] something non-living that serves to preserve life. We might say that this need for self-preservation is at the root of all contemporary forms of body modification: the body suspends itself—it interrupts and doubles itself—with the aim of extending its duration. It exposes itself to what lies outside it in order to save what it still bears inside. It enters into a problematic relationship with the other in order to protect itself from itself, from its natural tendency to be consumed. On these lines, from this perspective, once again the figure of the immune system rises out of the heart of biopolitics. Situated at the crucial point in which the body encounters what is other than itself, it constitutes the hub that connects

various interrelated entities, species, and genera such as the individual and the collective, male and female, human and machine. Precisely because of this power to combine, the immune apparatus has become the point of tangency—of connection and tension—between all contemporary languages.[44]

Notes

1. See Giorgio Agamben, *The Use of Bodies*, trans. Adam Kotsko (Stanford, CA: Stanford University Press, 2016).
2. See Jean-Luc Nancy, *The Experience of Freedom*, trans. Bridget McDonald (Stanford, CA: Stanford University Press, 1993).
3. See Jean-Luc Nancy, *Being Singular Plural*, trans. Robert Richardson and Anne O'Byrne (Stanford, CA: Stanford University Press, 2000).
4. Roberto Esposito, *Persons and Things*, trans. Zakiya Hanafi (Cambridge: Polity, 2015), 115–16.
5. See Roberto Esposito, *Bios: Biopolitics and Philosophy*, trans. Timothy Campbell (Minneapolis: University of Minnesota Press, 2008).
6. See Roberto Esposito, *Immunitas: The Protection and Negation of Life*, trans. Zakiya Hanafi (Cambridge: Polity, 2011).
7. See Jean-Luc Nancy, *Corpus*, trans. Richard A. Rand (New York: Fordham University Press, 2008).
8. See Stefano Rodotà, *La vita e le regole: Tra diritto e non diritto* (Milan: Feltrinelli, 2006).
9. See Enrica Lisciani-Petrini, *Vita quotidiana: Dall'esperienza artistica al pensiero in atto* (Turin: Bollati Boringhieri, 2015).
10. Esposito, *Immunitas*, 147.
11. Nancy, *Corpus*, 168.
12. Esposito, *Immunitas*, 14.
13. Esposito, *Immunitas*, 15.
14. Esposito, *Immunitas*, 17.
15. Esposito, *Immunitas*, 17.
16. Esposito, *Immunitas*, 8.
17. Roberto Esposito, *Common Immunity: Biopolitics in the Age of the Pandemic*, trans. Zakiya Hanafi (Cambridge: Polity, 2023).
18. Esposito, *Common Immunity*, 156.
19. Esposito, *Common Immunity*, 190.
20. See Alfred Tauber, *The Immune Self: Theory or Metaphor?* (New York: Cambridge University Press, 1994); and, the most recent, *Immunity: The Evolution of an Idea* (New York: Oxford University Press, 2017).

21. Donna Haraway, *Simians, Cyborgs and Women: The Reinvention of Nature* (New York: Routledge, 1991).

22. Esposito, *Immunitas*, 17–18.

23. Jean-Luc Nancy, *Hegel: The Restlessness of the Negative*, trans. Jason Smith and Steven Miller (Minneapolis: University of Minnesota Press, 2002), 57.

24. Jean-Luc Nancy, *A Finite Thinking*, ed. Simon Sparks (Stanford, CA: Stanford University Press, 2003), 315–16.

25. Maurice Merleau-Ponty, *The Visible and the Invisible*, ed. Claude Lefort, trans. Alphonso Lingis (Evanston, IL: Northwestern University Press, 1968), 261.

26. See note 33 below.

27. Maurice Merleau-Ponty, *Phenomenology of Perception*, trans. Colin Smith (London: Routledge and Kegan Paul, 1962; rev. 1981), 107.

28. Esposito, *Immunitas*, 118–19.

29. Esposito, *Immunitas*, 119–20.

30. Esposito, *Immunitas*, 120.

31. Esposito, *Immunitas*, 121.

32. Esposito, *Immunitas*, 121.

33. In this regard, reference is made to verse 14 of the prologue of the Gospel of John: "And the Word became Flesh" (*Kai o Logos sarx egeneto*).

34. Nancy, *Corpus*, 5.

35. Nancy, *Corpus*, 15.

36. Nancy, *Corpus*, 119.

37. Esposito, *Immunitas*, 152.

38. Nancy, *Corpus*, 28.

39. Nancy, *Corpus*, 167–68.

40. Esposito, *Immunitas*, 151.

41. Esposito, *Persons and Things*, 123.

42. Nancy, *Corpus*, 163.

43. Esposito, *Immunitas*, 148.

44. Esposito, *Immunitas*, 149.

Seven

The Impersonal between Ethics and Politics

Roberto Esposito and Emmanuel Levinas on the Third Person

Silvia Dadà

Esposito's Political Impersonal

The theme of the impersonal plays a central role in contemporary debate. It occupies many fields: from bioethics to politics, literature, and the figurative arts.[1] Esposito describes it as "a shifting border: that critical margin, one might say, that separates the semantics of the person from its natural effect of separation; that blocks its reifying outcome."[2] The emergence of this theme is, in fact, mainly due to the need to rediscuss the related notion of "person," which has proved inadequate to represent the complexity of human reality that it claimed to define.[3] The person in fact has always been a fundamental category of thought: it developed from the fusion of the Roman legal tradition with the Christian doctrines of the Incarnation and the Trinity.[4] In these two contexts, however different, it plays the same legitimizing role, for it is a "exclusionary dispositif,"[5] which acts performatively. In the case of Roman law this is particularly evident, since the status of person immediately defines what a person is not, for instance children, or slaves. Through the practices of *manumissio* and *mancipatio*[6] one could in fact either stop being considered as a person and thus slip into reification, or be freed from slavery and become a free man. Even in philosophical thought, being a subject and being a person become almost synonymous:[7] this happens for the first time with the Bohetian definition of the person as *naturae rationalis individua substantia*, and it increases in the early modern philosophy,[8] especially in Cartesianism.

The notion of person tends to distinguish and hierarchize one part, considered authentic, over the other, inauthentic. This is the case, for example, with the dualism between soul and body, in which only the soul is worthy of being considered as a person, while the body is rather seen as an object to be subjugated.

The failure of the discourse on human rights, which following World War II (with the 1948 Universal Declaration of Human Rights) had prompted the affirmation of the person, of its philosophical, religious, ethical, and political value, demonstrates the inadequacy of this category: "At no time more than today do human rights, beginning with the right to live, seem so utterly denied. No right more than the right to live seems contradicted by the millions of victims who die because of hunger, sickness, and war."[9]

The use of the idea of the person fails to universalize the concept of citizenship that for Arendt[10] was the cause of the discrimination of various groups of people (those who, in Butler's words, we might call "ungrievable"[11]). The reason for this failure, in Esposito's opinion, is not so much the insufficient affirmation of this theory of the protection of the person, but rather the fact that the distinction between person and non-person justifies the objectification and the sacrifice of a part of the human species. Even in the dramatic case of Nazism, although there is an inverse process of valorization of race and the biological (and therefore not spiritual) components of life of human being, nevertheless here too there is a process generated by the discriminatory character of the idea of person. It is not so much the soul that commands the body, but the body that determines the spirit.

The person, this "Two in the One, the imposition of one that seeks to eliminate the other,"[12] always draws a clear line of demarcation with what is not a person, both within the individual, in the case of his animal and bodily part, and within society, between persons with rights and non-person without rights. In order to overcome this split and breathe new life into the values expressed by human rights, Esposito therefore proposes the category of the *impersonal*. In particular, in *Third Person*, but also in later works, he explores this notion through various vectors. Esposito's aim is not to eliminate the idea of the person, but rather to deconstruct it and bring forth an alternative space to overcome its dichotomous and exclusionary logic.

Why "third person"? "The 'third person' is still a person, but deconstructed to the point of incorporating an impersonal dimension."[13] As the linguist Emile Benveniste shows in his studies on personal pronouns, the third person *he/she/it* is profoundly different from the first two (*I* and *you*).[14] It paradoxically escapes personal logic and is therefore defined as "non-person." This is found, for example, in medieval Arabic, where the first person indicates "the one who speaks," the second "the one who listens," and the third person represents "the one who is absent"; similarly, in the Jewish grammar, a distinction is made between second-person speech, understood as "language of presence," and third-person speech, called "language of absence."[15] What is absent, as Esposito notes, "is always the subjective quality of the person or, better perhaps, the personal identity of the subject."[16] We can see it with some impersonal expressions found in many languages, such as "it rains" and other expressions related to the weather.

As much as philosophy has preferred the person to the impersonal, there are various authors who have instead realized the deconstructive potential of the third person. Esposito analyzes them and finds three main directions in which a philosophy of the impersonal can be fruitfully developed: justice, writing, and life. Especially the latter, *life*, seems to be, in his opinion, the most successful path.

This is not surprising since his interest in biopolitics and the attempt to elaborate an immunitary paradigm for an affirmative biopolitics had already been the focus of his most important works.[17] Esposito finds in Foucault and Deleuze the principal philosophers for thinking the impersonal as life, or, rather, as *a* life. Without falling into Nazi thanatopolitics, in which the biological datum suppresses everything else, for Esposito life is an event that is never identified with the subject but manifests itself as a continuous resistance to subjectivation and subjection, "a realm of pure intensities—as Davide Tarizzo defines it—devoid of specific affiliations and stripped of essential qualities."[18] With the concept of life, distinctions and discriminations between *bios* and *zoe*, human and animal, soul and body are neutralized in favor of the virtuality and the power of the event.

Before reaching these conclusions, Esposito also dwells on Levinas and shows what he sees as the strengths and weaknesses of this perspective.

Esposito's attitude toward the French philosopher oscillates between admiration and criticism, as if Levinas's perspectives were for him a kind of unfinished revolution. In fact, according to Esposito, Levinas understood the importance of the third person. While for the dialogical philosophy of Buber and Jankélévitch the third person (*Autrui*) can be absorbed into the first and the second, Levinas showed its absolute and its irreducibility to the first two. However, this awareness also became the aporia of his thought: "The entire work of Emmanuel Levinas is traversed and troubled by the question of the third person. It constitutes both the theoretical apex of his thought and its point of internal crisis, its problem and the limit it strikes up against without ever arriving at a solution."[19]

In Esposito's view, the Levinasian third person, called *illeité* (noun form of the French *il*, "he") takes on two modes: "internal" and "external."

The internal is that third person who is at the bottom of the face-to-face relationship with the other man. For although Levinas is the thinker of the dual relationship between the Self and the Other and theorizes this relationship in terms of ethical responsibility, nevertheless what makes it possible is precisely the third person. In fact, this relationship of responsibility is asymmetrical: the subject is "in the accusative,"[20] and responds to the call of the Other to the point of substitution. This asymmetry is always caused by a *diachrony*, as the Other comes from an immemorial past that precedes being and ontology. This absolute transcendence at the (an-archic)[21] origin of the relationship allows the Other to survive as other and not to become pure object of subject's knowledge. This absolute transcendence is described both in divine terms, as the presence of God in me, and in negative terms of absence, of trace, of enigma: it is the limit, the intangible threshold within the denucleated self. Indeed, God "comes to mind"[22] in the face of the other, but in the form of a trace and erasing Himself.

Thus, this first sense of the impersonal seems to coexist with Levinasian subjectivity. Indeed, it grounds the dual relationship in which it is involved. This is not the case, however, for the "external" sense of the impersonal, which, according to Esposito, undermines the entire architecture of Levinasian thought. Especially from *Otherwise Than Being*, Levinas introduces the theme of *justice* through the notion of "third party."[23] The exclusive, ethical relationship, in fact, runs the risk of wronging the other of the other, that is, the third: equality and calculation are therefore necessary.

The diachrony of face-to-face is complemented by the synchrony of "togetherness in the same place."[24] On the one hand, justice makes society possible; on the other, ethics remains its fundamental inspiration. According to Esposito, the entire Levinasian philosophy is undermined by the intrigue between *illeité* (internal impersonal) and the third party (external impersonal). This intrigue also includes the relationship between love and justice, between individuality and generality, between "logic of superabundance" and "logic of equivalence."[25] Thus, Esposito's first criticism of Levinas is that he did not break out of the aporia between the logic of Two and the logic of Three. The second criticism concerns the lack of radicality of his idea of justice. According to the Italian philosopher, Levinas failed to grasp the potential of the impersonal neutrality of the third party: "The neutrality of justice, justice as neutrality—which he also refers to in one of his (Levinas') final essays—does not found a new discourse based on the neutral. It does not inaugurate a crosswise gaze on that 'anyone' or 'anyone at all' in which a truly third person can be reflected on its originary impersonal ground."[26]

So, Levinas does not take that step further, "*le pas au dela*," as Blanchot[27] writes, toward a philosophy and politics of the impersonal. Which is instead done, for example, by Weil, Blanchot, and Deleuze.

Levinas's Ethical Impersonal

Let us now turn directly to the analysis of the Levinasian perspective. Indeed, although Esposito captures many central aspects of the Levinasian idea of the impersonal, some others are not examined.

First, it should be noted that Levinas understood as early as the 1930s the danger of Hitlerism and its connection to a specific idea of the body and life. In his 1934 article "Reflections on the Philosophy of Hitlerism" he states:

> The mysterious urgings of the blood, the appeals of heredity and the past for which the body serves as an enigmatic vehicle, lose the character of being problems that are subject to

> a solution put forward by a sovereignly free Self. [. . .] Man's essence no longer lies in freedom, but in a kind of bondage [*enchainement*]. To be truly oneself does not mean taking flight once more above contingent events that always remain foreign to the Self's freedom; on the contrary, it means becoming aware of the ineluctable original chain.[28]

Martin Heidegger's involvement in Nazism was an event that profoundly marked Levinas's life and philosophy, but, for Levinas, however tragic was, this was also understandable, as Heidegger's perspective also responds to a similar logic of *enchainment*, in which the *Dasein* is completely subservient to the neutrality of Being.[29] If for Nazi thought the biological dimension is what we are chained to, for Heidegger Being is our destiny: for Levinas, in both cases an *escape* is necessary.[30]

Thus, the recent historical facts, Levinas's personal experience of war and imprisonment,[31] but also his philosophical criticism of Heidegger—all these elements come together and give rise to the concept of *il y a*. What is *il y a*? This term first appeared in the 1948 text, *Existence and Existents*, in which it is described as an "existence without a world."[32] Levinas performs a phenomenological *epochè*: in the face of the negation of the world, "something would happen, if only night and the silence of nothingness."[33] This anonymous background, impossibility of nothingness or coincidence between being and nothingness, is the *il y a*. He describes this concept using images from art, literature, and the sacred.[34] In particular, he explicitly refers to Maurice Blanchot's novel *Thomas l'Obscur*,[35] in which "the presence of absence, the night, the dissolution of the subject in the night, the horror of being, the return of being to the heart of every negative movement, the reality of irreality are admirably expressed."[36] It is therefore a reality in which the subject finds himself immersed and loses his identity, crushed by the tragic weight of being.

The first appearance of the impersonal, therefore, in Levinas is undoubtedly negative, associated with the danger and horror of the indeterminate as a tragic fate to which the existents are chained. Levinas's subsequent philosophical work seems to develop precisely in order to abandon this impersonal dimension. However, this overcoming of *il y a* does not take place with a renewed personalism. Besides the fact that it is rare that Levinas uses this term, he carries out a deconstruction of the modern subject and main person's attributes. In fact, for Levinas as well as for Esposito, even the category of the modern subject ends up being complementary or rather functional to this perspective. Even on the political dimension, the idea of human rights was not sufficient to save man from brutality and injustice, and simply revealed Europe's "bad conscience":

> A bad conscience after thousands of years of glorious Reason, of the triumphant Reason of knowledge; but also after thousands of years of political—and bloody—fratricidal wars, of imperialism in the guise of universality, of contempt for human beings and exploitation, including, in this century, two world wars, oppression, genocides, the Holocaust, terrorism, unemployment, the never-ending poverty of the Third World, the ruthless doctrines of Fascism and National Socialism, and even the supreme paradox in which the defense of the person is inverted into Stalinism.[37]

The Levinasian strategy carried out on the idea of subjectivity does not, therefore, lead to an abandonment of this notion, but rather to a radical transformation that, on closer inspection, in discarding certain attributes of the traditional idea of "person," such as that of substance, rationality, and independence, it maintains certain aspects in common with it, redefining them. For example, responsibility remains a sort of *principium individuationis*, no longer, however, founded on the subject's freedom of action and decision but on the subject's ability to listen to the Other and take charge of him. Precisely because of this passive character of responsibility, subjectivity seems to accentuate the link with the concept of subjection, no longer of one part (the soul) over the other (the body), or in a sense of subjection in the political sphere, but as subjection to the Other, who obliges and accuses the Self, infinitely. Moreover, the idea of uniqueness continues to constitute a character proper to the human, although no longer indicating its value as atomic individuality, but rather its impossibility of ignoring the face of the Other.

Hence Levinas in *Totality and Infinity* states: "We have thus the conviction of having broken with the philosophy of the Neuter: with the Heideggerian Being of the existent whose impersonal neutrality the critical work of Blanchot has so much contributed to bring out, with Hegel's impersonal reason, which shows to the personal consciousness only its ruses."[38]

Despite these statements, the impersonal continues to have a central role in later works, so much so that it can be seen as the very Levinasian "temptation."[39] However, it is no longer configured as the *il y a* but as the *illeité*. This notion, as Esposito clearly understood, is used by Levinas to describe the trace of God at the bottom of the relationship between the Self and the Other. Although it is not the *il y a*, the *illeité* is also impersonal, precisely a third person. Both are described through a lexicon that refers to the semantic field of impersonality, but in the former case it excludes the subject and annihilates it, in the latter case it is the very foundation of the ethical relationship and the possibility of an ethical subject:[40] "*Beyond being is a third person*, which is not definable by the oneself, by ipseity. It is the possibility of the third direction of radical *unrightness* which escapes the bipolar play of immanence and transcendence. Through a trace the irreversible past takes on the profile of a 'He.' The *beyond* from which a face comes is in the third person."[41] To these two forms of the third person is added *the third party*, that is, justice. It is at this level that laws and institutions take place: not so much to limit the violence by means of a social contract but to curb the exorbitant responsibility. Indeed, an absolute face-to-face relationship would lead to crushing the subject under the weight of responsibility, but also to forgetting the other of the other, the third party.[42]

Just as ethics needs justice, justice also needs ethics. In fact, politics comes *after*, and is always guided by ethics, which asks it to go beyond itself and beyond calculation and equity. There is a need for measurement, but without this entailing the dissolution of the difference and uniqueness of individual faces. Although justice comes from a ground that transcends ontology, that is, the encounter with the face of the other, it cannot remain suspended outside the world of sociality, community, institutions, and history: "Justice requires and establishes the state. There is, to be sure, the indispensable reduction of human uniqueness to the particularity of an individual of the human genus, to the condition of citizen. A derivation. But still its imperative motivation is inscribed in the very right of the other man, unique and incomparable."[43]

Justice rests on responsibility, but the face-to-face relationship has always been in the social dimension. In Levinas's perspective, therefore, there is no responsibility without equity, because the third party is always present and demands justice, but also because the Other needs to become member of a society.[44]

Conclusions

As I have tried to show here, there are many points in common between Esposito's and Levinas's idea of the impersonal. First of all, both need to overcome the dualistic perspective of the person and the idea of the modern subject that underlies human rights theory. Both think that this vision is insufficient: it has failed to stop the tragedies and dramas that have taken place in the twentieth century.

Moreover, neither Esposito nor Levinas uses the third person and the impersonal in order to abandon the category of person, but rather to deconstruct it, to modify its attributes, and to show its internal contradictions.

Levinas excludes certain aspects of the person, such as the egocentric character, the rationality and independence, proposing instead a subject who is responsible, vulnerable and decentered on the other and who finds in the third person, in *illeity*, its meaning. Esposito, on the other hand, critiques the exclusionary traits of the person and its capacity for reification, valuing the more dynamic aspects of life (*bios*).

There are also profound differences between the two perspectives. The most obvious one concerns biopolitics. Whereas for Esposito an affirmative biopolitics based on the impersonal is possible and desirable, for Levinas the reference to biopolitics is always negative, in terms of *enchainment* (to the body or to the Being) and *il y a*. Moreover, Esposito addresses the issue of the impersonal on an ontological-political level, while Levinas does so from an ethical point of view.

Esposito, as I've already shown, explicitly criticizes Levinas's perspective in several respects, especially about justice (i.e., "external sense of impersonal"). Although Esposito sees in this dimension of the impersonal the aporia of Levinas's philosophy, in my opinion this is instead the point of greatest closeness between the two thinkers, for two reasons.

The first one is that Levinas, without reducing the logic of Three to the logic of Two, affirms the need of "comparison between incomparables"[45] and thus to continually relate Second and Third, the particular and the universal. There is a kind of universalization of uniqueness. For without eliminating the uniqueness of the ethical relationship, in justice it is extended to the other, as the subject becomes "another for the other."[46] Only in this way does the other also become unique as responsible. Counterintuitive as it may seem, then, it is justice that is the site of the highest realization of ethics. The transition from Two to Three allows for the coexistence of the singular and the universal. Far from being an aporia, justice in Levinas is rather the bridge between ethics and politics and enables the fruitful relationship between them. Indeed, justice is a paradoxical dynamic,[47] a "*mouvement pendulaire de la générosité et de la justice*" that Pierre Hayat defines as "*intuition du social.*"[48]

Although starting from a more explicitly political intent, in my opinion Esposito is also driven by a similar goal. As Laura Bazzicalupo states: "There is a strong ethical drive [. . .] toward a world and politics-to-come, in Roberto Esposito. This means reformulating the assumptions of political action, abandoning the perspective adopted even by critical thinking of the inevitable division between government and the governed, making room for the multiplicity of singularities. Singularities, not individuals."[49] The second reason can be found in more recent works, particularly in *The Instituting Thought*.[50] In this book, Esposito goes beyond the affirmative biopolitics that was the core of *Third Person*, while still maintaining the centrality of the category of impersonal.

While still interested in the biopolitic perspective,[51] Esposito argues that it risks nullifying the difference between ontology and political. Avoiding even the opposite risk, that of difference and the denial of a common foundation, he therefore proposes an "instituting paradigm" by referring to Lefort's thought and his reading of Machiavelli. According to this model, the political is traversed by conflict, which is an irreducible relationship between parties for power. It is precisely this instituting dynamic that constitutes the unfounded foundation[52] of society: the institution or, better, *instituting*, has the task of avoiding any fixed determination of these mobile configurations of the social: "Rather than referring to a consolidated order of rules and laws, instituting refers to a task that coincides with that of politics and is destined to continually change the normative framework in which it operates—and to do so without either deactivating it in a salvific mode or dissolving it in the name of a creativity so accelerated that it destroys what was just created."[53] In this work, Esposito returns to themes already addressed in *Third Person*, and argues that the logic of the instituting is impersonal, and irreducible to the idea of the person: "Unlike those philosophies that look to dialogue as the archetype of all possible social relationships, even face-to-face interactions are made possible only by the presence of institutions aimed at protecting them from an excess of immediacy. One does not pass immediately from I to you, from one to the other, without transitioning through the 'non-person,' which relates them via impersonal institutions."[54] It's not difficult to spot some similarities with Levinas's role of third person, both the internal and the external.

According to Levinas, just as *illeité* guarantees ethical asymmetry in the dual relationship and avoids reduction to the One, so too does justice, in which the value of institutions is precisely that of mediation.

This is why Ciaramelli defines Levinas's justice as the "original necessity of the instituting mediation."[55] The sociality is based on the rejection of the immediacy of the face, but at the same time cannot renounce it. This "hyperbolic thought of instituting"[56] creates a dynamic of foundation for the political, which cannot be fixed in static institutions. The legitimacy of institutions depends on their ability to always question themselves on the basis of the an-archical principle of ethical responsibility: "Justice is always a revision of justice and the expectation of a better justice."[57] Although there is no explicit confrontation on this point, it thus seems that both Esposito and Levinas interpret institutions as dynamic structures that have their legitimacy in the ability to question themselves. The inextinguishability of this task, far from being sign weakness and vulnerability of the political, is the very possibility of justice.

Notes

1. See Vincenzo Cuomo, *Del corpo impersonale: Saggi di estetica dei media e di filosofia della tecnica* (Naples: Liguori, 2004); Enrica Lisciani-Petrini, "Verso il soggetto impersonale," *Filosofia politica*, no. 1 (2012): 39–50.

2. Roberto Esposito, *Third Person: Politics of Life and Philosophy of the Impersonal*, trans. Zakiya Hanafi (Cambridge: Polity, 2012), 4.

3. Roberto Esposito was already interested in the deconstruction of the concept of person in several of his works preceding *Third Person*, such as *Bios: Biopolitics and Philosophy*, trans. Timothy Campbell (Minneapolis: University of Minnesota Press, 2008); *Communitas: The Origin and Destiny of Community*, trans. Timothy Campbell (Stanford, CA: Stanford University Press, 2010); and *Categories of the Impolitical*, trans. Connal Parsley (New York: Fordham University Press, 2015).

4. Roberto Esposito, *Persons and Things: From the Body's Point of View*, trans. Zakiya Hanafi (Cambridge: Polity, 2015).

5. Esposito, *Third Person*, 14.

6. See Esposito, *Persons and Things*.

7. See Alain De Libéra, *Archéologie du sujet*, vol. 1, *Naissance du sujet* (Paris: Vrin, 2007).

8. See Ugo Thiel, *The Early Modern Subject: Self-Consciousness and Personal Identity from Descartes to Hume* (New York: Oxford University Press, 2011).

9. Roberto Esposito and Timothy Campbell, "For a Philosophy of the Impersonal," *New Centennial Review* 10, no. 2 (2010): 123.

10. Hannah Arendt, *The Origins of Totalitarianism* (New York: Penguin, 2017).

11. Judith Butler, *Precarious Life: The Power of Mourning and Violence* (London: Verso, 2004).

12. Roberto Esposito, *Two: The Machine of Political Theology and the Place of Thought*, trans. Zakiya Hanafi (New York: Fordham University Press, 2015), 3.

13. Roberto Esposito, *Dall'impolitico all'impersonale: Conversazioni filosofiche* (Milan-Udine: Mimesis, 2012), 143.

14. Emile Benveniste, *Problems in General Linguistics*, trans. Mary Elizabeth Meek (Coral Gables, FL: University of Miami Press, 1978), 217–22.

15. Stephane Moses, "Autour de la question du tiers," in *Emmanuel Levinas et les territoires de la pensée*, ed. Danielle Cohen-Levinas (Paris: Puf, 2007), 237.

16. Esposito, *Third Person*, 107.

17. Esposito, *Bios*; Esposito, *Communitas*; Roberto Esposito, *Immunitas: The Protection and Negation of Life*, trans. Zakiya Hanafi (Cambridge: Polity, 2011).

18. Davide Tarizzo, *La vita: Un'invenzione recente* (Rome-Bari: Laterza, 2010), 174.

19. Esposito, *Third Person*, 119.

20. Emmanuel Levinas, *Otherwise Than Being and beyond Essence*, trans. Alfonso Lingis (Dordrecht: Kluwer Academic, 1994), 110.

21. On the "an-archy" in the thought of Levinas, see Miguel Abensour, "An-archy between Metapolitics and Politics," *Parallax* 8, no. 3 (2002): 5–18.

22. Emmanuel Levinas, *Of God Who Comes to Mind*, trans. Bettina Bergo (Stanford, CA: Stanford University Press, 1998).

23. Levinas, *Otherwise Than Being*, 157.

24. Levinas, *Otherwise Than Being*, 158. On this theme, see Rita Fulco, *Essere insieme in un luogo: Etica, politica, diritto nel pensiero di Emmanuel Levinas* (Milan-Udine: Mimesis, 2013).

25. Paul Ricoeur, *Love and Justice*, in Werner G. Jeanrond and Jennifer L. Rike, eds., *Radical Pluralism and Truth: David Tracy and the Hermeneutics of Religion* (New York: Crossroad, 1991).

26. Esposito, *Third Person*, 125.

27. Maurice Blanchot, *Le pas au-delà* (Paris: Gallimard, 1973).

28. Emmanuel Levinas, "Reflections on the Philosophy of Hitlerism," *Critical Inquiry* 17, no. 1 (1990): 69.

29. In a 1938 article titled "The Understanding of Spirituality in French and German Culture," right after discussing the Heideggerian perspective, Levinas notes that "it is no coincidence that extremist political parties, which are presently so strong in Germany, are enchanted with this notion of spirit. They do not trust reason because reason opposes their vitality; they do not listen to reason which says 'yes' when their existence screams 'no.'" Emmanuel Levinas, "The Understanding of Spirituality in French and German Culture," *Continental Philosophy*, no. 31 (1998): 6.

30. Emmanuel Levinas, *On Escape: De l'évasion*, trans. Bettina Bergo (Stanford, CA: Stanford University Press, 2003).

31. Levinas's philosophical activity and his life experience can be seen in the writings of his prison notebooks, *Carnets de captivité*. Emmanuel Levinas, *Oeuvres:* book 1, *Carnets de captivité suivi de Ecrits sur la captivité et Notes philosophiques diverses* (Paris: Grasset, 2009). On this theme, see Howard Caygill, "Levinas's Prison Notebooks," *Radical Philosophy*, no. 160 (2010): 27–35.

32. Emmanuel Levinas, *Existence and Existents*, trans. Alphonso Lingis (The Hague: Nijhoff, 1978), 52.

33. Levinas, *Existence and Existents*, 57.

34. On this theme, see Francesco Paolo Ciglia, "L'essere, il sacro e l'arte negli esordi filosofici di Emmanuel Levinas," *Archivio di Filosofia*, no. 1–2 (1982): 249–80; and Silvia Dadà, "L'oscurità del reale: Levinas poeta dell'*il y a*," *Bollettino filosofico*, no. 32 (2017): 232–54.

35. Maurice Blanchot, *Thomas l'Obscur* (Paris: Gallimard, 1941). Levinas met Blanchot at the University of Strasbourg and became close friends with him. He writes several essays on Blanchot's thought. Emmanuel Levinas, "Sur Maurice Blanchot," *Revue Philosophique de la France et de l'Etranger* 167, no. 1 (1977): 112–13.

36. Levinas, *Existence and Existents*, 63.

37. Emmanuel Levinas, *Entre nous: Thinking-of-the-Other*, trans. Michael B. Smith and Barbara Harshav (New York: Columbia University Press, 1998), 161.

38. Emmanuel Levinas, *Totality and Infinity: An Essay on Exteriority*, trans. Alphonso Lingis (Dordrecht: Nijhoff, 1991), 299.

39. "The il y a is one of Levinas's most fascinating propositions: but it is also his temptation, since, being the inverse of transcendence, it is also indistinct from it"; Maurice Blanchot, *Political Writings, 1953–1993*, trans. Paul Zakir (New York: Fordham University Press, 2010), 151. On the same opinion, see also Rocco Ronchi, *Bataille, Levinas, Blanchot: Un sapere passionale* (Milan: Spirali, 1985); and Simon Critchley, *Very Little . . . Almost Nothing: Death, Philosophy, Literature* (New York: Routledge, 1997).

40. On this theme, see Silvia Dadà, "La doppia negazione del senso: Levinas contro il nichilismo," *Teoria* 40, no. 1 (2019): 183–94.

41. Emmanuel Levinas, "The Trace of the Other," in *Deconstruction in Context*, ed. Mark C. Taylor (Chicago, IL: University of Chicago Press, 1986), 356.

42. This way of understanding the origin of sociality and the political dimension is very different from Thomas Hobbes's description of the state of nature. The state and institutions do not arise to limit the uncontrolled violence of individuals, but to limit exorbitant responsibility. Miguel Abensour, in this regard, describes Levinas as a "contra Hobbes"; Miguel Abensour, *Le contre-Hobbes d'E. Lévinas*, in *Difficile justice: Dans la trace d'E. Lévinas*, ed. Jean Halpérin and Nelly Hansson (Paris: Albin Michel, 1998), 120–33.

43. Levinas, *Entre nous*, 196.

44. "The neighbour that obsesses me is already a face, both comparable and incomparable, a unique face and in relationship with faces, which are visible in the concern for justice" (Levinas, *Otherwise Than Being*, 158).

45. Levinas, *Otherwise Than Being*, 16.

46. Levinas, *Otherwise Than Being*, 158.

47. Silvia Dadà, *Il paradosso della giustizia: Levinas e Derrida* (Rome: Inshibboleth, 2021).

48. Pierre Hayat, "Emmanuel Levinas: Une intuition du social," *Le Philosophoire*, no. 39 (2009): 134.

49. Laura Bazzicalupo, "La politica e le parole dell'impersonale," in *Impersonale. In dialogo con Roberto Esposito*, ed. Laura Bazzicalupo (Milan: Mimesis, 2008), 75.

50. Roberto Esposito, *Instituting Thought: Three Paradigms of Political Ontology*, trans. Mark Willian Epstein (Cambridge: Polity, 2021).

51. Even later, especially after the experience of the COVID-19 pandemic, the topic of biopolitics remains central. On this issue, see Roberto Esposito, *Immunità comune: Biopolitica all'epoca della pandemia* (Turin: Einaudi, 2022).

52. Despite some differences (Esposito, *Instituting Thought*, 13–15), Esposito's paradigm can be compared to Marchart's notion of "post-foundational political thought"; Olivier Marchart, *Post-Foundational Political Thought Political Difference in Nancy, Lefort, Badiou, and Laclau* (Edinburgh: Edinburgh University Press, 2007).

53. Esposito, *Instituting Thought*, 12.

54. Esposito, *Instituting Thought*, 126.

55. Fabio Ciaramelli, *La legge prima della legge: Levinas e il problema della giustizia* (Rome: Castelvecchi, 2016), 44.

56. Rita Fulco, "Levinas: Al di là delle istituzioni, nelle istituzioni," in *Istituzione: Almanacco di Filosofia e Politica 2*, ed. Mattia Di Pierro, Francesco Marchesi and Elia Zaru (Macerata, Italy: Quodlibet, 2020), 176.

57. Levinas, *Entre nous*, 196.

Eight

Assurance and Community

The Far Proximity between Esposito and Heidegger

Sandro Gorgone

Biopolitics of Immunity

In his recent book *Immunità comune: Biopolitica all'epoca della pandemia*,[1] Roberto Esposito, referring to his 2002 volume *Immunitas: The Protection and Negation of Life*,[2] in which he had shown the centrality of the immune paradigm, notes how his analysis has been confirmed by the experience of the pandemic: "But contemporary society's propensity to immunize itself has certainly exceeded all imagination, becoming the most significant phenomenon of our time."[3] He therefore identifies, in the mass vaccination policies implemented by most European governments, an example of "affirmative biopolitics" that outlines the "unprecedented silhouette of a *common immunity*."[4]

Esposito therefore claims, starting from the philosophical experience of the pandemic, a rigorous continuity of his thought on immunity: it is no coincidence that the last paragraph of his 2022 book *Immunitas* was titled "Common Immunity" and, through the analysis of immunological tolerance, focused on the positive value of immune processes in defining the identity of the subject and its relationship with otherness. The consequent philosophical challenge that Esposito poses in this study is to not only find the immune mechanism at the center of contemporary biopolitics but also to recognize it as the general horizon of meaning of the founding philosophical texts of modernity. The political ontology of modernity would therefore be permeated from top to bottom by the immune paradigm. Esposito intends to trace it in a complex implication with the category of negativity. Emblematically, in Nietzsche "immunization reveals itself as a negation of life that is necessary for life's facilitated survival. Like the Pauline figure of the *katechon*, it protects from evil, by incorporating rather than excluding it."[5]

The affirmation of the immune paradigm sanctioned by the recent pandemic has, moreover, posed with new force the question of the relationship between community and immunity: the demand for global immunization, put forward by individual institutions but also by governments and political forces, leads to a redefinition of the relationship between these two intimately related concepts, albeit in perennial tension with a view to their possible overlapping, which Esposito expresses precisely with the pregnant expression of *common immunity*.

Immune processes are, in fact, necessary for the existence of any community, since it is precisely certain external and internal boundaries that define its physiognomy in relation to other communities—the borders—and its own social and economic articulation. Immunization, therefore, "cuts through the community along lines of inclusion and exclusion that, by qualifying its members socially and politically, make them different from one another."[6] The immunization paradigm does not, therefore, establish sharp and disjunctive fractures but delineates osmotic thresholds of contact from which political bodies take shape. In particular, Esposito sees one of the main theoretical merits of this perspective in the fact that it represents a balancing point in the opposition introduced by Foucault between the terms "life" and "politics" within the notion of biopolitics. In contrast to the absolutely negative declination of biopolitics whereby life is completely subjugated by power and the opposite but specular declination whereby, instead, life absorbs power in its affirmative dynamic, the immune logic manages to connect these two terms in a nonoppositional manner through a nonabsolute characterization of the negative. Indeed, within the immunitary perspective, it stands as "the way in which life survives, taking distance from its own internal energy, which could be disintegrative. When we define immunity as a negative protection of life, we mean that immunity does not protect life directly—in an immediate, frontal fashion—but by subjecting it to a constraint that diminishes its vital potency, channeling that power within certain borders."[7]

This particular immune declination of the negative can be interpreted in an ontological-existential sense as a presupposition of the relationship between identity and otherness that underlies the community bond. And it is precisely at the existential roots of this relationship, in the Heideggerian thematization of the *Mit-Dasein* contained in the existential analytics of *Being and Time*, that, according to Esposito, lies the possibility of a conception of the common and the community in an immune sense. It is, therefore, from here that we must start in order to outline the theoretical challenge of a thought that wants to hold together the need for the common and the need for the immune and that, through this problematic connection, is able to think about the immune character of contemporary societies.

Mit-Dasein and Worldliness

In the chapter dedicated to Heidegger in his earlier text on community, Esposito characterizes his thought as a thought of community and not as a political philosophy, since the starting point of his reflection is not the individual but the "relationship of sharing," the "with" on which the very constitution of *Dasein* as *Mit-Dasein* is based: "Existence is the being whose essence is the 'with,' the '*mit*,' the '*avec*'; or existence is 'with,' with-existence [*con-esistenza*], or doesn't exist. The *cum* isn't something that is added from without to the being of existence. It is that which makes being that being that it is."[8]

That the being of *Dasein* is, to use Jean-Luc Nancy's fortunate expression, *singular-plural*, can already be deduced from Heidegger's phenomenological analysis of the Who of *Dasein*: analogous to the impossibility of a subject without a world, "as insolated I without the others is in the end just as far from being given initially."[9] The "others" doesn't mean "everybody else but me—those from whom the I distinguishes itself";[10] rather, they are those "among whom one is, too."[11] This "being-there-too" nominates an existential trait of being-in-the-world of *Dasein*, in such a way that being-in turns out to be constitutively a Being-with-Others (*Mitsein mit Anderen*) and the very innerworldly Being of Others is identified with being-with (*Mitdasein*). *Dasein* meets others in caring (*Besorgen*) and in the prescient *circumspection* (*Umsicht*) in which its worldliness is unfolded and in which it can "find itself." Insofar as *Dasein* encounters Others in the being-with of the world, it finds itself: "Da-sein in itself is essentially being-with."[12] Against the existentialist vulgate that wants existence consigned to an irredeemable solitude, here Heidegger is asserting, with a radicality that has often been silenced or downplayed in his reception, that the absence of others and the loneliness of *Dasein* are defective and nonoriginal modes of its being-with. The "property" of *Dasein* (*das eigene Dasein*)[13] is revealed in the encounter with the other as a being-with since *Dasein* has the existential structure (*Wesensstruktur*) of being-with.

As being-with, *Dasein* is, moreover, essentially in-view of others [*umwillen Anderer*]. This assertion is to be understood in an existential sense and does not indicate any original altruistic vocation of man; rather, it refers to the constitutive openness toward others—*among whom Dasein is already to be found*—that contributes to articulating the worldliness of the world. Together with the usable thing, that is, of which it takes care (*besorgt*), *Dasein* always encounters the being-with of others of which it is concerned (*fürsorgt*).

The fact that others appear in the mode of mere presence as subjects to whom one must relate first and foremost through knowledge and psychological investigation, as *alter egos* whose original extraneousness must be overcome through a process of progressive familiarization and rapprochement, descends, according to Heidegger, from the prevalence of the defective modes of caring whereby being-together (*Miteinander-sein*) is reduced to mutual neglect or, at best, to the pursuit of a sentimental attunement—the empathy so emphasized today by social psychology—and of a common interest. The dominance of the theoretical and practical-economic traits of being-together derives from the inauthenticity, literally from the "impropriety" (*Uneigentlichkeit*) of the relationship between *Dasein* and the others; this relationship, however, is always based on the authenticity, literally on the "property" (*Eigentlichkeit*) of the existential mode of being-with and not on the relationship of merely present entities: "Being-toward-others [*das Sein zu Anderen*] is ontologically different from being toward objectively present things. The 'other' being itself has the kind of being of Da-sein. Thus, in being with and toward others, there is a relation of being from Da-sein to Da-sein."[14]

This relationship is also not to be understood as a possibility of the narcissistic mirroring of being in the other understood as *alter ego*, that is, as a "double of the self."[15] Rather, it is the relation of *Dasein* to itself that opens up the relationship with the other as other.[16] These passages seem to indicate that the relation with the otherness of others is internal to *Dasein* itself not in the manner of dialectical recognition but insofar as *Dasein* is originally outside itself, extraneous to itself, exposed and delivered to its own impropriety.[17] The *Sein zum Anderen* is thus configured as "an autonomous and irreducible relation of being" which as being-with "already exists with the being of *Da-sein*."[18]

As Esposito states, refering to these passages from *Being and Time*, there cannot be an I that is not already a We: "Existence, in other words, cannot be declined except in the first-person plural: we are."[19] Against the prevailing approach of the following philosophies of otherness and of the dialogical relationship[20] that place the relationship between the subject and the other, which can be defined in various ways, at the center Heidegger's aim would therefore be that of a radical deconstruction of the concept of individual, that is, of the idea of a monolithic identity, accomplished and closed in itself that only relates to another closed identity. *Dasein*, therefore, could not be individual, insofar as it is already split and open, outstretched and exposed to the outside: "Heidegger refers to the originally singular *and* plural character of a shared existence, which is properly ecstatic: each [*ciascuno*] opens to all, not despite of but *inasmuch* as single, the contrary of the individual. The other cannot be brought near, nor can it be absorbed or incorporated by the one, or vice versa, because the other is already *with* the one given, on account of the fact that there is no one without the other."[21] This is why, as Esposito also argues, Heidegger's starting point is not the me but the *cum*. We are not, that is, points of identity that, according to various processes of a moral, social, and political nature aggregate or disintegrate, rather, we are always the-ones-with-others and the-ones-of-others.

And yet, if *Dasein* identifies with the world it cares for and relates to others as elements of the *Mitwelt*, it risks dispersing itself and no longer being itself. The world, that is, becomes a kind of danger for *Dasein*, the occasion of a possible gnostic "perdition" insofar as it brings others together only as a mirroring of itself; the world, that is, becomes a horizon of intersubjectivity from which Heidegger resolutely wishes to distance his philosophy. This danger is, however, ineradicable since there is no other place of encounter with others than the *Mitwelt*. In this aporia the genuine basis of the objection that has repeatedly been made to Heidegger also lurks, suggesting that he has never sufficiently articulated the understanding of the *cum*, that he has failed to delineate the thought of the *Mit*, of the *Mit-Dasein*, and of the being-with in a way that is as structured and accomplished as that of the *Jemeinigkeit* of *Dasein*. Esposito argues however that this failure is not to be attributed to Heidegger's neglect or inability to understand, but belongs to the very "thing" of the thought of the commune. The *cum*, in fact, is impossible to comprehend and, consequently, to fully realize, just as, consequently, the community is necessarily incomplete; but this constitutive incompleteness of the community indicates, according to Esposito, the constitutively defective essence of its historical existence.

Esposito radicalizes this character of incompleteness of the community by grasping, albeit without making its meaning explicit, a decisive trait of existential analytics, that is, the constitutive exposure of Dasein to its impropriety, or rather, with a lexical hyperbole, to its most proper impropriety. The original *vulnus* of community, its structural deficit, would constitute, that is, the very object of communitary sharing: "What human beings share is just this impossibility to 'make' the community that they already 'are,' which is to say the ecstatic opening [*apertura*] that destines them to a constitutive lack. [. . .] We are not joined by a fullness but rather by an emptiness, by a defect, by a fall [*caduta*]."[22]

Through the interpretation of Heidegger's *Mit-Dasein*, Esposito, therefore, can verify the assumption already set out in the introduction to *Communitas*, namely that community is founded on *munus* as debt, pledge, and gift giving and thus on the lack and constitutive impropriety of the subject that opens itself up to the relationship with others: "The common is not characterized by what is proper but by what is improper, or even more drastically, by the other; by a voiding [*svuotamento*], be it partial or whole, of property into its negative; by removing what is properly one's own [*depropriazione*] that invests and decenters the proprietary subject, forcing him to take leave [*uscire*] of himself, to alter himself."[23] In the community, therefore, we encounter only an emptiness, a distance, an extraneousness in which its members find themselves lacking and involved in a circuit of reciprocal donation, destined, in the sharing of a radical nonbelonging, to the exteriority that, by dispossessing them, brings them together.

The Disposition of Community

In the introduction to the 2001 Italian edition of Jean-Luc Nancy's *Being Singular Plural*, Esposito affirms the inevitability of the question of community precisely in such a defective, lacking, and unfinished form. Referring to some statements in Nancy's *Inoperative Community*, Esposito in fact states: "Community [. . .], anything but a common body, essence or subject, refers precisely to this game of relation and distinction [between the self and others], to the 'proximity of the gap and proximity.' It is therefore that [. . .] community remains our question. One might go so far as to say, our *only* issue, that which makes the flight of sense still and still our sense, the sense of 'us.' "[24]

Esposito, moreover, links the inevitability of the question of community and being-in-common with the need, shared by Nancy himself, of a reformulation of "first philosophy," that is, ontology, in the sense of plural singularity; this would allow a radical deconstruction of all traditional political philosophies. Central to this is the articulation of the "consistency" of *Dasein* in the form of being-in-common. Like Esposito, Nancy is also convinced that this perspective, indicated by Heidegger's existential analytics, was then rejected by Heidegger himself at the moment in which the phenomenological *Destruktion* of the human being, through above all the existential coordinates of care and *Angst*, gave way in the 1930s to a new substantiation of the common destiny of *Dasein* as the destiny of the German people.[25] And yet, both Nancy and Esposito agree on the necessity of resuming this deconstructive path, that is, to start writing fundamental ontology again, as well as the history of being and the thought of the *Ereignis*, "that starts from the plural singular of origins, from being-with."[26]

Nancy too, in fact, is convinced that being-with is inherent, in its various declinations (*Mitsein, Mitdasein, Miteinandersein*) to the very existential constitution of *Dasein*. It is never "one," but is always *every one*, in the sense of one-*with*-another, even though Heidegger—as we have noted above—never arrives at explicitly and definitively ascribing such an exposition of *Dasein* to its most proper constitution, remaining the victim of a sort of vertigo of the proper and origin aimed at grasping *Dasein* in itself. In the ontological interpretation of *Dasein* as being-with, however, according to Nancy, the same fundamental intention of Heidegger is at stake, namely that of bringing being back to the word and thus reproposing the long-forgotten question of the meaning of being. That is, no understanding of being of *Dasein* is possible that is not already in itself an understanding of others: "The themes of being-with and co-originarity need to be renewed and need to 'reinitialize' the existential analytic, exactly because these are meant to respond to the question of the meaning of Being, or to Being as meaning."[27]

The very existential structure of the understanding and, therefore, the possibility of the unfolding of the sense of being—as Heidegger would later explicitly state through Hölderlin's figure of the *Gespräch*—is realized as dislocation (deferment[28]) and dis-position[29] in relation to others. By revealing itself as a place (*Lichtung*) of manifestation of the sense of being, *Dasein* has already revealed itself as being-with. Being itself, consequently, necessarily reveals itself as being-with: "From now on, this is the minimal ontological premise. Being is put into play among us; it does not have any other meaning except the dis-position of this 'between.'"[30]

The structure of the "between," the spacing of the "we," which Nancy interprets as weave, network, and reticle, is a figure of the origin of our unfinished and fragmented communitary condition; it discloses, therefore, the dimension of our singular plurality. But the dis-position of the "between" is also the place of each individual's openness to his or her other, of his or her ecstatic exposure to his or her out-of-self. This exposure is, moreover, a constitutive character of the very singularity of being, or rather, of being as singularity. Every act of existence would be, as Nancy again notes, an act of exposure to the original singularity of being.[31] The being-*in* of *Dasein* cannot, therefore, be interpreted as being inside a given environment but as a relation to one's exteriority, whereby the world is "the proper space of its being-out-in-the-world."[32] It is the nonobjective and nonhuman sphere to which the human being is exposed, and which it in turn exposes in saying and thinking. In an attempt to radically overcome any anthropocentric and subjectivist temptation, Nancy proposes the following formula: "*Humanity is the ex-posing of the world; it is neither the end nor the ground of the world; the world is the exposure of humanity; it is neither the environment nor the representation of humanity.*"[33]

In consonance with such statements by Nancy, we can read the passages that Esposito dedicates to the relationship between *communitas* and exposure as opposed to the traditional interpretation of community as a fusion body or sphere of mirror recognition: "The community isn't a mode of being, much less a 'making' of the individual subject. It isn't the subject's expansion or multiplication but its exposure to what interrupts the closing and turns it inside out: a dizziness, a syncope, a spasm in the continuity of the subject."[34]

The exposure of the world and the disposition of the "between us" thus identify the two constitutive traits of what, following both Esposito and Nancy, we might call the "ontology of being-in-common." The constitutive impoliticity of community is rooted in them: starting from such a conception of the common and of *munus* as debt and gift, the subject deflects[35] from any historical-empirical realization and from any claim to foundation. Only, therefore, in the renunciation of our role as active subjects can we remain faithful to the infinite task of being-in-common in the continuous spacing and alteration of *cum*: "The community cannot have 'subjects' because it is the community itself that constitutes—that deconstructs—subjectivity in the form of its alteration."[36]

Immunity and Tolerance

Foreshadowing the immunitary logic fully outlined by Esposito, Nancy addresses the question of the "we" not from the perspective of a social or merely communitary dimension that would be added to a primitive individual datum or an intersubjective structure that would integrate the individual subjects; nor is it simply, as much of the so-called philosophy of otherness would like, an external instance that would alter and complicate the subject understood as *solus ipse*. According to Nancy it is something more and it is, also, something different: "It does not so much determine the principle of the *ipse*, whatever this may be [. . .], as it codetermines it with the plurality of *ipses*, each one of which is co-originary and coessential to the world, to a world which from this point on defines a coexistence that must be understood in a still-unheard-of sense [. . .]. It is not a nearness [*voisinage*] or community of *ipses*, but a co-ipseity."[37]

This co-ipseity—Nancy himself also defines it as "hetero-ipseity"—corresponds to the duplicity of *munus* and *immunus* that Esposito develops through the recovery of the immune mechanism in an ontological perspective. Esposito's declared intention in *Immunitas* is, in fact, to develop a philosophy of immunity that situates the immune paradigm in a relationship that is not merely exclusionary with its communitary reverse.[38] The prerequisite for this is, however, an alternative conception of the living organism to that of classical medicine, according to which the relationship between the self and the other, between health and disease—between the immune and the common—is conceived in terms of a radical opposition that does not tolerate contamination. Through the analysis of the decisive phenomenon of the coexistence of the unborn child with the mother's body, Esposito can affirm, instead, that the immune system "cannot be reduced to the simple function of rejecting all things foreign. If anything, the immune system must be interpreted as an internal resonance chamber, like the diaphragm through which difference, as such, engages and traverses us."[39]

The immune element is, therefore, stripped of its negative and potentially deadly power; that is, the immune is not simply the enemy of the common but something that internally implies and constitutes it, not, however, as if the antigen were a destructive germ that could lead to the collapse of an organism—or more generally of a system—as in the case of autoimmune diseases. If, in contrast, as some studies on the functions of the immune system seem to suggest, the tension between the communal and the immune is not crystallized in the destructive form of an internal *stásis* but takes on the features of a productive polemic, then it is possible that the intrinsically exclusionary immune logic gives rise to new communal semantics. Refering mainly to Alfred Tauber's studies, Esposito can state that "maintaining organic integrity is only a secondary, derivative function of the immune system, while its main function is to define the identity of the subject."[40] The main task of the immune mechanism would thus be not to defend an already given bodily identity but to produce it through the management of a dynamic and competitive interaction with the external environment, thus allowing a historical-processual conception of identity to emerge.

In order to understand, however, how the immune system does not primarily exercise a defensive and exclusionary function but is at the origin of the very definition of the bodily self and its relations with the outside world, it is necessary to interrogate the mechanism of immunological tolerance, and, more generally, the semantic spectrum of the concept of tolerance, which is fundamental to all modern thought and liberal-democratic culture.

The etymological meaning of the Latin verb *toleràre* refers in the first place to the action of carrying, lifting, and supporting, and only secondarily indicates the bearing of an extraneous element by repressing the instinct to suppress, expel, or, in any case, depower it. The idea of tolerance, enshrined in Voltaire's treatise of 1763[41] as the leading idea of Enlightenment culture and then at the center of the social and political claims of nineteenth-century liberalism, does not, therefore, only want to propose as a model that of a repression of the exclusionary impulse but intends also to promote an acceptance of the other that is also a welcome and responsibility toward him.

In the medical sphere, immunological tolerance seems to indicate, instead, a failure of the immune response induced by a previous exposure to the antigen. The decisive question that arises here, however, concerns how to understand this failure to respond: as a failure of the immune system, "or, conversely, as the active effect of its self-restraint? Should it be interpreted as a lack of recognition, or as a kind of recognition that is so sophisticated that it prevents a negative response to antigenic components belonging to the same organism?"[42] Esposito believes, on the basis of some studies on immunologic tolerance, that tolerance is not a defect of the system but its own product. The functioning of the immune system, therefore, would follow the univocal logic of rejection not of the other-from-itself but of its "tolerance." In other words, the organism, through immunological tolerance, would be able to incorporate the antigen and take it inside itself, accepting it and allowing it to persist in its difference, which, however, now no longer constitutes a danger to the survival of the organism itself but rather contributes to defining its identity by determining the osmotic balance in relation to the external environment.

Elevating these reflections to a properly philosophical level, we could affirm that the immune paradigm induces us to think of the processes of constituting identity not through exclusionary, dialectical, or speculative opposition to otherness but starting from the dynamics of self-definition of the ego that always take place in conjunction with the encounter with the other. Immunity would thus be the open and indefinite (infinite) process of production of the self and the other, of the I-in-the-other and the other-in-the-I. It is only on the basis of this interweaving of identity and otherness, whereby the presence of the stranger is detected and amplified only in the space of the familiar and intimacy, that it is possible to think of the common, the being-in-common as singular-plural being.

Common Singularity

The opposition between the self and the extraneous, between identity and otherness, between being-self and being-with is, therefore, replaced by a kind of ontological dis-position of an immune nature, in which the extraneous trait constantly feeds the processes of identification and configures the very relationship between the self and the other. Similarly, Nancy interprets the being-with no longer, in the traditional and fusional sense, as a com-position but also as a dis-position in the sense of the spacing of being *entre nous*, between us. This implies a sharing (*partage*) of being: it is equally shared between the different. This, according to Nancy, "makes Being as such a being-similar which circulates from being to being and which, thereby, implies the disparity, discontinuity, and simultaneity required for gauging a 'resemblance.'"[43] The being itself is determined, therefore, in its very being as being one-with-another, even in the irrepressible difference that separates beings from one another. Distinct, therefore, from the classical concepts of individuality, exceptionality, and particularity, singularity is inseparable from plurality: "The singular is primarily *each* one and, therefore, also *with* and *among* all the others. The singular is a plural."[44]

Each being, as well as each existent, is isolated and at the same time, simultaneously, with-others in an indissoluble interweaving of deferral and approach, separation, and relation. Insofar as there is this interweaving, being divides itself as event, as history and as world, dis-posing and dis-locating beings and existents in the spacing of what Heidegger had already named *Lichtung des Seins*, clearing of being. Nancy can affirm, in this regard, that the time proper to being that simultaneously dis-poses is that of the incidence,[45] of the coming and unfolding of the singular-plural.

What emerges here is an aspect of Heideggerian thought of being-with (and of *Mit-Dasein*) that runs through, albeit in a subterranean way, Esposito's pages on community in *Being and Time* as an ecstasy of *Dasein*. That is, it is not only a matter of thinking of the outside as the exposure of existing or existence as exposure but also of thinking of being and *Dasein* as incidence and "in-standing" in the spacing of the "between us."

In the *Introduction* to *What Is Metaphysics?* of 1949, Heidegger, in fact, with a retrospective critical intention toward *Being and Time*, writes: "What is meant by 'existence' in the context of a thinking that is prompted by, and directed toward, the truth of Being, could be most felicitously designated by the word 'in-standing' [*Inständigkeit*]. We must think at the same time, however, of standing in the openness of Being, of sustaining this standing-in (care), and of enduring in what is most extreme (being toward death); for together they constitute the full essence of existence."[46]

The connection that Heidegger makes here between the "in-standing" of *Dasein* and its capacity for resistance, a harbinger of further developments in an ethical-political sense, opens up a new possibility of interpreting being-with and being-in-common in terms of a common care and a common resistance to and on the limits of the constitutive finiteness of the human.

Assurance and Immunity

The relationship between proper and stranger is susceptible to an immune interpretation in the sense that it disposes and exposes the proper to the perturbations of the encounter with the stranger from which the very identity of proper takes shape. Therefore, another Heideggerian context in which it is possible, according to Esposito, to trace the immune mechanism at works is that of the diagnosis of the modern as an affirmation of subjectivity and the simultaneous reduction of the world to image. The privileged place in which Heidegger expounds this interpretation of modernity is the 1938 lecture *The Age of the World Picture*.[47] In fact, in the dynamics of the representation and objectification of the world outlined by Heidegger in this lecture Esposito believes he can trace a "thread of meaning related to the concept of immunization,"[48] identifying especially in the concept of *insurance* the bridge between the two paradigms of representation and immunization.

Assurance (*Sicherstellen*) is, in fact, the fundamental characteristic of representation (*vorstellen*) by which the real, reduced to an object (*Gegenstand*), is placed at the disposal of the subject in the sense that the latter can be "sure (*sicher*)—which means certain (*gewiss*)—of the being."[49] This need for assurance, according to Heidegger, does not only belong to modern science but also indicates the characteristic trait of modern metaphysics, which thinks of the real as an object of representation and truth as the certainty of the cognitive procedure.

The metaphysical presupposition of assurance constitutes, according to Esposito, a sort of "immune screen" of metaphysical subjectivity "via which *Dasein* escapes from its dependence on Being, by closing the opening in which Dasein is located and replacing it with a representational device."[50] By guaranteeing a stable orientation and a certain relationship with the world, the metaphysical assurance typical of representation, however, would preclude man from experiencing ontological difference: the being that meets the representative subject, insofar as it is objectified and available, no longer bears any trace of its origin in the ontological movement of being. The experience of being is, that is, precluded by modern metaphysics—and, according to Heidegger, by all metaphysics as "oblivion of being"—insofar as it conceals the essential provenance of man and the world from the openness—the *Lichtung*—of being.

Metaphysical immunization would also act by depotentiating the exposure inherent, as we have seen, in the very constitution of *Dasein* as *Mit-Dasein*, insofar as it would exempt it from the *munus* that, in the meaning of gift, exists in the disposition of one-with-another, in the spacing of "between us." The immune screen of assurance would, that is, cover the abysmal movement of giving and sending (*Geschick*) of being itself to which all Heideggerian reflections of being as an event are dedicated.

According to Esposito, Heidegger has the merit of grasping the intrinsically violent character of insurance processes, since in them—as happens in every immune process—"the securing act of self-defense spills over into a preventative attack against anything that puts the self in danger."[51] While remaining within his own conceptual lexicon, Heidegger would push his analyses of modernity to the point of intuiting the immune mechanism that, precisely in the second half of the 1930s, was tragically being realized in the politics of the Nazi regime and that would later impose itself as a decisive biopolitical device even in postwar liberal democracies.

Notes

1. Roberto Esposito, *Common Immunity: Biopolitics in the Age of the Pandemic*, trans. Zakiya Hanafi (Cambridge: Polity, 2023).
2. Roberto Esposito, *Immunitas: The Protection and Negation of Life*, trans. Zakiya Hanafi (Cambridge: Polity, 2011).
3. Esposito, *Common Immunity*, 4.
4. Esposito, *Common Immunity*, 5.
5. Esposito, *Common Immunity*, 11.
6. Esposito, *Common Immunity*, 18.
7. Esposito, *Common Immunity*, 20.
8. Roberto Esposito, *Communitas: The Origins and Destiny of Community*, trans. Timothy Campbell (Stanford, CA: Stanford University Press, 2010), 93.
9. Martin Heidegger, *Being and Time*, trans. Joan Stambaugh (Albany: State University of New York Press, 1996), 109.
10. Heidegger, *Being and Time*, 111.
11. Heidegger, *Being and Time*, 111.

12. Heidegger, *Being and Time*, 113.

13. Authenticity thus has an essential relation to being-with. Heidegger connects *Eigentlichkeit* to the possibility of *Dasein*: "It *can* choose itself in its being, it can win itself, it can lose itself" (Heidegger, *Being and Time*, 40). Authenticity is ultimately connected to *Jemeinigkeit* of *Dasein*, but it is also true that *Dasein*, "the Being which I myself always am" (Heidegger, *Being and Time*, 49), can choose itself only if, through the ability of "resoluteness" [*Entschlossenheit*], it frees itself from the scattering of the Self and decides for the authenticity of care (see Heidegger, *Being and Time*, 267), that is, for the relationship with others: "It is from the authentic being a self of resoluteness that authentic being-with-one-another first arises, not from ambiguous and jealous stipulations and talkative fraternizing in the they and in what they want to undertake" (Heidegger, *Being and Time*, 274).

14. Heidegger, *Being and Time*, 117.

15. Heidegger, *Being and Time*, 117.

16. See Heidegger, *Being and Time*, 117.

17. In the celebrated section 40, the treatment of *Angst* as *Grundstimmung* refers back to *Uneigentlichkeit* as the most proper and original existential condition of *Dasein*, but only apparently does anguish isolate beingness, because, in fact, it authentically refers it back to its constitutive being-in-the-world, delivering it, however, to the original and insuperable nonfamiliarity of this condition, that is, to the impropriety that runs through and constitutes it: "Anguish [. . .] goes on to take Essence back from its identification of the objective with the "world." Everyday intimacy dissolves. Beingness remains isolated, but nevertheless as being-in-the-world. In-being assumes the existential "mode2 of not-being-in-its-own-home [*Un-zuhause*]. Nothing else is alluded to when one speaks of 'bewilderment' [*Unheimlichkeit*]" (Heidegger, *Being and Time*, 237). On the relationship between distress and authenticity, see Markus Höfner, "Autentisce Angst: Eine Skizze zum Zusammenhang von Angst, 'Eigentlichkeit' und Religion bei Martin Heidegger," *Hermeneutische Blätter* 26, no. 1 (2021): 53–70.

18. Heidegger, *Being and Time*, 117.

19. Esposito, *Communitas*, 93.

20. I refer here especially to dialogical thinking, the most significant text of which is undoubtedly Martin Buber's *Die Schriften über das Dialogische Prinzip* (Heidelberg: Schneider, 1954).

21. Esposito, *Communitas*, 94. Jean-Luc Nancy theorized the opposition between singularity and individuality in *Being Singular Plural*, trans. Robert Richardson and Anne O'Byrne (Stanford, CA: Stanford University Press, 2000), 8–9.

22. Esposito, *Communitas*, 95.

23. Esposito, *Communitas*, 7.

24. For an analysis of the German folk community, especially in the *Rektoratsrede*, and in the course on Hölderlin of 1934–35, in which Heidegger links

this theme to death and the willingness to sacrifice in a substantial sharing of the ideology of *Kriegsideologie*, see Roberto Esposito and Jean-Luc Nancy, "Dialogo sulla filosofia a venire," in Jean-Luc Nancy, *Essere singolare plurale* (Turin: Einaudi, 2001), XIX.

25. See Domenico Losurdo, *La comunità, la morte, l'Occidente: Heidegger e "l'ideologia della guerra"* (Turin: Bollati Boringhieri, 1991), 36. Debatable, however, is the connection Losurdo establishes between the concept of destiny (*Geschick*) in *Being and Time*, by which Heidegger understands essential historicity, and the *deutsches Schicksal* of the *Rekotoratsrede*; similarly, the community prefigured in the work of 1927, on the basis of the analysis of *Mitdasein*, is quite distinct from the *deutsche Gemeinschaft* Heidegger will speak of in the 1930s.

26. Nancy, *Being Singular Plural*, 26. On the issue of community and of being-with in Nancy, see Michel Gaillot, *Jean-Luc Nancy: La communauté, le sens* (Paris: Galilée, 2021); Daniela Calabrò, *Dis-piegamenti: Soggetto, corpo, e comunità in Jean-Luc Nancy* (Milan: Mimesis, 2006), 101–24; Fausto De Petro, *Comunità, comunicazione, comune: Da Georges Bataille a Jean-Luc Nancy* (Rome: DeriveApprodi, 2010), 149–62; Erika Marcantonio, "Comunità e co-esistenza," in *Intorno a Jean-Luc Nancy*, ed. Ugo Perone (Turin: Rosenberg & Sellier, 2012), 23–27.

27. Esposito, *Communitas*, 27.

28. It seems to me that the nondialectical relation between *Dasein* and others can also be read from the concept, central to the unpublished texts in the second section of the *Gesamtausgabe*, of *Austrag* used by Heidegger to indicate the diverging of difference, but also the threshold, the fragment (*das Inzwischen*) that separates but at the same time brings the elements of difference into relation by differing from one another; see Martin Heidegger, "Die onto-theo-logische Verfassung der Metaphysik," in *Gesamtausgabe*, vol. 11, ed. by Friedrich-Wilhelm von Herrmann (Frankfurt a.M.: Klostermann, 2006).

29. This is how Nancy expresses the decisive link between plural singularity of being and dis-position: "Being consists in nothing other than the existence of all existences [*tous les existants*]. However, this consistency itself does not vanish in a cloud of juxtaposed beings. What I am trying to indicate by speaking of 'dis-position' is neither a simple position nor a juxtaposition. Instead, the *co-* defines the unity and uniqueness of what is, in general. What is to be understood is precisely the constitution of this unique unity as *co-*: the *singular plural*" (Nancy, *Being Singular Plural*, 39).

30. Nancy, *Being Singular Plural*, 27.

31. See Nancy, *Being Singular Plural*, 17–18.

32. Nancy, *Being Singular Plural*, 18.

33. Nancy, *Being Singular Plural*, 18.

34. Esposito, *Communitas*, 7.

35. It was precisely in the "outflow" of and from subjectivity that Esposito had identified, in the wake of Nancy's analysis, the challenge of a community

to come: "The wound that we cause or from which we emerge when we ourselves are changed when we enter into a relationship not only with the other but with the other of the other, he too is the victim of the same irresistible expropriative impulse. This meeting, this *chance*, this contagion, more intense than any immunitary cordon, is the community of those that manifestly do not have it, when not losing it, and losing themselves in the very same process of flowing away from it" (Esposito, *Communitas*, 18–19).

36. Esposito, *Communitas*, 97.

37. Nancy, *Being Singular Plural*, 44.

38. Esposito recently addressed the inseparable link between the notions of immunity and community and the urgency of finding a balance between these two instances, especially since the pandemic of recent years, as well as on the relationship between immunity and philosophy in *Common Immunity*.

39. Esposito, *Immunitas*, 18.

40. Esposito, *Immunitas*, 166.

41. Voltaire, *Treatise on Tolerance*, trans. Brian Masters (Cambridge: Cambridge University Press, 2000).

42. Esposito, *Immunitas*, 166.

43. Nancy, *Being Singular Plural*, 46.

44. Nancy, *Being Singular Plural*, 32.

45. Nancy had already stated that "the essence of Being is the shock of the instant [*le coup*]. Each time, 'Being' is always an instance [*un coup*] of Being [. . .]. As a result, it is also always an instance of 'with': singulars singularly together" (Nancy, *Being Singular Plural*, 33).

46. Martin Heidegger, "Introduction to 'What Is Metaphysics?'" (1943), in *Pathmarks*, trans. William Mcneill (Cambridge: Cambridge University Press, 1998), 284.

47. Martin Heidegger, "The Age of the World Picture," in *Off the Beaten Track*, trans. Julian Young and Kenneth Haynes (Cambridge: Cambridge University Press 2002).

48. Esposito, *Common Immunity*, 121.

49. Heidegger, *Age of the World Picture*, 66.

50. Esposito, *Common Immunity*, 122.

51. Esposito, *Common Immunity*, 123.

Nine

Roberto Esposito and Reiner Schürmann
A Political Ontology after Heidegger

Alberto Martinengo, translated by Sarah De Sanctis

The publication of *Instituting Thought: Three Paradigms of Political Ontology* (2021) and *Institution* (2022) is of great importance in Roberto Esposito's theoretical journey, as well as in its reception on both sides of the Atlantic. It was not only that Esposito rethought certain key labels—above all, that of "Italian thought"—and refined certain interpretative models of his political philosophy. Those works are much more relevant than that, and contain a set of novelties that pave the way for the recent release of *Common Immunity: Biopolitics in the Age of the Pandemic* (2023).

Esposito's renewed discourse is centered on a radicalization of the concept of *political ontology* through the comparison of various theoretical paradigms, as evidenced by the subtitle of *Instituting Thought*. This area has become the laboratory in which Esposito has situated himself in recent years; it is his "*Sache des Denkens*," as Martin Heidegger would say. After all, Heidegger's work plays a crucial role in Esposito's model, as it provides an effective definition of political ontology and serves as the primary reference against which Esposito contrasts his own ideas. Heidegger's influence on Esposito's writing, however, takes two forms: direct, in the analysis of his texts, or mediated through broader interpretations and discussions. Reiner Schürmann plays a crucial role in this context. Despite the limited space Esposito devotes to him, his reading of Heidegger is decisive for the construction of the political ontology Esposito has in mind.

Heidegger's Political Ontology

Schürmann's work is currently experiencing a renewed surge of interest in both America and Europe. This renewed attention can be attributed, in large part, to the release of previously unpublished works that were preserved at the New School for Social Research in New York, where Schürmann taught from 1975 to 1993, succeeding Hannah Arendt. The publishing company Diaphanes has made a significant contribution to this effort, with translations and reissues in English, French, and German starting in 2013. Additionally, an ambitious archival project, spearheaded by editors Francesco Guercio, Michael Heitz, Malte Fabian Rauch, and Nicolas Schneider, began publication in 2019, further fueling interest in Schürmann's work.

Schürmann's thinking follows a complex trajectory, and its reception has not always been linear. Its early fortunes date back to the publication of *Heidegger on Being and Acting: From Principles to Anarchy* (1987). It was an immediate hit, aided by the fact that Schürmann himself edited the English publication of the text, originally released in French in 1982. But this popularity was destined to fade within a decade, with the posthumous publication of *Broken Hegemonies*, released in French in 1996. It is not easy to establish correlations, causes, and effects of this first wave of interest: what's certain is that it coincides and ends with the golden years of Continental philosophy. Similarly, the current resurgence of interest in Schürmann's texts is linked to, and has been somewhat fueled by, the reopening of the philosophical and political discussion surrounding Heidegger's work, which has been spurred by the publication of the first *Black Notebooks* (1931–38, 1938/39, 1939–41, and 1942–48). These have been very contentious debates, unraveling over a number of years, from 2014 onward. Their focus is not solely Heidegger's affiliation with Nazism, nor the examination of his life and ideas. Rather, they are more broadly concerned with the *political implications* of his thinking (as well as philosophy in general).

Schürmann's analyses on the theme of acting in Heidegger gain great significance in the new context opened by the *Black Notebooks*.

They not only offer an innovative articulation of the problem compared to when the Notebooks were first published but are also relevant in light of Heidegger's unpublished works and their problematic nature. Of course, the point is not to credit Schürmann with predictive skills or the fortuitousness of having guessed something that time would confirm. If anything, it should be acknowledged that Schürmann's interpretation of Heidegger's already published works in Heidegger on Being and Acting, as well as his interpretation that would form the basis of Broken Hegemonies, is capable of addressing questions that would not arise until a few decades later. This interpretive capacity is especially significant given that the Black Notebooks appear to challenge the mainstream view on Heidegger that prevailed in the 1980s and 1990s.

To put it concisely, Schürmann's originality can be attributed to two key elements. Firstly, he argues that the problem of praxis, along with related issues that touch on politics, are not at all absent from Heidegger's understanding of being. Rather, they are not located where one would typically expect to find them, namely as secondary reflections compared to his ontology. This is the topic of Heidegger on Being and Acting. For Schürmann, acting is not relegated to what the Aristotelian tradition characterizes as secondary philosophies. On the contrary, in a complete reversal of Aristotelianism, acting is the principle of ontology: esse sequitur agere.

The second element of Schürmann's originality emerges in Broken Hegemonies. The pages dedicated to Heidegger in this extensive volume aimed at reconstructing the "history of metaphysics" focus on a specific goal: to demonstrate that his entire thought (rather than certain moments, as previous interpretations would have it) is divided between a desire to transcend metaphysics and a relapse into a kind of metaphysics of the second order. This interpretive model is highly ambitious, particularly in its attempt to identify a constant thread through the intricate path of Heidegger's philosophy. However, what is of particular interest here is a more limited yet more significant aspect: according to Schürmann, this same fissure is present in Heidegger's political thought, with repercussions that are both biographical and philosophical.

In Heidegger on Being and Acting, Schürmann speaks of the need to articulate a different "phenomenological understanding of truth,"[1] a genuine phenomenological task that reveals these correspondences and reversals. It is crucial to proceed step by step and meticulously reconstruct these connections. Schürmann's notion of phenomenology refers to the one clarified in section 7 of *Being and Time*, which does not express Heidegger's affiliation with Edmund Husserl's model but rather a reference to the conditions under which a phenomenon shows itself. This definition forms the basis of Schürmann's political ontology, a notion that he does not explicitly use but that appears to be entirely appropriate to his reading of Heidegger.

In chapter 2 of *Heidegger on Being and Acting*, Schürmann states: "The political is the surface where the code that rules a historical field becomes visible. This visibility can be described as the emergence from the private: when speech becomes public persuasion instead of merely private expression, when doing becomes action instead of mere activity, and when things become products instead of mere artifacts, then each time the political order is constituted."[2] Although implied, this is probably one of the best definitions of political ontology in the post-Heideggerian debate. Schürmann argues that the network of things, words, and actions that constitutes the essence of reality is an invisible fabric, which remains so until viewed against the light of politics. The term "politics" has a specific meaning here that only partially overlaps with its usage elsewhere in twentieth-century philosophical debates. According to Schürmann, politics is the realm where "speech becomes public persuasion," "doing becomes action," and "things become products."[3] The political is thus the arena where a particular configuration of things, words, and actions becomes an "economy" or system of laws. Phenomenology, in short, is the method by which a given "economy" becomes visible.

The references to the ruling code and the political order, which are semantically rich in Schürmann's writing, contain an important ambiguity that should not be overlooked. The point is not simply that there exists a network of things through which one can read the structure of the world, also including its political dimension. Rather, for Schürmann, reality and being are inherently political, and metaphysics itself is a model of governance. Therefore, when Schürmann asserts that the aim of *Heidegger on Being and Acting* is to show "the identity between the manifest order of an epoch and the political,"[4] he means it literally: the way in which an epoch is ordered by a metaphysical principle is fundamentally political, and, conversely, the way in which politics functions as a governing principle is essentially metaphysical. Not only does "the political exhibit the epochal principle,"[5] but politics and metaphysics are, in a sense, the same dispositif. In this sense, the "phenomenological understanding of truth" that Schürmann advocates is a political ontology in its full sense. As Schürmann delves deeper into Heidegger's philosophy, his goal becomes clearer: to demonstrate that the analysis of the political nature of ontological structures is a fitting interpretation that aligns with Heidegger's thought in its entirety. However, Schürmann's discourse becomes more complex and nuanced as he focuses on Heidegger's contradictions. Thus, in *Broken Hegemonies*, he posits that Heidegger's trajectory is characterized by an oscillation between post-metaphysical and doubly metaphysical ontologies. This ambiguity does not eliminate the preexisting ontological-political background, but rather makes it more intricate. The title, *Broken Hegemonies*, reflects this ambiguity: this intentional oxymoron conveys the fragile nature of the hegemonic principles that govern thought, existence, and values in a given era. A hegemony determines what one can think, do, believe, or not in a certain historical context, but it bears fractures that can undermine it from within and eventually collapse it.

In the case of Heidegger, Schürmann argues that the oscillations or ambiguities inherent in his thought intensified sharply in the 1930s. The writings from that period thus become a kind of construction site where different designs and projects, even two different philosophical paradigms, coexist. This strongly resembles a *speculative laboratory*,[6] with the *Contributions to Philosophy* being the best example according to Schürmann. In *Broken Hegemonies*, he writes: "In jumping from strategy to strategy, the *Contributions* not only thematize the monstrous passage to the normative limits, but they carry it to completion."[7] In short, the writings of the 1930s would offer glimpses—this is the sense of Schürmann's title—of a philosophical system revealing its *monstrous* face, that of absolute norms that are transfigured and exhausted. This reversal is evidenced by Heidegger's own "textuality," the texture of his arguments and the style of his writing. Schürmann, wondering where the author of the *Contributions* speaks from, adds: "Heidegger does not leave the terrain where the substitutes for the Platonic sun continue to rule—and how could one?"; if anything "he speaks from that blank place [. . .] that has been gaping in consciousness from the time of its referential institution. He speaks from the place of the innermost rent [. . .] in the modern theticism of the same, [. . .] where night erupts into the obviousness of the blazing midday sun."[8]

In Schürmann's lexicon, this is a good definition of the *Destruktion* of metaphysics: not a leap beyond the limits of metaphysics but a deepening of the rift—the discovery of the double bind between different principles that hold up the fabric of a waning age. Which, Schürmann concludes, "is something quite different from declaring cheerfully that metaphysics has ended and that one has only to decide to change terrain by abruptly placing oneself outside."[9] In short, to him *Destruktion* is the reversal of the metaphysical tendency to posit principles. In this reversal, the functioning of principles comes to the fore—and it is a *political* functioning, just as the metaphor with which *Destruktion* speaks of metaphysics as the government of being is *political*. Heidegger explains this well when talking about the Greek notion of *arché*:

> The Greeks ordinarily hear two meanings in this word. On the one hand, *arché* means that from which something has its origin and beginning; on the other hand it means that which, *as* this origin and beginning, likewise keeps rein *over*, i.e., restrains and therefore dominates, something else that emerges from it. *Arché* means, at one and the same time, beginning and domination. On a broader and therefore lower scale we can say: origin and ordering. In order to express the unity that oscillates between the two, we can translate *arché* as originating ordering and as ordering origin. The unity of these two is *essential*.[10]

In short, *archein* certainly means "to initiate," but it also means "to dominate" and, above all, "to govern"—that is, to hold the entity under a principle.

In *Broken Hegemonies*, Heidegger's episode is the final chapter in a series that begins with Parmenides. However, the same words that Schürmann applies to Parmenidean philosophy can be seen as relevant to the entire history of metaphysics:

> The promotion of this or that representation to the highest rank—which are ways of identifying a being and being—is a political affair *par excellence*. The word *polis* suggests this, at least if its root is the same as that of *polos*, the "pole" around which all names circulate, and also that of *pelein*, "being." The first political act, in the sense of assuring the cohesion of a collectivity into a community, thus amounts to declaring what is. There is no need for a social contract to do this. One agrees to elevate one being—a natural one like

the cosmic order, a divine one like Zeus, or a human one like an ideology—to the level of a standard.[11]

This is the crux of what we can specifically identify as Heidegger's political ontology—or rather, the political ontology that Schürmann, while employing other terminologies, endeavors to uncover in Heidegger. It is also the theoretical framework that enables him to grasp the ambiguity of Heidegger's texts from the 1930s. The question that remains is to what extent this interpretation of the *Contributions to Philosophy* can be applied to the *Black Notebooks*, especially those written during the same period.

The *Black Notebooks*

A comprehensive analysis of the ontological-political scope of the *Black Notebooks* from 1931–38, 1938/1939, and 1939–41, building on Schürmann's work, would require more space than the intentions of this chapter allow. Nevertheless, it is possible to briefly demonstrate the continuity of motivations and arguments with Schürmann's observations regarding the *Contributions to Philosophy*, particularly with the double bind between metaphysics and its overcoming. In fact, by their very form, the *Black Notebooks* stage a sort of play between opposing tensions and contradictions, texts and off-texts, theoretical thrusts and rhetorical counterthrusts. Heidegger blends philosophical analysis and political language into a common metaphoric, which is an innovative feature of his thinking. These linguistic entanglements can be followed step by step, revealing the tension I previously mentioned: the *anarchic-emancipatory*, antimetaphysical *project* versus the *totalizing counterpush* that seeks a new ground for thought to take root in.[12]

What emerges is a sort of ontology of actuality. Indeed, the *Notebooks* propose a way of understanding the present by using philosophical categories that must be validated through actuality. Besides, the placement of the first two volumes during the 1930s is very significant, since it was a time when Heidegger's philosophy was focused on the development of the antimetaphysical "turn." But the same period also includes the most biographically difficult moment of his political involvement: his public support of the Nazi regime and his appointment as rector in Freiburg. This period encompasses texts in which Heidegger envisages liberation from a conception of truth that he perceives as oppressive and violent, but also includes the pages of *The Self-Assertion of the German University* and the pro-Hitler content of his *Address to German Students* (1933).

In this context, the *Black Notebooks* resemble a foray "off the beaten track," to quote the English title of another collection, *Holzwege*, dating from the years 1935 to 1946. Or, rather, it is a labyrinthine path where finding an overall pattern is not easy. How, then, to proceed? The two sides of the discourse can be summarized easily and produce distinct lexicons: the overcoming of metaphysics is expressed in different ways, but all refer to the notions of end (*Ende*), completion (*Vollzug*), and sometimes demolition (*Abbau*). On the opposite side, the semantic constellation of the new ground to be sought speaks of foundation (*Gründung, Begründung* . . .), of the beginning or new beginning (*Anfang*), of rootedness that fights uprooting (*Verwurzelung/Entwurzelung*), and of the empowerment (*Ermächtigung*) of being or essence. The meeting point between the two lexicons is undoubtedly the *happening of being* (*Geschehnis*): a key notion of Heidegger's mature reflection that can be read here, as early as the 1931–38 volume, in its delicate—sometimes feverish—elaboration.

In the opening pages of the first volume, the question "Why does being happen?" is in fact one of the fundamental themes from which philosophy must start again.[13] In Heidegger's vocabulary, this question takes the form of the noun *Wesung* or, more rarely, the verb *wesen*. The end of metaphysics thus coincides with the abandonment of the language of substance, and the rereading of metaphysics itself as the history of *Wesung*, the essential unfolding of being. Being is no longer conceived as a stable foundation underlying what we are, what we know, how we act, and how we live but rather as the horizon within which things—and us as subjects—are situated.

The transformation of metaphysical vocabulary is an important aspect of Heidegger's proposed *Verwindung* or overcoming. The latter is not understood as a step beyond Western philosophy, but rather as its acceptance and deepening—its *Durcharbeitung*, as Schürmann would say. Indeed, in the *Black Notebooks*, Heidegger engages in a kind of "self-reflexive" *Verwindung* by reworking his own categories. One example of this is his treatment of the notion of existence, which is a cornerstone of *Being and Time* but undergoes a profound resemantization in later years. In the first volume of the *Black Notebooks*, Heidegger outlines the evolution of this transformation as follows: "*against* anthropologism, *for* mankind; against the 'existentiell,' *for* existence—standing-out as the standing-forth endurance (persistence) of beings—*against* existence, for

Da-sein; 'against' Dasein, for being; | against being, for the essence. In the essentially occurring essence toward the *uniqueness* of the *isolation* of being in nothingness."[14] All of these notions—man, *Dasein* (with or without the hyphen), Being (with or without the capital), existence, essence, nothingness—are theory-laden. However, each indicates a different moment in the transformation undergone by Heidegger's initial project. The incompleteness of *Being and Time*, the need to abandon basic philosophical notions, and the awareness (or claim) that this relates to the very history of being are all recurring themes throughout his diaries of the 1930s. What is surprising is the clarity with which he elaborates on these themes, rather than the themes themselves. What is even more surprising is that these pages do not clearly mark a single moment of transition or split in Heidegger's thought into two distinct phases, before and after a "turning point."

Heidegger's evolution is in fact uninterrupted, and it affects language, treating it in a malleable way and infusing it with gradually new meanings. In this process, poetry frequently emerges as a reference point, as already clear in Heidegger's published works. Poetry is a linguistic form that facilitates the transition from metaphysical language to its overcoming, surpassing what philosophical language can achieve. This is particularly evident in the case of Hölderlin, to whom *Ponderings* VI in the 1931–38 volume attributes both a place within the metaphysics of idealism and the ability to transcend it: "As much as Hölderlin himself does seem to move yet within the 'metaphysics' of German Idealism, so essentially is his poetry the first overcoming of all 'metaphysics.'"[15]

However, the poetry that Heidegger refers to is not just language in verse (*Dichtung*); if anything, it is *poetry of being*, in the sense of the construction (the Greek *poiesis*) of a specific form of what exists. It is the consolidation of different "orders of being," as the German term *Dichte* (density) suggests. As Heidegger states, "The poetry of being earlier than beings (for us) and yet only in order to propound beings as older. The bursting forth of being in the packings of its poetry."[16] In short, the emphasis on the poetry of being implies that reality is not objectivity, but is "to admit beings—let them through 'through' Da-sein. Ambiguity of the 'through' ['*Durch*']."[17] Heidegger's discourse suggests that entities founded on the secure support of substance are replaced by the poetic word, which cannot provide a metaphysical basis for beings. Instead, the poetic word structures the latter according to linguistic arrangements that are historically situated.

Emphasizing the *poetic foundation* clarifies the copresence of a theoretical-political strategy and its counterstrategy: the less "substantive" the founding poetry is, the stronger the *other foundation* becomes, drawing a completely different solution. This new context is outlined by the metaphorical vocabulary of the root: the search for a foundation is translated into a call for rootedness, for "com[ing] again onto a soil,"[18] and into a stigmatization of uprootedness.[19] In short, to grasp the new beginning Heidegger envisions for philosophy, we are called to take root in truth and its essence, as he writes in the 1931 notebook: "We are becoming mindful of everything the truth requires to take it up and to take a stand within it—to become ones who are indigenous, who stand on native soil."[20]

The question remains of where and how post-metaphysical humanity should take root. In the *Black Notebooks*, as well as in Heidegger's previously published works, the new beginning coincides with the originary beginning (*ursprünglich Anfang*) of Greek thought.[21] However, the reformulation of the notion of origin can be traced word for word in the *Notebooks*. The noun "beginning" remains ambiguous regarding the alternative between metaphysics and its overcoming; the juxtaposition with the adjective "originary" typically implies a reference to the premetaphysical origin. However, in the *Black Notebooks*, the search for the beginning requires an enhancement of the foundation. Hence the question of what constitutes the premetaphysical ground (*Grund*): "Which courses must a transition tread in order to arrive at that developing and developed ground from which the leap into the other beginning becomes possible?"[22] However, unlike what typically occurs in Heidegger's work, preclassical Greece no longer appears capable of guaranteeing this foundation. The ideal of Greek philosophy is transformed into the rootedness of *another* people in *another* soil. Heidegger asserts that the German people must now cast down their roots. In a note from the fall of 1932, he expresses his desire to grasp the "awakening actuality of German Dasein,"[23] which is also a philosophical awakening, because "only someone who is German" can "poetize being and say being" and will "finally create *logic*."[24]

The fact remains that the political dimension is the most relevant aspect for interpreting the ontology presented in the *Black Notebooks*, and vice versa. Schürmann makes this clear from the outset of *Heidegger on Being and Acting*, regarding Heidegger's thought more broadly: "The political is that domain, that *dominium*, which most clearly marks an epochal principle's scope of rule."[25] This means two things: firstly, what philosophy calls *arché* is always also a political principle, a dispositif for governing things (as well as thought, action, language, value systems, and so on); secondly, not only its functioning but also its malfunctioning can be read in the political realm. In other words, if an *arché* works or stops working, it is because its capacity to govern a given sphere of reality is activated or interrupted.

This definition draws on the Heideggerian thesis on the "essential ways in which truth establishes itself in the beings" contained in the essay on *The Origin of the Work of Art* (1936) and shifts the focus from the "setting-itself-to-work of truth" to the "act which founds a state."[26] However, it does so with an additional trait that makes the political *dominium* not only the place where the foundation appears but also the very nature of the foundation itself. The metaphysical *principium* around which an epochal economy is organized reveals itself as a *princeps*, that is, a governing principle on the basis of which ontology assumes the force of law.

Esposito on Heidegger (and Schürmann)

The space that Roberto Esposito devotes to Schürmann in *Instituting Thought* is very circumscribed. In his perspective, Schürmann is one of the interpreters of Heidegger who take the destituting paradigm to its extreme consequences. The starting point of *Instituting Thought* can be summarized as follows: political ontology expresses the "essential relationship that conjoins being and politics." This correspondence holds true in both senses: on the one hand, the "necessarily ontological configuration of political praxis," and, on the other, the "ultimately political character of every event." More explicitly, Esposito says that "any political action implies a conception of space, time, and human beings—and therefore of being"; and vice versa "every philosophical definition of being entails presuppositions and effects of a political nature."[27]

This approach to the ontological-political problem intersects with the other leading theme of *Instituting Thought*, namely, postfoundationalism: "Ancient politics [. . .] was still bound to metaphysical presuppositions, whether theological or natural." Instead, "modern politics begins with and is constituted precisely starting with their revocation." Nevertheless, albeit in the form of the negation of transcendence (however it is understood), the question of the foundation remains and modern political philosophy is firmly set within its logic.[28] In contrast, the postfoundationalist scenario presents a further break from modernity: "not only a negative foundation, one already theorized by modern political philosophy, but a non-foundation, a lack of foundation."[29]

In turn, this is not simply the consequence of a different kind of event. The crisis of the foundation is not a fact (or a presupposition) that also concerns political ontology; instead, it is primarily an onto-logical-political phenomenon that consequently upends all the domains in which the philosophical constellation of the foundation is expressed. In this regard, Schürmann's perspective is crucial for Esposito, extending beyond what is apparent in *Instituting Thought*. Schürmann, in fact, is the author to whom Esposito owes the radicalization of Heidegger in a destituting sense, which, in *Instituting Thought*, serves as the authentic model to oppose in order to define the instituting paradigm. In other words, the three-paradigm model proposed by Esposito implies that both ways out of Heidegger's ontology—the Deleuzian "constitutive paradigm" and the neo-Machiavellian "institutive" one—depend, if only by opposition, on how that first paradigm is defined. All the postfoundationalisms examined in *Instituting Thought* are based on the principle that, after Nietzsche, "attempts at restoration notwithstanding, the hypothesis of grounding politics in the sphere of a substantive being seems to be definitely exhausted, a process tied to the ongoing deconstruction of the notion of substance itself."[30] But it is Heidegger—as reinterpreted by Schürmann—who represents the turning point toward ontological-political postfoundationalism.

Instituting Thought reconstructs in detail the genesis and structure of destituting power in Heidegger's thought. The main stages that Esposito considers decisive are the *Introduction to Metaphysics* (1935), parts of the *Black Notebooks* (1931–38 and 1939–41), and the 1942 summer course *Hölderlin's Hymn "The Ister"* as well as the following one (WS 1942/43) on *Parmenides*. Along this path, in fact, the development of the destituting model has its telltale sign in the way the discourse on politics mostly unfolds: through the register of negation. According to Esposito, the impolitical—the negation of the efficacy of action, and of political action in particular—is the true keyword of Heideggerian political philosophy.

Instituting Thought makes this case by mainly analyzing how the notion of *polis* is constructed. Esposito's discourse centers on the texts of the mid-1930s, where the lexical constellation of the *polis* overlaps with the same set of phenomena as the conflict between World and Earth. The temporal proximity between the *Introduction to Metaphysics* and the essay *The Origin of the Work of Art* (1935/36) is certainly not accidental: the *polis*, like the work of art, is the site where ontological difference takes shape. In relation to Heidegger's commentary on the first chorus of Sophocles' *Antigone*, Esposito writes: "The *polis* is the context in which history occurs—to which belong essentially—in other words, in what they are—kings, temples, gods, poets, thinkers, armies, ships."[31] He then goes on to say: "*Polis* is not a political regime, as a philosophical tradition that culminated in Hegel always imagined, but rather that from which the political originates. [. . .] The *polis* constitutes the most appropriate place for the wrangling of violence with itself, because it delineates the margin that both divides and conjoins inside and outside."[32] Thus, the *polis* is both a margin and a site for the continuous creation of forms. However, this perspective of infinite "constituting," or form production, is only apparent. Heidegger's margin, as discussed in his commentary on *Antigone*, does not draw the line between the inside and outside of the *polis* but instead runs through the *polis* itself. The "outside," which would ensure the stability and constitutive capacity of political forms in the "inside," does not truly exist, or rather—Esposito explains—it is a part of the inside.[33]

The question of the ontological difference that runs through—rather than around—the *polis* is subtle but decisive: the eminently creative function of the political can be maintained only on the condition of tracing a perimeter (so far, the *polis*; further on, the impolitical) and always going beyond it. Esposito continues: "Those who inhabit it [the *polis*] are defined by the mobile relationship they entertain with the border they themselves instituted through the act of foundation. It is the limit they establish, so as to then go beyond it, before tracing it anew. Only in this manner can they maintain the role of creators to which Heidegger ties the function of the political."[34] In the *Introduction to Metaphysics*, this balance between the political and the impolitical thus plays a productive role much like the aforementioned equilibrium between World and Earth. But things change rapidly over the years: starting with the *Contributions to Philosophy* (1936–38), the lexicon of action loses its positive connotation, gradually adhering to the semantic region of *techne* and *Machenschaft*. Just as *techne* becomes a political issue, so "politics begins to increasingly assume technology characteristics, which pervert its so originary affirmative meaning."[35]

At this juncture, which is even more evident in the *Black Notebooks* than in the *Introduction to Metaphysics* and the *Contributions to Metaphysics*, we can see the rupture that clears the way for Heidegger's definitive response to the theme of the *polis*. This leads to another fissure: having assigned the original sphere of action to *techne*, the only option left to the political domain is that of "unworking," or the impolitical.[36] This last passage will be fully accomplished in the course on Hölderlin's *Der Ister* and the subsequent one on Parmenides, also through a rereading of the historical events of those months translated into a metaphysical key. In the first case, the discourse unfolds along the thread of logic: if the *polis* is the place from which the political is thought (or is), one cannot affirm the opposite, namely that the political is the foundation of the *polis*. Indeed, Heidegger writes that the *polis* is not a political concept[37] and—as he reiterated just a few months earlier in the *Überlegungen* collected in the *Black Notebooks* (*Ponderings XII–XV, 1939–41*)—politics is now entirely complicit in the machination.[38]

In short, as Esposito demonstrates, the *polis* is essentially *polos*, an "intrinsically restless *status*," the barycentre of all that relates to the entity in ancient Greek thought.[39] Thus, the *polis* acquires a structure that can be fully overlapped with *aletheia*: as the locus of the manifestation of the entity, it is in turn founded on withdrawal, self-negation, its own opposite—that is, the impolitical. The course on Parmenides confirms this overlap and, as it were, historicizes the original contrast between the political and the impolitical. This opposition arose from the "Romanization" undergone by the Latin and modern understanding of the Greek *polis*, which removed concealment and conflict from it. According to Esposito: "From that point on, the sphere of the political, dragged in a technico-operational direction by its Romanization, drastically separates itself from the essence of the *polis*, understood as a site starting from which humans address the Being of what is."[40]

This is the dominant feature of Heidegger's later philosophical-political reflection: if political action can be salvaged, it is through deactivation, the deconstruction of the illusion of politics as doing. Esposito finds this appeal largely unsatisfactory because it effectively excludes the possibility of philosophically guiding political action. Instead, Schürmann claims that it is the only way to save action—albeit in a sense that Esposito would no longer consider "political"—from the violence of metaphysics. As the conclusions of *Broken Hegemonies* argue, only this type of action is capable of dismantling the conditions under which violence is legitimized in the name of a metaphysical universal.

Notes

1. Reiner Schürmann, *Heidegger on Being and Acting: From Principles to Anarchy* (Bloomington: Indiana University Press, 1987), 150.
2. Schürmann, *Heidegger on Being and Acting*, 37.
3. Schürmann, *Heidegger on Being and Acting*, 37.
4. Schürmann, *Heidegger on Being and Acting*, 37.
5. Schürmann, *Heidegger on Being and Acting*, 38.
6. This expression belongs to Alessandra Iadicicco, editor of the Italian edition of the *Black Notebooks, 1931–1938*. See Martin Heidegger, *Quaderni neri, 1931–1938* (Milan: Bompiani, 2015), V.
7. Reiner Schürmann, *Broken Hegemonies* (Bloomington: Indiana University Press, 2003), 539.
8. Schürmann, *Broken Hegemonies*, 540.
9. Schürmann, *Broken Hegemonies*, 540.
10. Martin Heidegger, "On the Essence and Concept of Physis in Aristotle's Physics B, 1," in *Pathmarks* (Cambridge: Cambridge University Press, 1998): 189.
11. Schürmann, *Broken Hegemonies*, 69. See also Heidegger's *Parmenides*: "The *polis* itself is only the pole of the *pelein*, the manner in which the being of beings is combined, through its unconcealment and concealment, in a place where the history of a community is gathered"; see Martin Heidegger, *Parmenides*, trans. André Schuwer and Richard Rojcewicz (Bloomington, Indiana University Press, 1992), 142. On the same subject, see Martin Heidegger, "Hölderlins Hymne 'Der Ister,'" in *Gesamtausgabe*, vol. 53 (Frankfurt a.M.: Klostermann, 1984), 88, 100.
12. I discussed this interpretation of the *Black Notebooks* in more detail in "La metafisica dei *Quaderni neri*," in *I "Quaderni neri" di Heidegger*, ed. Donatella Di Cesare (Milan: Mimesis, 2016), 41–60. I refer the reader back to that text, whose analysis I am merely resuming here.
13. "What should we do? Who are we? Why should we be? What are beings? Why does being happen? Philosophizing proceeds out of these questions upward into unity." Martin Heidegger, *Ponderings II–VI: Black Notebooks, 1931–1938*, trans. Richard Rojcewicz (Bloomington: Indiana University Press, 2016), 5.
14. Heidegger, *Ponderings II–VI*, 53.
15. Heidegger, *Ponderings II–VI*, 311. On the ambiguity of Hölderlin's position, Heidegger writes: "Accordingly, the concealed backward turn of the history of truth and of humanity and of being will become even more pressing and enduring than we—who are already standing in the transition—would like

to admit. The fact that Hölderlin must still further await his future is a sign which is more seldom seen the more univocally it shows itself" (Heidegger, *Ponderings II–VI*, 297).

16. Heidegger, *Ponderings II–VI*, 12.
17. Heidegger, *Ponderings II–VI*, 9.
18. Heidegger, *Ponderings II–VI*, 45. See also 123, 196, 204.
19. See Heidegger, *Ponderings II–VI*, e.g., 24, 47–48, 52–53, 58, 214, 252–53, 264–65, 269, 283.
20. Heidegger, *Ponderings II–VI*, 29.
21. Heidegger, *Ponderings II–VI*, 14.
22. Heidegger, *Ponderings II–VI*, 268.
23. Heidegger, *Ponderings II–VI*, 80.
24. Heidegger, *Ponderings II–VI*, 21.
25. Schürmann, *Heidegger on Being and Acting*, 36.
26. "One essential way in which truth establishes itself in the beings it has opened up is its setting-itself-into-the-work. Another way in which truth comes to presence is through the act which founds a state. Again, another way in which truth comes to shine is the proximity of that which is not simply a being but rather the being which is most in being. Yet another way in which truth grounds itself is the essential sacrifice. A still further way in which truth comes to be is in the thinker's questioning, which, as the thinking of being, names being in its question-worthiness." Martin Heidegger, "The Origin of the Work of Art," in *Off the Beaten Track*, trans. Julian Young and Kenneth Haynes (Cambridge: Cambridge University Press, 2002), 37.
27. Esposito, *Instituting Thought*, 2.
28. Esposito, *Instituting Thought*, 2–3.
29. Esposito, *Instituting Thought*, 3.
30. Esposito, *Instituting Thought*, 3.
31. Esposito, *Instituting Thought*, 37.
32. Esposito, *Instituting Thought*, 37.
33. For a more in-depth analysis, let me refer to my essay "Paradigms for a Political Ontology Family Resemblances in the Contemporary Philosophical Debate," in Federica Pedriali, ed., *Italian Thought from Machiavelli to Esposito* (Edinburgh: Edinburgh University Press, 2023). Here I summarize its main elements.
34. Esposito, *Instituting Thought*, 37.
35. Esposito, *Instituting Thought*, 43.
36. "Once the entire political horizon is occupied by technology or sucked up into its *dispositifs*, the thought of the political contracts into the space of the impolitical. One will have to wait for the collapse of Nazi Germany [. . .]: only subsequently will this option become irreversible in Heidegger's reflections" (Esposito, *Instituting Thought*, 47). The indirect reference here is to Jean-Luc Nancy, both for his interpretation of *Dasein* as unworkable action and for his

model of the inoperative community: see in particular Nancy's essay "The Decision of Existence" and his book *The Inoperative Community*.

37. Heidegger, *Hölderlin's Hymn "The Ister,"* 80.

38. Martin Heidegger, *Ponderings XII–XV: Black Notebooks, 1939–1941*, trans. Richard Rojcewicz (Bloomington: Indiana University Press, 2017), 34.

39. Esposito, *Instituting Thought*, 54.

40. Esposito, *Instituting Thought*, 58.

Ten

Immunity and Community

A Note of Discord between Roberto Esposito and Jacques Derrida

Valentina Surace

The 2020 COVID outbreak has dramatically revealed that the individual and the nation state are "ekstatic," in the sense that they are structurally exposed to outside. The society's efforts to eliminate every external threat resulted in the appearance of viruses that prompted unforeseen chain reactions.[1] The virus, whether biological or cyber, is a metaphor for the global age, one that is characterized by the unexpected relations that arise between people because of technology. The coronavirus is not, therefore, an invention or an exception, but a physiological effect of globalization, which tragically reveals the alterity that underpins the structure of all identities, both individual and collective. It also reveals the fragility of any kind of self-protection, as it relates to the urgency of the *Globale Zeit*, in which the dis-location of a communitary belonging has given rise to a protective reaction and rejection.[2] The viral-politics, which was needed to contain the pandemic, fed power based on fear (*phobocratia*)—fear of the external (*exophobia*) as much as fear of the stranger (*xenophobia*). Moreover, the pandemic has made biopolitics fashionable again. To this extent, *physical bodies* have become objects of intense medical and political discussion. The protection of the *social corpus* is the only way out. Within this context, the development of biopolitics into death-politics (*thanato-politics*) appears as a structural issue, rather than a racist deviation, directed against a minority. In the most dangerous moments of the pandemic, governments were forced to introduce "the break between what must live and what must die."[3] A similar logic prompted calculations about the cost and the benefits of vaccines, which are both a remedy and a poison.

Nowadays when immunity has become practical politics as well as a genuine cornerstone of society, Roberto Esposito and Jacques Derrida's thoughts are more relevant than ever. Although they both agree that immunity is an important means to understand the political paradigm, the approach they take as well as the outcomes they arrive are nevertheless *discordant*. Esposito, reflecting on the recent events, sees the pandemic as having disrupted the equilibrium between immunity and community, because the priority is the immunity. Even if an excessive focus on immunity reduces life to biological data, Esposito thinks that the measures adopted to contain the coronavirus are adequate. He adds that "after being activated, by necessity, the immunitary principle [. . .] needs to activate the communitary principle."[4] Derrida, who did not live through the pandemic, was convinced that it was necessary to deconstruct the communitary principle that characterizes our ideas of democracy and the political categories associated with it. He thought that an autoimmunitary *threat* pervades every community, affording them an opportunity of another *chance*.[5] Both Esposito and Derrida recognize, although in different ways, that the immunitary paradigm characterizes immuno-democracies, in which citizens expect protection rather than participation. Moreover, they agree that its logic is ambivalent: excessive immunity leads to death, and yet the immunitary system protects the body. Immunity is not negative, because no body, whether individual or social, can exist deprived of protection. However, once a certain limit is surpassed, it results in a negation of life.

Com-munity

According to Derrida, "no region of being, *phúsis* or history would be exempt"[6] from immunity. He remarks that "it is especially in the domain of biology that the lexical resources of immunity have developed their authority."[7] Nevertheless, he recognizes immunity within the domains of law as exemption: *immunis* is who is exempted from the obligations, *munus*; and he sees an immunitary tension behind all "co-immunity." Derrida uses this term to highlight the complex intersections of *communitas* and *immunitas*. The comm-unity, for him, constitutes an immuntary identity that can be both national and global.[8] According to this line of thinking, the word "community" "resounds with the 'common' [*commun*], the as-one [*comme-un*],"[9] as well as the neutralization of alterity and the reduction of the other to the self. Nevertheless, a death drive is silently at work in every auto-co-immunitary system, "no community 'is possible' that would not cultivate its own auto-immunity, a principle of sacrificial self-destruction ruining the principle of self-protection (that of maintaining its self-integrity intact)."[10] This autodestructive power, if excessive, inevitably leads to death but, to a certain extent, it maintains the life of the community. It opens the community towards something else, something that no longer implies "the motifs of community, appurtenance or sharing, whatever the sign assigned to them."[11]

Esposito maintains that the category of immunity can be understood as having two meanings—one that refers to the community and the other in terms of biopolitics, and he believes that Derrida fails to connect the idea of immunity to neither one nor the other, even though he recognizes the double medical-juridical meaning of the concept.[12]

Esposito introduces the notion of immunity as the *opposite* of community. *Communitas*, for him, is the *relationship* of "persons united not by a 'property' but by an obligation or a debt; not by an 'addition' (*più*) but by a 'subtraction' (*meno*)."[13] *Immunitas*, by contrast, is the absent *state* of this obligation. The *communis* is, accordingly, a person who engages in this *compensatory* exchange; they are obligated to give a gift (*munus*), which is a mutual gift (*mutuus*). This interaction expropriates their most intimate property—their subjectivity. The *immunis*, by contrast, is the person who is excused (*dispensation*) from such obligations; they are free from "the contagion of the relation with others"[14] and are therefore able to maintain the integrity of the self. Immunity interrupts the circuit of mutual obligations, it sacrifices the "with." Nevertheless, community and immunity share a semantic root—the *munus* (a gift but also an obligation and service), which they both relate to, one in a positive fashion and the other in a negative fashion. The immune is the "non-being" or "not having" anything in "commune." Nevertheless, it "presupposes that which it also negates. Not only does it appear to be derived logically, but it also appears to be internally inhabited by its opposite."[15] Between the "commune" (the "outside ourselves") and the immune (one's own space) there is an "unconcluded dialectic,"[16] in which "neither term is limited to negating the other but instead implicates the other, in subterranean ways."[17] The immunity is a private notion, but it is also comparative as it denotes an *exception* to the rules and the condition of others. It is therefore a "chiasmatic" conceit, which operates by "exclusionary inclusion or exclusion by inclusion."[18] The immunitary system is not a secondary element. Rather, it constitutes the community. Every community is always immunized. It is *externally* delineated by confines that set limits to an infinite space. It is also *internally* protected by devices that are essential to its survival, such as the law. Nevertheless, as immunity is necessary to the preservation of the life of the individual and the community, if it surpasses a threshold, it leads to death, as in the case of autoimmune diseases, or when a community is locked inside. A surplus of immunity entails the end of the sense of existence, that is to say, it is exposed to the outside (the commune).[19] So, community and immunity coexist in an "originary co-belonging."[20]

Immuno-Democracies

As regards modern politics, Derrida analyzes "the autoimmune *double bind* of the democratic."[21] On one hand, democracy relates to a "vocation for hospitality,"[22] while on the other, it is ready to attack itself in order to guarantee its own preservation, as in the case of the September 11 attacks against the symbolic leader of the free world (*caput mundi*). The attacks did not come from the outside but from *the inside*, from those who had been internally accommodated and were able to find the means to get hold of an American weapon in an American city on the ground of an American airport.[23] The subsequent counteroffensive of American democracy consists of attempting to retreat back into itself, at the cost of undermining its own legal system of protection.[24] Nevertheless, democracy can survive in the future only by adhering closely to its own "essence more autoimmune than ever,"[25] which exposes it to the other. If democracy, as all living organisms, were capable of calculating this filtration in advance, it "would have to die in advance [. . .], for fear of being *altered* by what comes from outside, by the other."[26] If an event worthy of this name is to happen or arrive, "it must touch an exposed vulnerability, one without absolute immunity, without indemnity; [. . .].

In this regard, autoimmunity is not an absolute ill or evil. It enables an exposure to the other, to *what* and to *who* comes [. . .]. Without autoimmunity, with absolute immunity, nothing would ever happen or arrive."[27] There would therefore no longer be any to-come.

Esposito, in turn, observes that nowadays democracy "speaks a language that is opposed to that of community insofar as it always has introjected into it an immunitary imperative."[28] Democracy consequently risks imploding on itself—as in the case of America following the September 11 attacks[29] and, more recently, because of the pandemic. For Esposito, the idea of *communitas* moves in a direction that is radically opposed to the push toward immunitary interiorization and to community understood as a belonging of identity. *Communitas* recalls an interpretation of existence as ecstasy, "as the subject's escape from himself or herself or as his or her originary opening to otherness that constitutes the subject from the beginning in the form of a 'being-with' (*essere-con*) or a 'with-being' (*con-essere*)."[30] Esposito is convinced that it is still possible to open the time of originary community, which is subtracted from the whole substantialism as it is not characterized by ownership; rather, it is based on a debt. Esposito also believes that it is still possible to conceive of a democracy that is not immunizing or immunized, considering that immunitary devices risk provoking a type of autoimmune illness. He nevertheless recognizes that "another possibility remains—that of employing degeneration as a productive force."[31] Such thinking intimates an immunization that immunizes itself.

Pharmaco-Logic

Derrida observes that the immunitary logic has two sources—faith and the drive to remain unscathed. Religion is, in this sense, "allergic to contamination."[32] In the etymological framework proposed by Benveniste, "*religio* is a hesitation, a misgiving that holds back, a scruple which prevents."[33] So too, Derrida observes a reticence "before that which should remain sacred, holy or safe: unscathed, immune."[34] The sacrosanct, or the immune, however, secretes an additional autoimmunitary antidote within itself. The law of indemnity is twofold. It is an immunitary law that protects the body from the profane. At the same time, it is also an autoimmunitary law that protects "against its own protection, its own police, its own power of rejection, in short against its own."[35] Religious self-immunity is transported into the field of biology: "The immunitary reaction protects the 'indemnity' of the body proper in producing antibodies against foreign antigens. As for the process of auto-immunization [. . .], it consists for a living organism [. . .] of protecting itself against its self-protection by destroying its own immune system."[36] The autoimmunitary response can take the form of an autodestruction (autoimmune sicknesses) or of a destruction of one's own means of protection (immune-depression). Biomedicine suggests that autoimmune sicknesses are caused by the body's *erroneous* rejection of its own cells, which are misidentified as foreign antigens. Immuno-depression, by contrast, is an *insufficient* immunitary reaction that occurs when the body fails to properly recognize an antigen (as for example, in case of an immunodeficiency virus like HIV).[37] Derrida, however, remarks "the positive virtues of immuno-depressants destined to limit the mechanisms of rejection and to facilitate the tolerance of certain organ transplants."[38] It works by welcoming the other into oneself. The autoimmunitary logic is, in his view, a "strange illogical logic"[39] that is simultaneously positive and negative. In this regard, it recalls the logic of the *phármakon*,[40] which is both beneficial and harmful.[41]

Esposito, similarly, observes that the negative quality of immunity concerns not only the *state* but also the *processes* that safeguard someone or something from a great evil by means of a minor one. The immunitary process, therefore, "does not present itself in terms of action, but rather in terms of *reaction*."[42] In his reflections on the performative force of the negative, Esposito extends the thinking of Hegel.[43] He considers the immunity/community pair as a "possible variant" of the Foucauldian polarity power/resistance. From this perspective, "immunisation has the same defensive attitude of reaction or resistance, but it is practiced in a much more sophisticated manner. Rather than a simply exclusion, it implements a sort of exclusionary inclusion—it includes part of what it seeks to exclude in order to thwart the force of its impact."[44] The immunitary procedure is therefore conceived as a counterforce that presupposes the force that it must contest. Its workings are apparent in the judicial, biomedical and the religious alike.

In order to safeguard the life of the community, the law must immunize it from its self-destructive tendencies. In fact, the community, by putting its members together in a reciprocal relationship, blurs its *own* boundaries. The corollary is that it generates its own internal threats.[45] The law acts against this confusion, as it needs to protect itself first in order to be able to immunize the community from its self-destructive tendencies, and—as it is demonstrated by Derrida—"it may do so only by relying on [. . .] the same force it must keep at bay."[46] As for the biomedical, Esposito writes that "the immune mechanism takes on the character of an out-and-out war: the stakes are the control and ultimately the survival of the body in the face of foreign invaders who seek first to occupy it and then to destroy it."[47] Nevertheless, such methodology is, in his opinion, wholly aporetic as it operates not by elimination but by recognition, incorporation, and neutralization of the antigen. This is the way the *phármakon* acts, as Esposito highlights, extending what "Derrida has argued in a form that reinstates the logic and semantics of the immune lexicon."[48] The *phármakon* is that which opposes by inclusion of the other, rather than exclusion: it incorporates without assimilation, "it can prolong life, but only by continuously giving it a taste of death."[49] Its workings are apparent in the process of vaccination, when a portion of the virus is introduced into the patient's body in order to protect it.[50]

Such immunitary thinking is also apparent in religion. According to Esposito, this emerges by the means of the intersection of the sacred and the saintly, which are recognized by Benveniste, while Derrida "only hints [them] at or takes [them] in another direction."[51] The *sacred* is positive, as it operates healthy and saves life. The *saintly*, by contrast, is negative, as it prevents all contact with the profane. So too, the Pauline figure of the restrainer, the *katéchon* (2 Thess. 2:6–7), expresses the immunitary logic of religion better than anything else, as it "restrains evil by containing it, by keeping it, by holding it within itself."[52]

To summarize, the *law* safeguards the political body by incorporating the violence that is its opposite. In a similar vein, the *pharmakon* remedies by transferring small doses of the sickness that is trying to heal. Finally, the *katechon* impedes evil by absorbing it internally. All three modes are evidently immunitary. Esposito, nevertheless, recognizes that the operation of each is positive, but by means of the negative. The law, in order to protect the community, must be focused on the rights of the individual subject and in doing so, it risks destroying the sense of *munus*. In a similar vein, the *phármakon*, by healing parts of the body, may cause harm to another. So too, the *katechon* in its attempt to stem evil, slows the *parousia*. Esposito, therefore, concludes that immunity is a productive negation because it adopts a lesser evil in order to avoid a greater one. It does not therefore *abolish* the negative but *makes use* of it. It is not a question of immunizing oneself *against* the negative but *by means* of it.

Biopower

Esposito remarks that "the representation of the immune paradigm has remained predominantly negative, considering that Derrida, who made wide use of it, identified it primarily with autoimmune disorders. The turning point came when the *immunitas/communitas* dialectic was connected with biopolitical thought."[53] While Derrida explores the "positive virtues" of immuno-depressants, Esposito turns his attention to other biological phenomena such as transplants and pregnancy, which he sees as being linked to immunitary tolerance. In such cases, the immunitary system does not only have a negative function, that impedes invading germs, but also has another positive function, "it serves not as dividing wall, but as a diaphragm and filter in our communication with the external environment."[54] When the immune mechanism is transferred from biology into sociopolitics, it assumes a new affirmative capacity, while maintaining its defensive role. It operates in "a positive horizon, in which the negative, rather than being suppressed or excluded, could be affirmed as an element necessary to the development of individual and collective life."[55] Immunization, as a medico-biological and a juridical-political conceit, situates power and life inside the same semantic block; it is "not simply the relation that joins life to power, immunity is the power to preserve life."[56] For Esposito, the immunitary paradigm overcomes the sematic gap between affirmative biopolitics (the power *of* life) and negative biopolitics (the power *over* life). According to this logic, "the negation doesn't take the form of the violent subordination that power imposes on life from the outside, but rather is the intrinsically antinomic mode by which life preserves itself through power."[57] Immunization is the negative protection of life, because, by saving it, negates or reduces its power.

When Derrida refers to political autoimmunity, he recognizes the "relationship between the *politikon*, *physis*, and *bios* or *zoe*."[58] That is to say, he recognizes that biopolitics is originally the fundamental relationship among life, death, and power. It is important to remember that Derrida's thinking reiterates the thinking about auto-immunity in *Beyond the Pleasure Principle*, where Freud differentiates between conservative drives and the death drive. The conservative drives "are the guardians of life, but by the same token also the sentinels or satellites of death."[59] The drives that preserve life from external threats are secret agents in the service of a hidden will—the death drive. They "are *destined* to *insure* that the organism dies *of its own death*, that it follows its own proper path toward death."[60] According to Derrida, the impossibility of distinguishing the drive to life from the drive to death reveals the secret contract binding "life-death"[61] and the autoimmunitary law. Drawing on Freud, Derrida remarks that "there is no life present *at first*, which would *then* come to protect [. . .] itself."[62] The living I is therefore contaminated by alterity from the very beginning. It is different from itself, and is, for this reason, autoimmune. Thus, its defense is a type of boomerang, of "return to itself and against itself, in the encounter with itself and countering of itself."[63] In order to survive, the ego must welcome the other, "it must therefore take the immune defenses apparently meant for the non-ego, the enemy, the opposite, the adversary and direct them at once *for itself and against itself*."[64] In this sense, autoimmunity consists in auto-erasure, as well as in the erasure of the *autos*,[65] "the relentless law of self-destructive conservation of the subject or the egological selfhood."[66] This drive is almost suicidal, since the suicide presupposes an *ipse*.

Beyond the troublesome distinction between *biopolitics* and *deconstruction*,[67] Esposito and Derrida revel that the notion of immunity problematizes the boundary between inside and out, identity and alterity, life and death, pushing us to consider it as a threshold or passage. As we are fundamentally exposed beings, nothing can save us from the contamination by the other, neither immune defenses nor walls. In this respect, we should think more about institutions[68] to-come—even in light of recent pandemic experience. Esposito thinks of a planetary democracy, in which differences unite the world. Derrida regarded it as "a link of affinity, suffering, and hope."[69]

Notes

1. As Baudrillard remarks, years before the 2020 COVID outbreak, "the impossibility of exchange, of reciprocity, of alterity secretes that other invisible, diabolic, elusive alterity, that absolute Other, the virus"; Jean Baudrillard, "AIDS: Virulence or Prophylaxis?," in *Screened Out*, trans. Chris Turner (London: Verso, 2014), 2.

2. As Resta observes states react defensively to the process of world unification: "They try delusively to make their borders impenetrable and occlude their porosity, transforming the border from threshold and crossing place into a wall and a defensive impassable enclosure"; Caterina Resta, "Walled Borders: Beyond the Barriers of Immunity of the Nation-States," in *Debating and Defining*

Borders: Philosophical and Theoretical Perspectives, ed., Anthony Cooper and Søren Tinning (New York: Routledge, 2020), 213). The desire for walled boundaries is animated by the immune illusion that closure can preserve the identity of a community, "but a community, which is entrenched in itself—if that is possible—condemns itself to self-annihilation" (Resta, "Walled Borders," 217). In this sense, "it would be appropriate to lower the immune system, by building bridges and ports along the borders, in order to open narrow passages, to allow transit, crossings and encounters with 'the other,' without whom we could not know who we are" (Resta, "Walled Borders," 217).

3. Michel Foucault, *"Society Must Be Defended": Lectures at the Collège de France, 1975–76*, trans. David Macey (New York: Picador, 2003), 254. As Butler notes, this virus is democratic in transmissibility, but exacerbates social apartheid. On the one hand, by crossing borders, it spreads *indiscriminately*. On the other hand, by encountering social and economic inequalities, it *discriminates* between lives worth living and lives that are expendable; Judith Butler, "Capitalism Has Its Limits," *Verso Books*, March 30, 2020, https://www.versobooks.com/blogs/4603-capitalism-has-its-limits?fbclid=IwAR37F5XPfOjTQfBg5ayE082114diDODFa4jcsNAlAO5DRLT1Do37RGuocBY. I focus on Judith Butler's social ontology in Valentina Surace, *Soggetti precari: L'ontologia sociale di Judith Butler* (Milan: Mimesis, 2023).

4. Roberto Esposito, "Interview" by Torbjörn Elensky, *Svenska Dagbladet*, April 22, 2020, https://www.svd.se/a/wPQmbP/installning-i-sverige-de-bast-anpassade-overlever. According to Esposito, for limited periods some freedoms, which are harmful to health, can be suspended. Thus, what distinguishes the state of *emergency* from that of *exception* is precisely this objective element, at the same time necessary and contingent; see Roberto Esposito, "Immunitas: Oltre le feconde contraddizioni di Foucault," *Micromega*, no. 8 (2020): 55. For a further elaboration of this position, see Roberto Esposito, *Common Immunity: Biopolitics in the Age of the Pandemic*, trans. Zakiya Hanafi (Cambridge: Polity, 2023). Agamben, by contrast, thinks that the coronavirus containment measures establish a state of exception. According to him, once the pretext of *terrorism* is exhausted, governments assume that of the *virus* to suspend constitutional guarantees and establish a biosecurity regime. The provisions for terrorism prevention saw everyone as possible *terrorist*, the measures put in place to contain the pandemic similarly see all people as possible *plague spreader*. Such measures reinforce the idea that digital devices can replace any *contact-contagion*. See Giorgio Agamben, *Where Are We Now? The Epidemic as Politics*, trans. Valeria Dani (London: Eris, 2021).

5. Jacques Derrida, "Nietzsche and the Machine," in *Negotiations: Interventions and Interviews, 1971–2001*, ed. Elizabeth Rottenberg and trans. Richard Beardsworth (Stanford, CA: Stanford University Press, 2002), 248: "Threat is chance, chance is threat."

6. Jacques Derrida, *The Politics of Friendship*, trans. George Collins (London: Verso, 2005), 76.

7. Jacques Derrida, "Faith and Knowledge: The Two Sources of 'Religion' at the Limits of Reason Alone," in *Acts of Religion*, ed. Gil Anidjar (New York: Routledge, 2002), 80n27.

8. For Derrida, the word "world" is a construction, destined "to protect us against the infantile but infinite anxiety of the fact that *there is not the world*"; Jacques Derrida, *The Beast and the Sovereign*, vol. 2, trans. Geoffrey Bennington (Chicago, IL: University of Chicago Press, 2011), 266).

9. Jacques Derrida and Maurizio Ferraris, *A Taste for the Secret*, ed. Giacomo Donis and David Webb, trans. Giacomo Donis (Cambridge: Polity, 2001), 25.

10. Derrida, "Faith and Knowledge," 87.

11. Derrida, *Politics of Friendship*, 298.

12. Roberto Esposito, "A proposito di Derrida: Biopolitica e immunità," *Identities: Journal for Politics, Gender and Culture* 8, no. 1 (Winter 2011): 11.

13. Roberto Esposito, *Communitas: The Origin and Destiny of Community*, trans. Timothy Campbell (Stanford, CA: Stanford University Press, 2010), 6.

14. Esposito, *Communitas*, 13.

15. Roberto Esposito, *Bios: Biopolitics and Philosophy*, trans. Timothy Campbell (Minneapolis: University of Minnesota Press, 2008), 51.

16. Roberto Esposito, *Living Thought: The Origins and Actuality of Italian Philosophy*, trans. Zakiya Hanafi (Stanford, CA: Stanford University Press, 2012), 30.

17. Roberto Esposito, *Immunitas: The Protection and Negation of Life*, trans. Zakiya Hanafi (Cambridge: Polity, 2011), 5.

18. Esposito, *Immunitas*, 8. For Agamben the topological structure of the state of exception can be defined by the oxymoron "being-outside, and yet belonging"; Giorgio Agamben, *State of Exception*, trans. Kevin Attell (Chicago, IL: University of Chicago Press, 2005), 35.

19. Roberto Esposito, interview with Timothy Campbell, trans. Anna Paparcone, *Diacritics: A Review of Contemporary Criticism* 36, no. 2 (2006): 51. This issue of the review contains essays by several authors on the topic "Bios, Immunity, Life: The Thought of Roberto Esposito."

20. Roberto Esposito, *Terms of the Political: Community, Immunity, Biopolitics*, trans. Rhiannon Noel Welch (New York: Fordham University Press, 2013), 38.

21. Jacques Derrida, *Rogues: Two Essays on Reason*, trans. Pascale-Anne Brault and Michael Naas (Stanford, CA: Stanford University Press, 2005), 39.

22. Derrida, *Rogues*, 63.

23. The autoimmunity of democracy is intertwined with that of domestic terrorists, who incorporate "two suicides in one: their own [. . .] but also the suicide of those who welcomed, armed, and trained them"; Jacques Derrida, "Autoimmunity: Real and Symbolic Suicides," in *Philosophy in a Time of Terror:*

Dialogues with Jürgen Habermas and Jacques Derrida, ed. Giovanna Borradori, trans. Pascale-Anne Brault and Michael Naas (Chicago, IL: University of Chicago Press, 2003), 95).

24. Derrida analyzes the immune reaction of American democracy, which attacks itself, its own system of protection, and its rights in order to protect itself. Moreover, by neutralizing the effect of the trauma, which is produced by the threat of the worst *to come*, it regenerates the very thing it seeks to disarm. In the same way, military operations, which are put in place to repress the terrorist threat, "work to regenerate, in the short or long term, the causes of the evil they claim to eradicate" (Derrida, "Autoimmunity," 100).

25. Derrida, *Rogues*, 41.

26. Jacques Derrida, "Artifactualities," in *Echographies of Television*, ed. Jacques Derrida and Bernard Stiegler, trans. Jennifer Bajorek (Cambridge: Polity, 2002), 19.

27. Derrida, *Rogues*, 152.

28. Esposito, *Terms of the Political*, 39. For further details on this issue, see Donatella Di Cesare, *Immunodemocracy: Capitalist Asphyxiatrans*, trans. David Broder (Los Angeles, CA: Semiotext(e), 2021).

29. Esposito believes that "what exploded along with the Twin Towers was the dual immunitary system that until then had kept the world intact" (Esposito, *Terms of the Political*, 62): on the one hand, the Islamic extremism that is determined to protect its own religious, ethnic, and cultural purity from contamination by Western secularization, and, on the other, the West that is bent on excluding the rest of the planet from sharing in its own excess goods.

30. Esposito, *Terms of the Political*, 44. For Esposito the being-with [*Mitsein*], which is one of Heidegger's most important concepts, "means that all that exists, coexists; or that existence is the being whose essence is the 'with,' the '*mit*,' the '*avec*'; or existence is 'with,' with-existence (*con-esistenza*), or doesn't exist. The *cum* isn't something that is added from without to the being of existence. It is that which makes being that being that it is" (Esposito, *Communitas*, 93).

31. Roberto Esposito, *Politics and Negation: Toward an Affirmative Philosophy*, trans. Zakiya Hanafi (Cambridge: Polity, 2019), 190. On the Derridian matter of democracy's mortal struggle against itself, as in some cases it can only protect itself by negating itself, see Esposito, *Common Immunity*, 54–58.

32. Derrida, "Faith and Knowledge," 63. For further details, see Peta Mitchell, "Contagion, Virology, Autoimmunity: Derrida's Rhetoric of Contamination," *Parallax* 23, no. 1 (2017): 77–93. This special issue of *Parallax*, ed. Stefan Herbrechter and Michelle Jamieson, is focused on autoimmunities.

33. Émile Benveniste, *Dictionary of Indo-European Concepts and Society*, trans. Elizabeth Palmer (Chicago, IL: Hau Books, 2016), 530.

34. Derrida, "Faith and Knowledge," 68. *Indemnis* is that which has not suffered damage [*damnum*]; the word *damnum* "comes from *dap-no-m*, tied to

daps, dapis, that is, to the sacrifice offered the Gods as ritual compensation. In this latter case, one could speak of *indemni-fication* and we will use this word here or there to designate both the process of compensation and the restitution, sometimes sacrificial, that reconstitutes purity intact, renders integrity safe and sound" (Derrida, "Faith and Knowledge," 61n16). For Derrida, the field of sacrificial indemnity includes security policies (Derrida, "Artifactualities," 18) and the death penalty, which aim to preserve the purity and health of a community; J. Derrida, *The Death Penalty*, vol. 1, ed. Geoffrey Bennington, Marc Crépon, and Thomas Dutoit, trans. Peggy Kamuf (Chicago, IL: University Chicago Press, 2014), 254.

35. Derrida, "Faith and Knowledge," 80.

36. Derrida, "Faith and Knowledge," 80n27. On the basis of Plato, Derrida claims that "the natural illness of the living is defined in its essence as an *allergy*, a reaction to the aggression of an alien element"; Jacques Derrida, "Plato's Pharmacy," in *Dissemination*, trans. Barbara Johnson (London: The Achlone Press, 1981), 101. Mortality determines this allergic relationship with otherness: indeed, "the immortality and perfection of a living being would consist in its having no relation at all with any outside. That is the case with God [. . .]. God has no allergies" (Derrida, "Plato's Pharmacy," 101).

37. Derrida, "Faith and Knowledge," 62n17.

38. Derrida, "Faith and Knowledge," 80n27. Reflecting on Nancy's transplant, when his heart stopped working and needed to be replaced with the risk that immune system may reject the other strange heart (Jean-Luc Nancy, "The Intruder," in *Corpus*, trans. Richard A. Rand [New York: Fordham University Press, 2008], 166–67), Derrida remarks that "in 'normal' conditions [. . .], only a woman can feel the beat of someone else's heart in her. The word for it is 'pregnancy.'" Jacques Derrida, *On Touching—Jean-Luc Nancy*, trans. Christine Irizarry (Stanford, CA: Stanford University Press, 2005), 336–37n5.

39. Derrida, *Rogues*, 123.

40. Derrida, "Autoimmunity," 124: "The *pharmakon* is another name, an old name, for this autoimmunitary logic."

41. Derrida, "Plato's Pharmacy," 98: "The word *pharmakon*, even while it means *remedy*, cites, re-cites, and makes legible that which *in the same word* signifies [. . .] *poison*."

42. Esposito, *Immunitas*, 7.

43. For Esposito, "that Hegel is the greatest thinker of the negative is a fact that no one can dispute" (Esposito, *Politics and Negation*, 68). However, we need to understand what the subject of negation is. According to the classical interpretation of Kojève, the subject that negates is the human being insofar he negates his animal nature; for Nancy, instead, what presents itself as pure negativity is the becoming as the negation of every given presence. Esposito recognizes the merit of Nancy, who shifts the angle of inquiry from the action

of the subject to the activity of becoming. However, he believes that "the ontological interpretation can be described as leaving out Hegel's political or theological-political side" (Esposito, *Politics and Negation*, 70). For further details on this issue, see Jean-Luc Nancy, *Hegel: The Restlessness of the Negative*, trans. Jason E. Smith and Steven Miller (Minneapolis: University of Minnesota Press, 2002).

44. Esposito, *Politics and Negation*, 196.

45. Esposito suggests that law reproduces the logic of ritual sacrifice, which is described by Girard (Esposito, *Immunitas*, 36–45). See René Girard, *Violence and the Sacred*, trans. Patrick Gregory (London: Continuum, 2005).

46. Esposito, *Immunitas*, 26. Esposito refers to Derrida and his interpretation of Benjamin's *Zur Kritik der Gewalt* (Esposito, *Immunitas*, 180n25). In this text there is the distinction between two kinds of violence (*Gewalt*), the founding violence, the one that institutes law, and the violence that conserves the law. Derrida suggests that "for the sake of convenience, let us continue to translate *Gewalt* as violence"; Jacques Derrida, "Force of Law: The 'Mystical Foundation of Authority,'" in *Deconstruction and the Possibility of Justice*, ed. Drucilla Cornell, Michel Rosenfeld, and David Gray Carlson (New York: Routledge, 1992), 31. However, *Gewalt* means the sovereignty of legal power: the force of law. The law has an interest in monopolizing violence, in the sense of *Gewalt*, which is also to say authority. "This monopoly doesn't strive to protect any given just and legal ends [*Rechtszwecke*] but law itself" (Derrida, "Force of Law," 33).

47. Esposito, *Immunitas*, 154.

48. Esposito, *Immunitas*, 127.

49. Esposito, *Immunitas*, 9.

50. On the vaccination process and the new technology of the anti-COVID-19 vaccine, which does not introduce the live virus, see Esposito, *Common Immunity*, 34–48. On the generalized anti-COVID-19 vaccination, which allows us to imagine immunizing the whole world, making community and immunity coincide for the first time in history, see Esposito, *Common Immunity*, 185–90.

51. Esposito, *Immunitas*, 55.

52. Esposito, *Immunitas*, 63.

53. Esposito, *Politics and Negation*, 199. Wolfe shows that Esposito and Derrida share an "ecologised" understanding of the immune system; Cary Wolfe, "(Auto)immunity in Esposito and Derrida," in *Roberto Esposito New Directions in Biophilosophy*, ed. Tilottama Rajan and Antonio Calcagno (Edinburgh: Edinburgh University Press, 2021), 153–73. Wolfe remarks that "in rethinking the biopolitical, it is precisely this dynamic, ecological perspective on immunity that Esposito adopts in his attempt to move beyond the paradigm of sovereignty, and with it the ideologeme of the "person," the discourse of "rights," and so on" (Wolfe, "(Auto)immunity in Esposito and Derrida," 164).

54. Esposito, *Politics and Negation*, 199. About pregnancy as block that inhibits the normal immune reaction in order to host the other, see Esposito, *Immunitas*, 169–71.

55. Esposito, *Politics and Negation*, 199.

56. Esposito, *Bios*, 46. Esposito affirms that life has always been the framework in which politics has moved and politics has been an instrument of defense of life. However, it is only in modernity that immunity has become the main purpose of politics. Hobbes is responsible for inaugurating modern immune scenario, subordinating *conservatio vitae* to obedience to sovereign power. This power, in a vertical exchange, saves the lives of individuals, putting an end to their relationship. Nietzsche is the first to see the aporetic core of the immune strategy (see Esposito, *Immunitas*, 85), when he analyzes the ascetic ideal, which is "a trick for the preservation of life" as well as "a partial physiological inhibition and exhaustion against which the deepest instincts of life [. . .] continually struggle"; Friedrich Nietzsche, *On the Genealogy of Morality*, trans. Carol Diethe (New York: Cambridge University Press, 2006), 88.

57. Esposito, *Bios*, 46. Esposito notes that biopolitics is characterized by biotechnology, in which the human body is no longer a biological given but a hybrid figure (organism and machine). In this context, as Donna Haraway argues, extending Foucault's theses, the immune system is a map drawn to guide recognition and misrecognition of self and other (Esposito, *Immunitas*, 145–50).

58. Derrida, *Rogues*, 109. As Foucault asserts, biopolitics is the modern power "to *foster* life or *disallow* it to the point of death," which replaces the ancient sovereign power "to *take* life or *let* live"; Michel Foucault, *The History of Sexuality*, vol. 1, *An introduction*, trans. Robert Hurley (New York: Pantheon Books, 1978), 138). For Derrida, instead, "biopolitics is an arch-ancient thing (even if today it has new means and new structures)"; Jacques Derrida, *The Beast and the Sovereign*, vol. 1, trans. Geoffrey Bennington (Chicago, IL: University of Chicago Press, 2009), 330. Showing that the distinction between *zoé* and *bíos* even in the classical world was not "clear and secure" (Derrida, *Beast and Sovereign*, 1:316), Derrida also highlights the contradictions of Agamben's argument (Derrida, *Beast and Sovereign*, 330–31). Agamben asserts that "biopolitics is at least as old as the sovereign exception" (Giorgio Agamben, *Homo Sacer: Sovereign Power and Bare Life*, trans. Daniel Heller-Roazen [Stanford, CA: Stanford University Press, 1998], 4), but he also claims that "the entry of *zoe* into the sphere of the *polis*-the politicization of bare life as such-constitutes the decisive event of modernity" (Agamben, *Homo Sacer*, 4).

59. Jacques Derrida, *The Post Card: From Socrates to Freud and Beyond*, trans. Alan Bass (Chicago, IL: University of Chicago Press, 1987), 360.

60. Derrida, *Post Card*, 355.

61. Derrida, *Post Card*, 360.

62. Jacques Derrida, "Freud and the Scene of Writing," in *Writing and Difference*, trans. Alan Bass (London: Routledge, 2001), 254–55.

63. Derrida, *Rogues*, 109.

64. Jacques Derrida, *Specters of Marx: The State of the Debt, the Work of Mourning, and the New International*, trans. Peggy Kamuf (New York: Routledge, 2006), 177.

65. Derrida, *Specters of Marx*, 75.

66. Derrida, *Specters of Marx*, 88.

67. Derrida questions the metaphysics of presence, distinguishing *deconstruction* from *biopolitics*, which presupposes that life is identical to itself. Esposito accuses Derrida of neglecting the question of the living being and of thinking about life not in itself, but only in relation to death. However, as Resta demonstrates, Derrida has been concerned with the living being since his first writings. Between deconstruction and biopolitics, therefore, there is no clear alternative; deconstruction, indeed, has the ambition to deconstruct biopolitics in its essential terms, life and power. For Resta, contrary to the thought of *différance*, Esposito's biopolitics remains in the absolute immanence of the present and of a life that coincides with itself. See Caterina Resta, "Bio-thanato-politica: Una questione di vita e di morte," in *Decostruzione o biopolitica?*, ed. Elettra Stimilli (Macerata, Italy: Quodlibet, 2017), 43.

68. On this issue, see Roberto Esposito, *Instituting Thought: Three Paradigms of Political Ontology*, trans. Mark Epstein (Cambridge: Polity, 2021). For further details, see *Il problema dell'istituzione: Prospettive ontologiche, antropologiche, e guiridico-politiche*, a special issue of *Discipline filosofiche* 29, no. 2 (2019), ed. Enrica Lisciani-Petrini and Massimo Adinolfi; see also Rita Fulco, "A Political Ontology for Europe: Roberto Esposito's Instituent Paradigm," *Continental Philosophy Review*, no. 54 (2021): 367–86, open access: https://doi.org/10.1007/s11007-021-09542-z.

69. Derrida, *Specters of Marx*, 106.

Eleven

From the Neuter to the Instituting Praxis

The Role of Blanchot in Roberto Esposito's Thought

Massimo Villani

According to Hegel, the subject is the entity that retains within itself its own contradiction.[1] The reason why an essay devoted to the presence of Maurice Blanchot in Roberto Esposito's thought begins with a reference to the author of the *Enzyklopädie* is twofold. On the one hand, the underlying assumption of the present chapter is that the most recent phase of Esposito's work has taken him to theoretical positions that share many aspects of the Hegelian thought: the institution, a theme on which he has been working for some years now, is conceived by him not as a thing but as a process whose specific characteristic is that in it the contradiction between order and conflict is held within a form. On the other hand, it is interesting to note how the figure of Blanchot operates as a kind of catalyst in this approach to Hegel. He, in fact, plays a limited but decisive role in Esposito's evolution because it will be precisely the exploration of the Blanchotian dimension of the neuter that will bring the Italian philosopher, as if by a sort of kickback, toward the need for determinate negation.

Two Paradigms of Crisis

Let us begin with the first point: in what sense can we speak of a return to Hegel?[2] First of all, it should be made clear right away that if we speak of a "return" it is not because the German philosopher would have been the original motive for Esposito's analyses, from which the latter would later move away. On the contrary, as we shall see in a moment, the Italian philosopher elaborates a thought that in many ways is incompatible with the Hegelian dialectic. Nevertheless, this return is a topic of great interest because we can say, following Esposito, that it concerns not the thought of a certain author but an entire era: it is necessary, in our time, to rethink the instituting function of the negative. It is in light of this historical need that the place and function that Hegel occupies in Esposito's philosophical itinerary has profoundly changed, this is our thesis, in recent years.

It is not possible here to give an exhaustive account of the multiple changes of direction, often even self-critical, that have marked this path. At least five macro categories have in fact punctuated the evolution of Esposito's thought: the impolitical, the ontology of community, the biopolitics, the impersonal, and the institution. In the background of these, admittedly quite abrupt, changes of direction it is possible to identify a permanent conceptual nucleus that inspired all of the philosopher's work, and that consists of a lucid awareness of the crisis of modernity, and particularly of the modern concept of politics. This concept was based on the idea of a dialectic progress: each contradiction that would have arisen in the historic-empiric order would have merely been the prelude for a reconstruction on a higher level. Once this historical and conceptual linearity has been broken, Esposito's research has wanted first and foremost to explore those fields—that we could call "existential"—that a theory centered on the legal and formalist aspects of politics has ignored, deeming them insignificant. Therefore, at the heart of Esposito's research lies the intuition of this *crisis of the political*: not, however, a crisis that would have occurred at a certain moment, but a flaw, an interruption that constitutes the political itself.

It is the very idea of this crisis, that is, this original break that keeps Esposito away from Hegel. Far from thematizing the identity of the rational and the real, he tries to cast his gaze into the crack that divides them; indeed, we can say that the matrix of his entire reflection is exactly this unsalvageable rift between theory and praxis, between philosophy and politics. His whole reflection on the impolitical, in fact, is obviously not an attempt to identify a neutral zone, free from the political. On the contrary, it is about penetrating deep into it, to the point of digging out its hollow core, the outside that the political carries within itself; it is about observing a "'oltre' che, più che a una semplice esteriorità rispetto alla politica, allude a una decostruzione e a un ribaltamento dei suoi parametri tradizionali ['beyond' that, rather than a mere externality with respect to politics, alludes to a deconstruction and overturning of its traditional parameters]."[3] Against a whole Hegel-Marxist tradition, Esposito exposes thought to a unemployed negativity that spoils the linear and progressive image of history.[4]

However, this emphasis on the negative poses a problem. It is true that the idea of this not appropriable origin deconstructs the liberal idea that, setting a scene always inhabited by rational, accomplished subjects, completely removes the conflict through which this scene takes shape; in this sense, then, "the impolitical is in direct opposition to its every form of depoliticization."[5] However, the risk of this perspective is that of a gnostic outcome, in which, deepening the crack separating ontology and politics, the latter loses its specificity, blurring the lines with an ethical register.

It is precisely to escape this gnostic outcome that Esposito will attempt to fill the hollow heart of the impolitical. First, in the phase inaugurated by the book *Communitas*,[6] he accentuates the relational density of historical-empirical communities. Above all, then, beginning with *Bíos*,[7] he tries to unbalance in an affirmative direction the biopolitical paradigm that Foucault had enigmatically formulated, leaving it suspended between a politics over life and a politics of life. In this phase of his work, anticipated by an important text such as *Immunitas*,[8] his authors of reference are mainly Foucault and Deleuze, that is, still authors who participate in a very radical way in the anti-Hegelian temperament of the second half of the twentieth century.

It is especially their legacy, in fact, that he uses to sabotage or, as Deleuze would say, "to convert"[9] the machine of political theology that precisely in Hegel "extends its scope beyond the regional or methodological to the global and ontological."[10] At this stage, Hegel is regarded as the one who thinks "the disjunctive connection of the One and the Two."[11] Esposito, thus, does not simply view the dynamic of *Aufhebung* as sublating or overcoming, that is, as the movement that takes what it erases to a higher level. He rather interprets it as an exclusionary selection procedure. In its historical-dialectical development, in fact, the Spirit includes in itself something that, at the same time, excludes, in the sense that it uses it only as a point of support or, as Esposito says, as "propellant": "the history of the world includes a nonhistorical portion inside it that constitutes both its dialectical driving force and the excluded remainder. This happens because one part—defined as the West—is at the same time also considered the whole, to the point of reducing the other to an inner propellant of its own expansion. Hegel's philosophy of history rotates around the axis that divides and separates outside and inside, whole and part, present and past, in a process aimed at functionalizing the second term to develop the first."[12] At the heart of the One, then, is the Two, namely an inexorable split that, however, Esposito, at this stage of his thought, distinguishes from that inoriginal crisis that he seeks to revive as the "essence" of the political. Or, more precisely, he finds in Hegel an obstacle toward the fully affirmative manifestation of that original rupture. In Hegel, in fact, universalism is always the reverse of exclusion: one part is always sacrificed to the other which stands as the whole, as One.

The author of *Bíos*, on the other hand, intends to subtract life, all life, from any sacrificial dynamic and make it, its expansive power, the driving center of the political: "That such a unique process crosses the entire extension of life without providing a continuous solution—that anything that lives needs to be thought in the unity of life—means that no part of it can be destroyed in favor of another: every life is a form of life and every forms refers to life. This is neither the content nor the final sense of biopolitics, but is at a minimum its presupposition. Whether its meaning will again be disowned in a politics of death or affirmed in a politics of life will depend on the mode in which contemporary thought will follow its traces."[13] That is why he will devote himself to deconstructing the device of the person that constitutes the fundamental pivot of the theological-political machine. The person, in fact, is the category that brings the fundamental performance of that machine all the way into the concrete life of each individual: it separates, in each living being,[14] a rational and voluntary part that attaches to itself another part that, at the same time, is excluded and sacrificed as corporeal and animal. So, even before directly confronting the theological-political machine, Esposito had devoted himself to dismantling the personalistic device, elaborating a long genealogy of it, starting from the Christian religion and the Roman law.[15] As mentioned, Foucault's thought of the outside[16] and Deleuze's impersonal[17] are the main resources Esposito brings to bear in his attempt at deconstruction.

However, Esposito will very soon abandon this position as well, and this will happen precisely because of the centrality in his thinking of the "crisis," the inoriginal principle, which we mentioned earlier. In fact, outlining an affirmative biopolitics—whose principle is, as we have seen, "every life is a form of life and every form must be referred to life—cannot mean making politics an emanation of ontology. Between the two there is not immediacy but articulation. In other words, fundamental for Esposito is to think of a force that can express itself immediately as form, or, in other words, a life that expresses itself without diluting itself.

Ultimately, the problem Esposito finds before him is to think of division neither as a gnostic split that precipitates existence into a condition of structural precariousness, a condition in which the sacrifice of one of the parties is equally necessary and structural, nor as the absolute immanence of politics in life. Neither *krisis*[18] nor vitalism. Well, Blanchot is exactly the author who allows him to think radically about this *neither . . . nor*, and, at the same time, to overcome it in the direction of a different, narrower, but politically more effective path.

Neutralizing Dialectics

Beyond a few sporadic and inconsequential occurrences, Blanchot plays a strategic role in Esposito's research at three key points. The first goes back to the phase of research on the impolitical: if in the book *Categories of the Impolitical* he figures mostly as an interpreter of Bataille, as well as the author who, together with the latter and Jean-Luc Nancy, elaborated in the most radical way the idea of a negative community, the anthology *Oltre la politica* hosts a short text of his *Le marxisme contre la Révolution*.[19] The great interest of this text lies in the fact that here Blanchot tears apart the concept of the political, taking it "beyond" itself. Indeed, he criticizes the Marxist idea, embodied in the Soviet state, that revolution is a necessary consequence of a certain socioeconomic development. Blanchot challenges exactly the idea that the political is *within* the processes: as a polemical moment of authentic rupture, it can only stand *outside* them, in an irreducible exteriority, which completely escapes any project. In fact, then, the revolution—or the political: it is the same here, since both refer to a moment of radical rupture—is beyond history, and the only possible representation of it, as of the community, is a negative one, never a historical and concrete one. Evidently, this gnostic separation between the actual and polemical planes, between history and event, or between politics and political, cannot but appeal to Esposito at a time when, as noted above, he is engaged in the exploration of the inoriginal, opaque, and inappropriable point of politics.

If the young Blanchot of the 1930s is an author who challenges the idea of a coincidence between the rational and the real, the mature Blanchot, from the 1950s onward, is even more radically antidialectical (and anti-Hegelian). It is precisely this Blanchot that Esposito resorts to in order to overcome the impasses of the impolitical in the direction, mentioned earlier, of a theory of the impersonal. In the long genealogical research conducted in *Third Person*, Blanchot occupies an eminent place—his second occurrence in the Italian philosopher's research—in which the deconstruction of "the personhood-deciding machine"[20] finds its climax, which in turn introduces an attempt at a positive, albeit fragmentary, definition of a different "practice that alters existence."[21]

As early as the long-simmering draft of the novel *Thomas l'obscur*,[22] in fact, at the center of Blanchot's reflection lies a dimension opened by a double negation, that "neither, nor" mentioned earlier: it is the neuter, a theme that Blanchot has relentlessly pursued, offering so many definitions of it, all of them, however, necessarily asymptotic. The approach to this dimension can only be "infinite," as stated in the title of a particularly important book of his,[23] because, being devoid of any property, it irretrievably escapes concept. As Esposito aptly notes, "What makes the neuter elusive is not any specific feature but, paradoxically, the fact that it does not have any: the way it evades in principle the traditional dichotomies that have marked the history of Western thought, such as being and nothingness, presence and absence, inside and outside. While the neuter does not belong in the sphere of being, this does not make it reducible to nothingness either."[24] So, what Blanchot describes is something very different from the process in which the Spirit finds itself. On the contrary, the neuter cannot but be ousted from philosophy, since it is absolute exteriority: "One can recognize in the entire history of philosophy an effort either to acclimatize or to domesticate the neuter by substituting for it the law of the impersonal and the reign of the universal, or an effort to challenge it by affirming the ethical primacy of the Self-Subject, the mystical aspiration to the singular Unique."[25]

In order to be remotely up to par, a genealogy of this concept would have to account at least for the relations between Blanchot's reflection and the suspensive method of Husserl's phenomenology,[26] the ontology of early Heidegger,[27] as well as the fruitful dialogue Blanchot had with Levinas.[28] Since we cannot carry out this work here,[29] we simply emphasize a fundamental point. The neuter that Blanchot seeks to focus on sets thought in motion, triggering, as noted above, its infinite movement. However, the purpose of this exposure of thought to what it irretrievably removes is to leave thought itself in an impasse: the experience of the neuter manifests itself as a pure shock of the heterogeneous, of the absolute Other that shatters the subject and intimates finitude as its unescapable condition. Where modern thought had imagined fully disposing of being—which presented itself without any opacity in the light of reason—here we are dealing with the experience of a limit, impacting against which subjectivity shatters. The philosophical tradition, particularly the modern one, has been mesmerized by "the temptation of the eternal," and has implemented "the concept as the instrument in this enterprise of establishing a secure reign";[30] thus the task Blanchot takes on is precisely to unmask this "Great Refusal"[31] of death, of finitude.

So the double negation inherent in the neuter has nothing dialectical about it. Whereas in Hegel we are dealing with real *work* of the negative (an expression to which we shall return in the conclusion), here we find an inert negative that is characterized precisely by its absence of the work: "Something is at work by way of the neuter that is immediately the work of worklessness (*désoeuvrement*): there is an effect of the neuter—this says something of the passivity of the neuter—that is not an effect *of the* neuter, not being the effect of a Neuter pretendedly at work as a cause or a thing."[32] Moreover, it is Blanchot himself who points out that the thought of the neuter has nothing to do with the Hegelian dialectic: "The Neuter [. . .] neutralizes (itself), thus evokes (does nothing but evoke) the movement of *Aufhebung*, but if it suspends and retains, it retains only the movement of suspending, that is, the distance it creates by the fact that, occupying the terrain, it makes the distance disappear."[33] The one Esposito refers to, then, is a Blanchot "whose intention is to protect his own perspective from the risk of a dialectical recovery implicit in every internal negative. While the term 'impersonal' remains on the horizon of meaning described by the person, albeit in a purely contrastive or privative fashion, the reference to the neutral opens up a whole new semantic field."[34]

As can be seen from this quote, the Italian philosopher uses Blanchot's reflection to imagine a political thought and praxis capable of dismantling the device of the person at its root. In this sense he recovers

Blanchot's attempts to translate the theory of the third person within a political practice. The most striking element in these attempts, Esposito writes, "is how he persistently strove to identify a public language corresponding to a philosophy of the impersonal. If you run through all the statements he made and the positions he took, what seems to unite them even more than the arguments he employed from one time to the next is the programmatic erasure of his name—or of any proper name—on behalf of the anonymous and the impersonal."[35]

In effect, for Blanchot it is a matter, through experiments in anonymous writing, of radically questioning the function of the intellectual: it is not enough to say that the latter should no longer show the way to those who would lack the means to find it for themselves. If this was a perspective acquired in the 1960s, and one that would explode in the movements of the Sixty-Eight, Blanchot goes further by asserting that the task of (philosophical) writing is to bring out the force of the impersonal, or, rather, the impersonal as *force*: "Intellectuals [. . .] have experienced [. . .] a way of being together, and I am not thinking of the collective character of the Declaration, but of its *impersonal force*, the fact that all those who signed it certainly lent it their name, but without invoking their particular truth or their nominal fame."[36] Very significantly, these words dating back to 1960 are addressed to Jean-Paul Sartre, with whom he would indirectly return to confront, many years later, about the question of intellectuals: in the short text *Les intellectuels en question* Blanchot states that the specific performance of intellectuals is not to produce works of ingenuity and beauty, but, on the contrary, it is precisely to *interrupt* this production: the intellectual—the writer, the artist, the philosopher—renounces his creative force, renounces his solitude and, ceasing to be what he is, stands as one among many, loses himself in the obscurity of anonymity.[37]

However, even at this level Esposito does not hide the difficulty and even the fallibility of Blanchot's project[38] and, consequently, also of his own attempt to situate the political in the impersonal. From this point of view, it is very interesting to note that the third occurrence of Blanchot in Esposito's work is found in a very important book that acts as a hinge between the latter's reflection on the impersonal and his more recent work on instituting thought. This is *Politics and Negation*,[39] a book that aims to recover the instituting force of the negative: an affirmative thought, the later Esposito tells us, cannot renounce confrontation with the negative, risking of exhausting itself in a politically ineffectual exercise.

In truth, already in the earlier A *Philosophy for Europe* Esposito distanced himself from the French thought that for many years had been a fundamental motive of his reflection: in this book in fact, a historical-dialectical path is outlined, starting from the *German Philosophy* and then culminating in the *Italian Thought*, the latter being a category that Esposito uses to refer to a tradition of (not only philosophical and not only Italian) thought that is characterized by a close contact with history and politics (where the outcome of the work of the Frankfurt School, and in particular of Adorno and his *Negative Dialektitk*, had been to leave philosophical discourse inexorably *outside* the real). What is important in the economy of our discourse is that the median point of this historical-conceptual path consists precisely of the *French Theory*, which, hegemonic in the last decades of the twentieth century, had been a fundamental source of inspiration for Esposito himself: if, in fact, *Communitas* admitted an "unpayable debt"[40] to Nancy, it was still to contemporary French thought that Esposito turned in order to bend biopolitics in an affirmative direction, reading above all Foucault and Deleuze. Well, in A *Philosophy for Europe*, Esposito points out the great influence that Blanchot's thought had on French Theory as a whole, particularly about the concepts of *neuter* and *outside*. In this context, however, the Italian philosopher no longer highlights the critical scope of these categories; rather, he stigmatizes that this theoretical approach—as mentioned earlier in quickly commenting on Blanchot's concept of revolution—dooms itself to remain inevitably outside history and the real. Now the neuter is no longer, for Esposito, what forces the limits of thought by opening it to what is external to it: on the contrary, by exacerbating this gap, it only *neutralizes*[41] thought itself, depriving it of any critical, polemical, political potential.

The goal of *Politics and Negation* is to think of a dialectical, and for that very reason productive, tension between negative and affirmative: each of these two polarities dissolves into abstraction if it does not meet the opposition of the other. The fundamental assumption of this research is that "what took place after Hegel, culminating in the last few decades, was not the further development of his perspective but its crumbling."[42] So the aim of this volume is to try to think of affirmative modes of negation, which Esposito identifies as: difference, determination, and opposition. Well, in this reflection Blanchot, who not coincidentally appears in the final pages of the text, represents the point of maximum tension in the discourse,[43] a tension destined to be dissolved in the following book, with a radical reshuffling of the theoretical framework.

Esposito comments on a text by Blanchot that, from its title,[44] insists on the lemma *pas*: it means "step" in French, but it is also a negative particle that in adverbial form can be translated as "not." Blanchot uses it as an operator capable of contaminating the positive with the negative, and thus preventing both from expressing themselves integrally, to the point of dissolution; hence Esposito can write that "event and non-event, noun and adverb, positive and negative are confused to the point of indistinguishability, in a contamination that drives the text beyond the confines of language itself. To come back to my underlying theme, we have here something that breaks down the dichotomous conflict between affirmation and negation by placing one inside the other. It is true that the action of taking a step, or several steps, is negated by something unfathomable, which blocks it. Still, this does not signal a victory of the negative, which is interrupted in its turn by the other meaning of *pas*."[45]

Commenting on another text by Blanchot, the short story *L'arrêt de mort*,[46] Esposito writes that "just as *pas* refers at the same time to that which moves and to that which stays still, in the same way *arrêt* stops that which, in another sense, it adjudicates. But just as the arrest of the step does not cancel out its possibility and alludes to a sort of reiteration of what has yet to take place, similarly, rather than definitively stopping death, the arrest of death consigns the pardoned person to a death that is always to come."[47]

As mentioned earlier, Blanchot represents, in this analysis by Esposito, the point of maximum tension in the discourse. On the one hand "the continual suspending of the positive in the negative and of the negative in the positive"[48] is exactly what the Italian philosopher was looking for; on the other hand, however, it is precisely this suspension that is problematic. Esposito states this here in a way that is still only symptomatic, but the critique is already extremely accurate: "Like the step that is arrested before being performed, *the dialectic power of the negative undergoes an arrest, which blocks not only negation but also the negation of negation*."[49] Blanchot's neuter, the double negation, resolves itself into an effect of generalized spectralization, into an unbounded sprawl of an infinite evil that can no longer be satisfactory to the philosopher who seeks a thought that not only emerges from the real but also makes friction with it. The obstinacy with which, instead, Blanchot holds fast to an idea of the neuter that is also undoing, the erasure of all work,[50] now appears to Esposito theoretically and politically unserviceable. It is time to abandon Blanchot.

Double Negation and Living Synthesis

Although in the first lines of this chapter the idea of the political as an inoriginary crisis was identified as the motif that consistently runs through Esposito's research in all its changes of direction, it is equally important to stress the importance of precisely these deviations. Indeed, they are not to be read as mistakes, swerves to be remedied by finding an internal coherence of discourse. On the contrary, they are the indicator of a theoretical posture that lets itself be stimulated by the constant new emergences. Esposito's is, as aptly pointed out, a living thought[51] that, rejecting any authorial pose, undergoes and registers the discontinuities and inconsistencies of current times. So, there was a long historical phase during which Esposito approached the thinkers of immediacy. These were the years in which neoliberalism, making itself hegemonic on a global scale, imposed the need to think politics outside the space that modernity had recognized as specific to it. Consequently, it was necessary to destroy the theological-political machine that practices toward living subjects only an extractive function. Esposito was fully inserted into this critical temperament, and in this long phase, which began in the early 1980s and lasted at least thirty years, he strategically made use of the conceptual arsenal of Blanchot, an author who, by shattering the fundamental device of modern politics, representation, could write: "I no longer represent, I am; I do not signify, I present [*je ne represente plus, je suis; je ne signifie plus, je presente*]."[52] But in the face of the populist wave that after imprinting a specific mode—in the musical sense of the term—to all contemporary politics, violently overwhelmed Western democratic institutions, up to the paroxysm of the attack on Capitol Hill on January 6, 2021, Esposito understood that that path was no longer viable. Indeed, a thought that wants to have a fruitful relationship with reality cannot remain monolithic and always identical to itself but must allow itself to be shaken by history.

Today, Esposito asserts, it is necessary to think not of the incessant undoing of all forms, the stubborn absence of work, rather it is necessary to be able to think, and to practice, the identity of form and force: the former should not be thought of to the detriment of life and its power of renewal. "Institution" is, for the Italian philosopher, the name of this overlap between force and form. It is, in fact, that which, while keeping open within itself that inoriginary split that gives the political its inalienable polemical character, does not renounce becoming a work. It is precisely for this reason that in the book following *Politics and Negation*, in which he attempts to delineate an instituting thought, Blanchot is absent and, more generally, the authors that the Italian philosopher had used for many years, such as Heidegger and Deleuze, reflux into opposite paradigms—the former is placed in the paradigm that Esposito calls "destituting," the latter in the "constituting" paradigm—but which are both considered "impolitical," that is, politically ineffective.[53] The only trait of Blanchot's reflection that will be retained in this last phase of Esposito's research is that relating to the impersonal: "Institutions are not the product of particular wills; they are the product of impersonal forces that precede individuals and determine their behaviors. Rather than forming institutions, individuals are formed by them through their upbringing, transmitted down the chain of generations."[54]

Let us return, in conclusion, to the relationship between neuter and double negation. Blanchot's is a negative that simultaneously addresses itself in two opposite directions: in doing so, it dismisses all the binary oppositions on which metaphysics was founded, but, more importantly, it forces experience into aporia, in the literal sense of roadlessness, blockage. The negative that Esposito seeks to rethink, in contrast, is *a process that turns back on itself*, and, in doing so, denies itself. In the last stages of his research, Esposito intuits that the only affirmative mode of negation cannot be the mutual contamination of two opposing polarities but rather, as we read in an earlier quotation, "the negation of negation,"[55] that is, a process that, in denying itself, is no longer just fading, but also form, and that holds within itself the split from which it takes its start.

The neither-nor that Esposito tries to think of is precisely the opposite of the aporia, the roadlessness: it is the difficult attempt to take a "narrow path,"[56] to quote a much-used expression of Hannah Arendt, a philosopher widely explored by Esposito. It is the path that avoids the polarization between order and conflict: *neither* pure vitalism, that is, politics as a direct emanation of ontology; *nor* the political as absolute, gnostic separation from the plane of the living. Esposito thinks the "articulation"[57] between dimensions—order/conflict, life/form, nature/history, work/inoperativity, *praxis* and *poiesis*—that, in the semantics of the neuter, are simply avoided, deactivated.

Esposito seeks this precise sense of a praxis that does not dilute in its making but produces forms that go beyond the level of immediacy, no longer or at least not only it in Machiavelli, that is, the author who more than any other thought the coextensiveness of order and conflict. It is especially toward Hegel that Esposito veers his thought, moved, as we have tried to show, by unavoidable historical needs.

The expression "*work* of the negative" was used above. This is the formula by which we chose to translate an expression that appears in the *Vorrede* of the *Phänomenologie des Geistes*: "die Arbeit des Negativen."[58] The choice fell on "work," rather than "labor," according to the English translation in use,[59] precisely to mark the coincidence, in Hegelian logic, of process and form, *Arbeit* and *Werk*. Very significantly, in Hegel this logical opposition is resolved not on an abstract and formal plane but in the concrete living process: it is here that *"vitam instituere"* is given in act, ceases to be an "unresolved question,"[60] and is used by Esposito as the point of articulation between *bíos* and politics.

Notes

1. "Ein solches, das den Widerspruch seiner selbst in sich zu haben und zu *ertragen* fähig ist, ist das *Subjekt*." Georg Wilhelm Friedrich Hegel, *Werke 9: Enzyklopädie der philosophischen Wissenschaft* (Frankfurt a. M.: Suhrkamp, 1970), 469.

2. To confirm an approach of Esposito to Hegel, we can consider his last book, titled *Vitam instituere: Genealogia dell'istituzione* (Turin: Einaudi, 2023). It proposes, as the title suggests, a genealogy of the institution that passes through three authors placed in an ascending trajectory, so to speak: Machiavelli, Spinoza, and Hegel. As the book was being published at the time of writing this essay, it was not possible to take it into account.

3. Roberto Esposito, *Oltre la politica: Antologia del pensiero "impolitico"* (Milan: Mondadori, 1996), 7.

4. See Roberto Esposito, "Anacronismi," *Filosofia Politica*, no. 1 (2017): 13–24.

5. Roberto Esposito, *Categories of the Impolitical*, trans. Connal Parsley (New York: Fordham University Press, 2015), 13.

6. Roberto Esposito, *Communitas: The Origin and Destiny of Community*, trans. Timothy Campbell (Stanford, CA: Stanford University Press, 2010).

7. Roberto Esposito, *Bíos: Biopolitics and Philosophy*, trans. Timothy Campbell (Minneapolis: University of Minnesota Press, 2008).

8. Roberto Esposito, *Immunitas: The Protection and Negation of Life*, trans. Zakiya Hanafi (Cambridge: Polity, 2011).

9. "This is the empiricist conversion." Gilles Deleuze and Felix Guattari, *What Is Philosophy?*, trans. Hugh Tomlinson and Graham Burchell (New York: Columbia University Press, 1994), 75.

10. Roberto Esposito, *Two: The Machine of Political Theology and the Place of Thought*, trans. Zakiya Hanafi (New York: Fordham University Press, 2015), 28.

11. Esposito, *Two*, 29.

12. Esposito, *Two*, 3.

13. Esposito, *Bíos: Biopolitics and Philosophy*, 194.

14. In each man, of course. But also, in each (living) being to whom the dignity of person is recognized.

15. It is a work that takes place mainly in the book *Third Person: Politics of Life and Philosophy of the Impersonal*, trans. Zakiya Hanafi (Cambridge: Polity, 2012), and then continued in different modulations in *Persons and Things: From the Body's Point of View*, trans. Zakiya Hanafi (Cambridge: Polity, 2015).

16. Michel Foucault, *La pensée du dehors* (Paris: Fata Morgana, 1986).

17. Gilles Deleuze, "L'immanence: une vie . . . ," *Philosophie*, no. 47 (1995): 3–7.

18. The critique of the crisis dispositif is at the heart of "The Crisis Dispositif," the first part of Esposito's volume, *A Philosophy for Europe: From the Outside*, trans. Zakiya Hanafi (Cambridge: Polity, 2018).

19. Maurice Blanchot, "Le marxisme contre la Révolution," *Revue française*, 1933. The Italian translation, titled *Il marxismo contro la rivoluzione*, can be found on pages 50–62 of the aforementioned anthology edited by Esposito, *Oltre la politica*.

20. Esposito, *Third Person*, 13.

21. Esposito, *Third Person*, 17.

22. Originally started in 1932, *Thomas l'obscur* was first published in 1941 (Paris: Gallimard), then in an extensively revised version in 1950 for the same publisher. On this novel, see Jean Starobinski, "Thomas l'Obscur, chapitre I," *Critique*, no. 229 (1966): 498–513.

23. Maurice Blanchot, *The Infinite Conversation*, trans. Susan Hanson (Minneapolis: University of Minnesota Press, 1993).

24. Esposito, *Third Person*, 129.

25. Blanchot, *Infinite Conversation*, 299.

26. See Edmund Husserl, *Ideen zu Einer Reinen Phänomenologie und Phänomenologischen Philosophie: Erstes Buch* (The Hague: Martinus Nijhoff, 1976), §§ 109–114.

27. See Blanchot, *Infinite Conversation*, 458.

28. There are many places where Blanchot, in describing the concept of the neuter, refers to Levinas's *il y a*. See, for example, Maurice Blanchot, "Notre compagne clandestine" in *Textes pour Emmanuel Lévinas*, ed. François Laruelle (Paris: Jean-Michel Place, 1980), 79–87: 86. In turn, Levinas recognizes in his

friend's work on the neuter, a "source" for his reflection on *il y a*. See Emmanuel Lévinas, *De l'existence à l'existant* (Paris: Vrin, 1947), 103. The irreducible difference between the two concepts is accounted for by Esposito in *Third Person*, 119–33.

29. We limit ourselves to mentioning at least Emmanuel Levinas, *Sur Blanchot* (Montpellier: Fata Morgana, 1975); Jacques Derrida, *Demeure: Maurice Blanchot* (Paris: Galilée, 1998); Marlène Zarader, *L'être et le neutre: À partir de Maurice de Blanchot* (Lagrasse, France: Verdier, 2021); and Francesco Garritano, *Sul neutro: Saggio su Maurice Blanchot* (Florence: Ponte alle Grazie, 1992).

30. Blanchot, *Infinite Conversation*, 33; quote slightly edited.

31. See Blanchot, *Infinite Conversation*, 33–48.

32. Maurice Blanchot, *The Step Not Beyond*, trans. Lycette Nelson (Albany: State University of New York Press, 1992), 75.

33. Blanchot, *The Step Not Beyond*, 75.

34. Esposito, *Third Person*, 128.

35. Esposito, *Third Person*, 132.

36. Maurice Blanchot, *Political Writings, 1953–1993*, trans. Zakir Paul (New York: Fordham University Press, 2010), 36; my emphasis.

37. See Maurice Blanchot, *Les intellectuels en question* (Paris: Fourbis, 1996). Blanchot's reflection on this topic intersects and overlaps with the clash that Maurice Merleau-Ponty and Jean-Paul Sartre had on the same subject during the 1950s and that had much resonance in France. Traces of this disagreement are three important letters addressed to Sartre by Merleau-Ponty, dating from 1953 but appearing only in 1994 in *Magazine littéraire* edited by François Ewald, then collected in the volume Maurice Merleau-Ponty, *Parcours deux, 1951–1961* (Paris: Verdier, 2000), 134–69. An important and comprehensive historical and philosophical reconstruction of the affair can be found in the *aut aut* issue edited by Enrica Lisciani-Petrini and Raoul Kirchmayr, titled "Sartre/Merleau-Ponty: Un dissidio produttivo," *aut aut*, no. 381 (2019).

38. "To what extent this 'communism of writing' is difficult, or even clearly impossible, to achieve would be made evident—even more than by the failure of this project—by the direction toward 'the disaster' that Blanchot's thought took in later years" (Esposito, *Third Person*, 133).

39. Roberto Esposito, *Politics and Negation: For an Affirmative Thought*, trans. Zakiya Hanafi (Cambridge: Polity, 2019).

40. Esposito, *Communitas*, 151.

41. This term returns several times throughout the third part of the book *A Philosophy for Europe*, titled precisely "French Theory."

42. Esposito, *Politics and Negation*, 3.

43. It should be noted that all Esposito's books are conceived in the form of a commentary on a series of theses. The order of the arguments set forth, however, does not follow a chronological sequence. Rather such order draws

a trajectory in which each thesis is "sublated," that is, refuted and taken to a higher level by the next one. It is in this movement, rather than in a formal exposition, that Esposito's thesis emerges. But this also means that the last author and conceptual figure that is expounded in his books has a particularly important strategic function.

44. Maurice Blanchot, *Les pas au-delà* (Paris: Gallimard, 1973). We have already quoted the English translation, *The Step Not Beyond*.

45. Esposito, *Politics and Negation*, 204.

46. Maurice Blanchot, *L'arrêt de mort* (Paris: Gallimard, 1948).

47. Esposito, *Politics and Negation*, 205.

48. Esposito, *Politics and Negation*, 205.

49. Esposito, *Politics and Negation*, 204; my emphasis.

50. This stubborn allegiance to the absence of work, to the limitless sweep of death (which, infinitely suspended, ends up spectralizing even life), is particularly evident in the reflection the French philosopher devotes to the myth of Orpheus. See Maurice Blanchot, *L'espace littéraire* (Paris: Gallimard, 1975), 167–196. On the theme of *mourir* as opposed to *mort* in Blanchot, see Aïcha Liviana Messina, "Apocalypse et croyance en ce monde: Monde, finitude et christianisme chez Nancy et Blanchot," in *Jean-Luc Nancy: Penser la mutation*, ed. Jérôme Lèbre and Jacob Rogozinski (Strasbourg, France: Presses Universitaires de Strasbourg, 2017), 153–68.

51. Daniela Calabrò and Giulio Goria, eds., *Les détours d'un pensée vivante: Transitions et changement de paradigme dans la réflexion de Roberto Esposito* (Paris: Mimesis, 2012).

52. Maurice Blanchot, *La part du feu* (Paris: Gallimard, 1949), 317, translated by Charlotte Mandell as *The Work of Fire* (Stanford, CA: Stanford University Press, 1995), 328.

53. See Roberto Esposito, *Instituting Thought: Three Paradigms of Political Ontology*, trans. Mark William Epstein (Cambridge: Polity, 2021).

54. Roberto Esposito, *Institution*, trans. Zakiya Hanafi (Cambridge: Polity, 2022), 23.

55. Esposito, *Politics and Negation*, 204.

56. Hannah Arendt, *Between Past and Future: Eight Exercises in Political Thought* (New York: Viking Press, 1968), 259.

57. "Articulation" is a keyword in Esposito's lexicon: it's the word he uses to title the paragraphs connecting the four parts of *A Philosophy for Europe*.

58. Georg Wilhelm Friedrich Hegel, *Werke 3: Phänomenologie des Geistes* (Frankfurt a. M.: Suhrkamp, 1970), 22.

59. See Georg Wilhelm Friedrich Hegel, *Phenomenology of Spirit*, trans. Arnold Vincent Miller (Oxford: Oxford University Press, 1977), 10.

60. Esposito, *Institution*, 1.

Appendix

Institutions, Conflicts, Common Immunity: In Dialogue with Roberto Esposito

Interview by Laura Cremonesi, Rita Fulco, and Valentina Surace

Translated by Tijana Okič

FULCO: This volume explores the relationship between your ideas and those of several other twentieth-century thinkers. Your focus on some of their categories is a method you consciously and willingly chose so as to allow your own thought to emerge and develop. A way of doing philosophy "in common" with those who preceded you and with your contemporaries, always gazing towards the present. Following Foucault, we could call it an "ontology of actuality." And yet, in contrast to previous centuries or even decades, which were altogether identified in relation to cultural or philosophical movements—think, for example, of the Enlightenment, idealism, or existentialism—our epoch isn't likely to be remembered by the name of a cultural or philosophical current. Philosophizing in an epoch as fragmented as ours is increasingly difficult and requires strong motivation. What has philosophy meant to you throughout your life and what does it mean for you today? What are some of the greatest responsibilities that you as a philosopher perceive in an era so saturated with fast news or short-lived, "fashionable" philosophical currents, which are immediately forgotten and replaced with others?

ESPOSITO: It is true that contemporary philosophy finds itself in a condition of great fragmentation. On the one hand is the often-misleading separation between analytic and continental philosophy. On the other, and internal to this division, is a series of "turns" or "moments" which fail to find a common denominator, to the point that the "postmodern," which during the seventies and eighties was strongly present in the philosophical reflection, theorized the productive combination of different styles. Deconstruction, biopolitics, new realism, immanentism, theories of the event are names which, more than others, have attempted to compress/encapsulate lines of research otherwise difficult to bring together. Nonetheless, finding a unitary background wherein these could find a common articulation remains difficult.

As for the meaning that the philosophical work has had and still has for me, I would leave the question of responsibility, which always risks slipping into an auto-gratifying rhetoric, in the background. Thought—for me but, I'd say, for anyone—is rather a necessity, a shockwave imposing itself irrespective of one's will. In many ways, as claimed by some Arab Aristotelians who, without much success, spoke about the 'agent intellect,' to think is not the expression of an internal choice but, rather, a 'foreign' element coming from the outside, absorbing us, sometimes despite ourselves. Like a presence or a burden that one cannot rid oneself of. Who is able to control one's own thoughts? Or even to erase them? Is it possible to decide not to think? Even if it were possible, such a decision would still be a thought, even if only negative. What is possible, to an extent at least, and if one doesn't suffer from innate obsessions (I myself am all but free of them), is to try and orient one's own thoughts in a non-destructive direction, perhaps by giving primacy to less traumatic ones over the unbearable ones. In this case—if one is able to do so—thought can even become a resource whose emergence distracts from the darkest evanescent nightmares. For me, in particular in recent years, the thought machine, precisely because I wasn't controlling it, has been an important tool, necessary for survival and, within certain limits, important for what, in a somewhat pompous way, is defined as the "life of the spirit."

Fashions? In general, one attributes fashions to others, proclaiming oneself to be the custodian of a non-fashionable, "consistent," and, in some respect, "eternal" thought. But nothing about us is eternal. The image of eternity, even if contrived, can be found in the classics. The classics have a hold which contemporary authors—including myself—lack.

This is not because the classics, as is often said, are immortal. The reason is rather the opposite, it is because they refer us to death, precisely because, at least to an extent, in the eyes of others, for a period, they survive death. Classics—including the most complex ones—have clarity in general outlook and expressive "simplicity"—a feature absent in most contemporary thinkers. In the course of time, I tried, though not always successfully, to make my writing and reasoning limpid. To write and also to think in a "simple" manner is the most difficult thing for anyone in our profession. I always advise my best students to try to explain to a non-philosophical audience in three or four propositions the arguments they will develop in longer and more complex texts. If they are not able to do this, it means that their ideas are confused. There is no such thing as something that would be entirely inexpressible. Naturally, like all specific languages, philosophical language too has its own technical formulations. But these too, in the end, are translatable in less complicated terms. Purity of such kind can be found in Latin. I would advise all students of philosophy to study Roman law so as to clarify their ideas.

FULCO: I think that it is necessary to return to the question of war, today more than ever. The recent war in Ukraine has once again brought death and destruction to the heart of Europe. Nonetheless, it is equally true that other bloody wars, fought in different parts of the world, hardly get any media attention across the globe. In reality, however, war—in the history of the West in particular—has a special status, as noted already by Hegel and as both Simone Weil and Hannah Arendt reiterate regarding the event of the "Trojan War." Referring precisely to the latter, you wrote: "It is the origin of our history. It is the origin of our history at least to the extent that it has assumed a truly political dimension. The event, in other words, opens up the time of politics and inevitably predetermines it."[1] If war is the origin of politics, how is such an origin to be thought? Should war be understood as an "external" event which gives rise to politics as something separate and different? Or, on the contrary, should it be understood as an original event, a "seed" whose mark politics will forever bear? In the case of the latter, however, such an identification would entail consequences so profound as to radically change the conception of politics, its *essence*.

ESPOSITO: There is a point of intersection between war and politics, discernible in the category of conflict. In this sense, it can be argued that war is at the origin of politics—a thesis, after all, held by conservative thought. For Hobbes, for example, it is a war of all against all that gives rise to or initiates politics. By retreating. Politics, for Hobbes is the exit from permanent war in favor of a different dimension ruled by the sovereign order. Of course, Hobbes's conception is problematic in other respects for it foresees the total cession of natural rights to the sovereign. Not only because of this, but because Hobbes excludes any type of conflict from politics, counterposing the civil order to it. But this is a different problem. What remains is the paradigmatic opposition between war and politics. War introduces politics, but negatively, ceding its place to it.

From this point of view, I feel like agreeing with Hobbes, thereby dissenting from Carl Schmitt, who, though he declares it, in reality never manages to truly separate war and politics, turning war not only into a negative, but also a positive beginning, and turning politics into a confrontation between friend and enemy. Having said this, I think that war is unlikely to disappear from history. Not because it is part of politics but, if anything, because it is part of our anthropology, at least the one we have known thus far, as Freud argued on more than one occasion. Far from deriving from war, politics has to aim at containing its invasiveness, transforming military conflict into a civic one. From this point of view, the classical thinker I feel closest to, considering of course the distance of six centuries, is Machiavelli. It is because Machiavelli, on the one hand, neatly distinguishes between war and political conflict and, on the other, unlike Hobbes, takes conflict to be a constitutive dimension of political order.

As for the unfathomable tragedy of the war in Ukraine, only politics can attempt a resolution, if not in a satisfactory, then at least in a way acceptable for both parties. Provided that both sides are interested in peace. Both must renounce something, accept not to take or obtain what each believes is completely "just." From this point of view, I would introduce the dimension of responsibility, one Weber dramatically tied to the ethics of conviction, unlike both the "no ifs or buts" pacifists and the warmongers "to the bitter end" who dream of the impossible military defeat of Russia. Besides, when the Nazis invaded France, Simone Weil, an author you know so well, grasped just how irresponsible an absolute pacifism would be and asked to be enlisted—obviously *against* the war and with the prospect of a future peace.

FULCO: In the face of the tragic events of recent years, from the economic collapse of 2008 to the pandemic to the environmental crisis up to the war in Ukraine, the term "crisis," as used in both economy and politics—to indicate the dynamic of the attempts of different politico-economic models to restructure and respond to continuous difficulties and blockages—seems insufficient. Not long ago, in several public speeches, you pointed out that such events should no longer be considered "crises" but real "catastrophes." In other words, as something affecting not only the form but also the very essence of humanity, whose survival is threatened and whose being-in-the-world is radically altered. It is then no coincidence that this chain of tragic events has further brought left-oriented politics into question worldwide. In this regard, you spoke of the inability of the left to mobilize due to its "extremism," which you contrast with "radicalism." Can you explain in what sense you intend the difference between "extremism" and "radicalism?"

ESPOSITO: As a matter of fact, the term "crisis," even when reinforced by the adjective "permanent," appears insufficient to characterize what has been happening—perhaps one ought to go all the way to September 11, 2001, and the events that followed—in the last fifteen years. The expression "crisis" has been used in the twentieth century in the sense of the crisis of growth and for growth. The capitalist system for a long time functioned and structured itself through the crises that it provoked. If one thinks about the first Italian Republic in particular, one sees how continuous crises of government always left the same parties in power, perhaps with slight internal shifts in balance. Obviously, it was all about changing a few elements in ways functional to the preservation of the system.

None of this returns in the 2000s crises—from the economic one of 2008, which radically changed the capitalist economy, to the current, pandemic crisis, which transformed all our styles of life, to the war, which is literally overturning the previous geopolitical horizon. Not to mention the environmental crisis, which is bound to change the geological sites of the planet. In all of these cases, the appropriate term is that of "catastrophe," understood etymologically, as the structural alteration of the state of things. Speaking of catastrophe, I do not allude to anything apocalyptical, but rather to a profound change, overturning the previous situation, which leaves nothing unchanged. From this point of view, a "catastrophe," in certain circumstances, can be a prelude to an innovative outcome. Of course, the innovation isn't something positive in and of itself; it always implies risks, and much depends on how it is put into effect. But it isn't necessarily something negative either.

Regarding the difference or, rather, opposition between extremism and radicalism, it is a matter of overturning, subverting a common place which assimilates two quite different phenomena. In the current literature, extremism is presented as the final stage of radicalism, as radicalized radicalism. Nothing could be further from the truth. Radicalism, as the word itself implies, refers to the deepest roots, to rootedness in the context of origins and the articulation of its polarities. Extremism, to the contrary, implies a separation from the roots and the divergence of seemingly opposing poles, which does not allow for the common horizon containing them to be recognized. As "your" Simone Weil—the most radical thinker of the twentieth century—writes in *Énracinement*, the typical expression of contemporary nihilism is the extremism of the uprooted who in turn uproot their victims, obliterating both identities and differences. To understand what uprootedness is, suffice it to read the beautiful pages of *Venice Saved* by Simone Weil. Saved precisely by the extreme uprootedness of the Venetians.

CREMONESI: In your recent works, you focused specifically on political ontology, defining its three major contemporary paradigms. In *Pensiero istituente*,[2] you argued that two of these paradigms, the destituent and the constituent one, are showing signs of exhaustion in terms of their political effectiveness. Even though these paradigms depart from radically different ontologies—the Heideggerian and the Deleuzian one—they both seem unable to provide an effective political praxis. This is because they fail to address the specificity of the political field: in the first case, the negative character of the political ends up permeating the entire sphere of politics, while in the second case, the overlapping between the plane of the real and the political prevents the emergence of the gap needed to define adequate political practices. Elaborating a new paradigm is therefore an urgent political and philosophical task today; precisely for this reason you have opened an important research field gravitating around the "instituting thought." Can you tell us more about your work up to this point, and the direction it is taking at the moment?

ESPOSITO: You have nicely reconstructed my initial assumption: the feeling that some of the theoretical paradigms dominant in the area of continental philosophy struggle to find a proper political expression and end up emphasizing the tendency leading to depoliticization. Obviously, I am talking about paradigms of a high or very high theoretical level, reducible to two of the major contemporary philosophers, namely Heidegger and Deleuze—both, however bereft of a possible translation into politics. We know how it ended when Heidegger tried to do it. But Deleuze's political trilogy too seems to result in auto-dissolution.

At this point, the only way I deemed open was to pave the way for an alternative paradigm, which I found in instituting thought. Recognizing and elaborating this wasn't and still isn't easy, in particular after the philosophy of the second half of the twentieth century—not only of the right but, above all, of the left—has pushed the category of the "institution" towards conservatism, if not exclusion altogether. From Sartre to Marcuse, from Foucault to Bourdieu, not to mention Deleuze, the institution has been overwhelmingly identified with the State and its offshoots, demonized precisely in an extremist manner that opposed it to free, anti-institutional protest movements. Let's be clear: few institutions—carceral or psychiatric asylums—did not exercise unacceptable forms of control, and these were rightly condemned. Far from abolishing medical institutions, Basaglia wanted to transform them, as indeed he did, showing that protest movements are not necessarily anti-institutional. On the contrary, they serve to change institutions, just as, if they want to have a political impact, they cannot remain eternally impolitical, in a way they must institutionalize themselves.

However, starting from the 1920s of the last century, we encounter three currents of institutional thought: philosophical in France, anthropological in Germany, and juridical in Italy. Within these, institutions find their relationship with life, with history, and with politics that they seemed to lack. On the one hand, they acquire a dynamic, which compared to the static noun "institution" foregrounds the dynamics of the verb "to institute." On the other, they assume autonomy with respect to the sphere of the state, a fact which situates them beyond the boundaries of the state. Today we are witnessing a proliferation of non-state institutions, which are occasionally even critical of states, such as NGOs. Compared to this disruptive process, instituting thought, reborn in Italy in the last couple of years, recognizes not only institutional change, but also the relationship between institutions and conflict intuited by Machiavelli, taken up above all by Claude Lefort and also, in a different way, by Paul Ricœur. Personally, I am trying to strengthen this kind of reflection, putting it into direct contact with the political situation of our time. For example, the recent pandemic has identified a new—and dramatic—horizon within which the role of national and international, public and private, governmental and non-governmental institutions is to be redefined.

CREMONESI: If in *Pensiero istituente* you defined the main features of the instituting paradigm, in your next book, *Vitam instituere: Genealogia del pensiero istituente*, you plan instead to outline a history of this paradigm, encompassing the Roman law and Machiavelli, Spinoza and Hegel, going all the way to contemporary authors addressed in *Pensiero istituente*, such as Claude Lefort. In describing your historical-philosophical methodology, you use a specific term, "genealogy," coined by Nietzsche and later taken up by Foucault, who used it as the method for the critical diagnosis of the present, starting from the historical elements that constituted it. In this regard, I would like to ask you: Why do you think a genealogy of instituting thought is either necessary or useful? Do you believe that tracing this line of thought in history is a fruitful method for a critical diagnosis of our present and for identifying more effective ways of action in the present?

ESPOSITO: At the beginning of my research, I stopped at the twentieth-century's French post-phenomenology, German philosophical anthropology, and Italian juridical institutionalism. Afterwards, I gradually became aware that despite their originality, these currents were rooted in classical and modern philosophy. At the same time, while unable to historicize its own categories—starting from the category of "nature"—or break with juridical formalism along political lines, Roman law, even if unclearly, grasps the relationship between institution and life. The first "instituting" thought, as I said, probably goes back to Machiavelli, who assigns politics the founding role in instituting civic life. The second author I place at the origin of the instituting practice is Spinoza. Notwithstanding his seemingly absolute immanentism, he understands the power of imagination as imbued with the capacity to renew, and even invent political institutions, as is the case in particular with the prophetic imagination in relation to the constitution of Hebrew theocracy. Finally, the author who can be said to inaugurate modern institutionalism is Hegel. I allude not only to the pages he dedicates to institutions in the *Philosophy of Right*, but to his entire anthropology and dialectics itself, understood as instituting power passing through the negative. It is not without reason that the majority of twentieth-century institutionalists, consciously or unconsciously, begin with the Hegelian objective spirit or what Hegel defines as "second nature," understood as artificial, indeed instituted nature.

On the one hand, the genealogical character of my research consists in the attempt to go back in time so as to find a key to access the present and, on the other, in the conscious impossibility of seizing an origin in continuous recession. Genealogy, both in Nietzsche's and Foucault's sense, implies a return to an origin that, as such, is inexistent because always in retreat in relation to the point that the researcher can reach. Each apparent "first" is, in reality, already a "second," preceded by something else which retreats continuously. Despite this or precisely because of this, genealogy, like—for other reasons—archaeology, is necessary in order to come closer to one part of the present which we are unable to see if we read it head on, directly. The tradition that accumulates upon it as an impenetrable layer prevents the phenomena from being directly grasped. The only way to get around or penetrate it is to reopen the relation with the origin which precedes that tradition, whilst knowing that it is inaccessible.

CREMONESI: A criticism often leveled at the genealogical method—a method that closely relates past and present—is that it risks anachronism. Carlo Ginzburg, for example, acknowledges that our questions directed to the past inevitably suffer from anachronism, but underlines that the answers we provide must respect the distance that separates us from our sources.[3] Do you think that genealogy really implies such a risk? Or do you think instead that anachronism can be philosophically productive? In your article dedicated to this topic,[4] you discuss a number of authors who have highlighted the importance of thinking the "contemporaneity of the non-contemporaneous" (Loraux, Kosselleck, Didi-Huberman, Bloch, and Benjamin, among others). Is there a relationship between the way you use genealogy and these reflections on anachronism?

ESPOSITO: In a certain way, Ginzburg is right. The anachronism of questions addressed to the past is inevitable, given that the language in which we formulate them is ours and nobody can ever escape their own language. The problem was posed already by Heidegger when he stopped writing *Being and Time* precisely because of a similar lexical difficulty. Today, the *Begriffsgeschichte* School that developed mainly in Germany, but also in Italy, assumes this difficulty as its point of departure. In reconstructing pre-modern concepts, the contemporary researcher has to presuppose an insurmountable semantic gap. For example, what the Greeks understood as "democracy" has nothing or almost nothing to do with what we understand by it. Likewise, to talk about the Greek *polis* or Roman *civitas* in terms of the state exposes the researcher to the risk of misunderstanding both the past and the present. That said, as you yourself point out, anachronism, if taken as what inevitably separates the contemporary interpreter and the ancient text, can also play a positive role, as the authors to which I refer to argue in different ways. At the same time, one ought to say that contemporaneity—one we define as such—itself has a constitutively anachronistic structure, in the sense that, in its literal meaning, it implies the co-presence of different times within time itself: hence the non-contemporaneity of any contemporaneous. As Koselleck maintains, the past and future do not mutually exclude one another but, in a way, overlap within any present. This insight is what constitutes the anachronistic foundation of Benjamin's entire quest. Only with this perspective is it possible to escape the historicism (*storicismo*) of progress and regress. History does not follow one single thread, it proceeds neither forwards nor backwards, but forms a constellation in which past, present, and future entangle in a new and unknown figure dominated by anachrony. Only the conscious assumption of the anachronism can, in principle at least, contest the dominion of what happened over what didn't, but which continues to suddenly appear in its absence in the present.

SURACE: The pandemic has brought biopolitics back into vogue. In particular, as you observe in *Common Immunity*, herd immunity reveals the reversal of biopolitics into *thanatopolitics*, social distancing reveals the negative while *vaccine prevention* reveals the positive character of biopolitics. Do you think that, other than the tragic triage choices that doctors face—which include saving those whose survival chances are judged to be highest—social distancing as a form of "social death" and cost/benefit calculations when it comes to vaccines reveal the thanatological character of biopolitics, the fact of its *structural* and not racist *deviation*? You observe that today "a new de facto racism"[5] has arisen from the ashes of old racism, as the difference between the biomedical resources of rich and poor countries clearly demonstrates.

ESPOSITO: In assessing historical phenomena, one should never lose a sense of proportion. At times, the differences are more important than the analogies. It is true that physical distancing has created a deficit in sociability, as we all have experienced in the last two years. One only has to look at schools or universities, profoundly damaged by long-distance learning. Nevertheless, to talk about it in terms of *thanatopolitics*—that is, a politics of death—seems to me to be exaggerated. The category of biopolitics—and continental philosophy on the whole—has paid an immense price for these kinds of exaggerations which, in the end, undermined its credibility. As for the new racism, the gap between biotechnological resources or disparity in vaccine distribution, the problem is in fact more serious. In this case too, rather than somebody's *thanatopolitical* choice to the detriment of the other, the current situation is a consequence of the long-term inequality of resources which separates the developed countries from the technologically and economically most underdeveloped zones. Of course, this outcome is not foreign to colonization nor to the sometimes-distorted form that decolonization took. Not to mention the capitalist primacy of economy over politics. Until now, politics has been unable to compel Big Pharma to give up the profits from pharmacological patents, thus bringing entire populations to their knees, condemning them to certain death. In this case, it is certainly possible to talk about *thanatopolitics* or about "necropolitics," as does Achille Mbembe. However, I repeat, one ought to look at these dramatic phenomena without losing sight of the historical events that led to them.

SURACE: In contemporary "immune democracy," the equality of the homogeneous corresponds to the exclusion of the heterogeneous—as Arendt noted concerning the nation-state. In *Common Immunity*, you emphasize that whereas in the earlier epochs "*immunitas* had the character of an exception, in modern democracy it extends, at least in principle, to all individuals."[6] Such an inviolability does not quite hold for the entire humankind, but only for one part, *the protected*, unlike and to the detriment of the other part, *the exposed*. To address this unequal distribution of humanity, you propose an analysis of *institutions*. Insofar as institutions are not equivalent to state, shouldn't the experiences of the pandemic and the current war in Ukraine prompt us to rethink international organizations?

ESPOSITO: Certainly. Institutions—national or international—ought to be profoundly changed, starting, for our part, with the European Union. But the World Health Organization itself has drawn attention to a significant number of criticisms. Even the work, however positive, of many NGOs requires a certain modification, at least in certain particularly sensitive places like Central and North Africa. Institutions can only function if they are modified depending on the context they arose in and the needs they were created to satisfy. Change isn't merely a possibility but rather a necessity of institutions. The latter, as instituted and precisely because instituted, have to keep alive the instituting principle that established them if they are not to be hollowed out and ultimately disappear. Already Machiavelli held that a political organism, threatened with extinction, has to return to principles, that is, to its own constituting principle. If the relationship between constituent and constituted power is a classical theme of political science, for instituting thought it is at the very center of the discussion.

In the book you mention, I related the polarity instituting/instituted to that of community/immunity. If it is not to be dissolved, the instituting principle has to solidify within permanent institutions; in the same manner, the community cannot do without an immunological dispositive which protects it from its inherent tendency towards entropy. Just as there are no individual bodies without immunological mechanisms of defense, there are no societies either. Of course, in order for these to have a positive effect, one must have a sense of proportion. If the immunological apparatus grows more than it should, it risks fighting against the body, biological or social, which it ought to defend, leading it thus to collapse. Institutions themselves are to be understood as living organisms. They are born, develop, and die when their function wanes. Their relationship to life—expressed in the ancient Latin motto "*vitam instituere*"—is to be understood not as a simple relation, but as a reciprocal integration: as life is always instituted and instituting—there is no life which would not at the same time be a form of life—the institution thus emerges and disappears on the basis of a vital principle. In its absence, the institution cannot but extinguish itself.

SURACE: In the "state of emergency," immunity is necessary, but outside of it, it neutralizes *conflicts*, the only thing capable of driving constituted power beyond itself, as Lefort teaches. Overcoming the dichotomy conflict/order—as Machiavelli and Luhmann suggest—you argue that the law should protect the community not *from*, but *through* conflicts. Is it possible to give a form to conflict? Conflict, albeit competitive and non-warlike, describes a dialectical relationship between opposing subjectivities. Does it not, therefore, risk legitimizing a violent political horizon? Why not insist on the concept of *friendship*, as a "nothing-in-common that unites in distance,"[7] a concept you deem compatible with *communitas*?

ESPOSITO: In normal conditions, immunization limits conflicts in the sense that it annuls or reduces the ratio of destructive aggressivity. The law, since time immemorial, is assigned this role. This is why Luhmann considers it the immunitary subsystem of social systems. Without it, we would risk auto-destruction. But, as you said, the law does not eliminate but civilizes conflicts, rendering them not only compatible with order, but productive of it. Something similar, expressed of course in a conceptually different language, was argued by Machiavelli, who understood the conflict between patricians and plebeians as the reason behind Rome's greatness. He argued that it was not only possible but necessary to give form to conflict, turning it into a dynamic generator of order. In this sense, it is possible to argue that Machiavelli anticipates the cornerstone of instituting thought. As Lefort argues centuries later, the political institutes the social in the sense of rendering it conscious of the conflict which, even though unconsciously, already cuts through it. It can also be said that the political is the space in which material conflicts are symbolized, becoming conflicts of power and mutual recognition between the sides. You are right, a political conflict can always escalate into a violent conflict. To contain such possibility, one needs precisely institutions, destined to keep it within certain limits compatible with the survival of social systems. Friendship is not a political concept if separated from enmity. As a matter of fact, it isn't even a category of *communitas*, at least the way I conceive of it. *Communitas* does not unite subjects-friends; rather, it expropriates subjectivity in the common *munus*. In any case, its dimension is impolitical. There is no politics of friendship, given that the category of friendship is not a political one. For there to be politics, there has to be a common front in which we mutually recognize ourselves and together enter into conflict.

SURACE: In your opinion, the logic of immunization can be applied to the regularization of migration flows. It is a matter of finding the point of equilibrium or sustainability up to which the system can hold, including as many people as possible without risking a breakdown or a collapse.[8] However, isn't the idea of admitting or taking in "the assimilable" the same idea that animates policies that aim to protect the state and safeguard the health of the national body? Is it possible, on the basis of this idea, to think the politics of hospitality?

Esposito: What is the alternative to admitting those who can be absorbed—that is, accepting all those it is possible to accept? To blow everything up, destroying everything and everyone? If we do not protect the state, what is there to be done? One thing is to criticize the authoritarian or exclusionary modalities of the principle of sovereignty; quite another though is to imagine a society without power. At the end of such reasoning, there is anarchy. Are we certain it is better than democracy? Affirming anarchy is a very good example of extremism contrary to political radicality. The latter consists precisely in the capacity to reconcile, with the maximum possible degree of openness, the ethics of conviction with the ethics of responsibility.

Naples, January 2023

Notes

1. Roberto Esposito, *The Origin of the Political: Hannah Arendt or Simone Weil?*, trans. Vincenzo Binetti and Gareth Williams (New York: Fordham University Press, 2017), 13.

2. Roberto Esposito, *Pensiero istituente: Tre paradigmi di ontologia politica* (Turin, Italy: Einaudi, 2020); *Instituting Thought: Three Paradigms of Political Ontology*, trans. Mark W. Epstein (Cambridge: Polity, 2021).

3. Carlo Ginzburg, *Le nostre parole, e le loro: Una riflessione sul mestiere di storico, oggi*, in *La lettera uccide* (Milan: Adelphi, 2021), 69–85.

4. Roberto Esposito, "Anacronismi," *Filosofia politica*, no. 1 (April 2017): 13–24.

5. See Roberto Esposito, *Immunità comune: Biopolitica all'epoca della pandemia* (Turin, Italy: Einaudi, 2022); *Common Immunity: Biopolitics in the Age of the Pandemic*, trans. Zakiya Hanafi (Cambridge: Polity, 2023), 111.

6. See Esposito, *Common Immunity*, 50–51.

7. See Roberto Esposito, *Comunità, immunità, biopolitica*, in *Spettri di Derrida*, ed. Carola Barbero, Simone Regazzoni, and Amelia Valtolina (Genoa, Italy: il nuovo melangolo, 2010), 147.

8. Marco Damilano, Donatella Di Cesare, and Roberto Esposito, *Dialoghi sul nostro tempo: Marco Damilano con Donatella Di Cesare e Roberto Esposito*, May 15, 2020, video interview, https://www.youtube.com/watch?v=2fwQOt1q3bo.

Contributors

Stefania Achella is full professor of moral philosophy at the University of Chieti-Pescara, where she teaches ethics. She is currently working on the relationship between philosophy and biology in the nineteenth century, the concepts of life and corporeity in classical German philosophy, and the contributions of feminism to the philosophical debate. On these topics she has published *Pensare la vita: Saggio su Hegel* (2020), in which she rereads Hegelian philosophy through Esposito's categories; "Gendering the Anthropocene?," *Itinerari*, no. 59 (2020): 137–156; and *Idealism and Science of Life: An Intersection between Philosophy and Biology*, in *Thinking: Bioengineering of Science and Art* (2022). She is also coeditor of *The Owl's Flight: Hegel's Legacy to Contemporary Philosophy* (2021).

Daniela Calabrò is associate professor of theoretical philosophy at Università of Salerno. She is the author of many books and articles and has edited many volumes, including *L'infanzia della filosofia: Saggio sulla filosofia dell'educazione di Maurice Merleau-Ponty* (2002); *Di-spiegamenti: Soggetto, corpo e comunità in Jean-Luc Nancy* (2006); *Les détours d'une pensée vivante: Transitions et changements de paradigme dans la réflexion de Roberto Esposito* (2012); *L'ora meridiana: Il pensiero inoperoso di Jean-Luc Nancy tra ontologia, estetica e politica* (2012); *Unlimit: Rethinking the Boundaries between Philosophy, Aesthetics, and Arts*, coedited with G. Bird and D. Giugliano (2017); *La tradizione dello Spirito: Eredità Hegeliane nel Novecento*, coedited with L. Scafoglio (2018); *The Correspondence: Jean-Paul Sartre and Maurice Merleau-Ponty* (2018); *Humanity: Tra paradigmi perduti e nuove traiettorie*, coedited with D. Giugliano, R. Peluso, A. P. Ruoppo, and L. Scafoglio (2020). Since 2017 she has been scientific director of *Shift: International Journal of Philosophical Studies*.

Laura Cremonesi is researcher in moral philosophy at the Scuola Normale Superiore (Pisa, Italy) and is "directrice de programme" at the Collège international de philosophy (Paris, France). She has a PhD in philosophy (University of Pisa and University of Paris XII–Créteil) and was Marie Curie Research Fellow at the University of Warwick (UK). Her major fields of research are contemporary French philosophy and Italian thought. She has widely published on Michel Foucault and Pierre Hadot. Her written works include *Michel Foucault e il mondo antico: Spunti per una critica dell'attualità* (2008); *L'esercizio della distanza: Foucault, Hadot, Ginzburg* (2024), and she has edited *Foucault and the Making of Subjects* (2016) and A. I. Davidson, *Gli esercizi spirituali della musica: Improvvisazione e creazione* (2020). She has published many essays in Italian, French, and English, and has translated some relevant books of Hadot from French into Italian: *Studi di filosofia antica* (2014) and *Studi di patristica e di storia dei concetti* (2018). Her current project revolves around the concept and the practice of "critique," starting from Foucault's way of conceiving it as a "critical attitude," and in relation to the ideas of alteration, transfiguration, and estrangement.

Silvia Dadà is post-doctoral researcher at the University of Pisa. She obtained her PhD from the University of Florence with a thesis on the theme of justice in the thought of Emmanuel Levinas and Jacques Derrida. Her research centers on the theme of care and vulnerability as ethical and political concept. On these themes she has written volumes and essays, which include *Il paradosso della giustizia: Levinas e Derrida* (2021), *Maternità e alterità: Per una bioetica della cura* (2021), and *Etica della vulnerabilità* (2022).

Mattia Di Pierro earned a PhD from the Scuola Normale Superiore and Université Diderot Paris VII in 2019. He currently is a research fellow at the Department of Philosophy, University of Milan, and editor of the *Almanacco di Filosofia e Politica*. His research interests include contemporary political thought, and theories of democracy and conflict, with a focus on the work of Maurice Merleau-Ponty, Claude Lefort, and Hannah Arendt. He is the author of *L'esperienza del mondo: Claude Lefort e la fenomenologia del politico* (2020) and of numerous essays around Lefort's thought and Italian workerism as well as contemporary readings of the works of Niccolò Machiavelli.

Rita Fulco is associate professor at the Department of Ancient and Modern Civilizations at the University of Messina, where she teaches philosophical hermeneutics and philosophies of the twentieth century. She was postdoc fellow in theoretical philosophy from 2016 to 2021 at Scuola Normale Superiore, Pisa. She qualified as associate professor in theoretical philosophy (2015 and 2018), political philosophy (2014, 2018, and 2023), and moral philosophy (2014). She works on the theoretical, religious, ethical, and political aspects of contemporary Continental philosophy. Her publications include *Corrispondere al limite—Simone Weil: Il pensiero e la luce* (2002); *Il tempo della fine: L'Apocalittica messianica di Sergio Quinzio* (2007); *Essere insieme in un luogo: Etica, politica, diritto nel pensiero di Emmanuel Levinas* (2013); and *Soggettività e potere: Ontologia della vulnerabilità in Simone Weil* (2020). She has edited the volume *Contemporanei della fine del mondo: Saggi su Manlio Sgalambro* (2023). She has also coedited various volumes, such as *L'Europa di Simone Weil* (2019), with T. Greco; *Sull'evento: Almanacco di Filosofia e Politica* 4 (2022), with A. Moresco; and *Martirio e testimonianza: Saggi di filosofia, storia, e teologia politica* (2023), with B. M. Esposito. Her recently published articles include "Emmanuel Levinas: A Philosophy of Exodus," in *The Pertinence of Exodus*, ed. S. Gorgone and L. Mackowitz (2019); "Life and Useless Suffering," in *Rethinking Life*, ed. S. Benso (2022); "Crítica y productividad de las instituciones: El quiasmo entre Roberto Esposito y Michel Foucault," in *Dorsal: Revista de estudios foucaultianos*, no. 14 (2023); and "Geofilosofia mediterranea: Pensiero e politica del 'mare di mezzo,'" *Logoi.ph—Journal of Philosophy*, no. 24 (2024).

Sandro Gorgone is associate professor of theoretical philosophy at the University of Messina. He is a scholar of twentieth-century German and French philosophy, and has especially investigated the thought of Martin Heidegger and Ernst Jünger. His main lines of research are temporality, ontology, technique, the crisis of humanism, and the relationship between modernity and secularization. He has also addressed the hermeneutics of religious experience and the relationship between theology and philosophy. A further current line of his research is related to geophilosophy and landscape philosophy for the purpose of a reproposition of the philosophy of nature and the earth in the context of ecological issues. He has participated in numerous conferences both in Italy and abroad and is the author of articles and essays in national and international volumes and journals. His recent monographs are *Nel deserto dell'umano: Potenza e Machenschaft nel pensiero di Martin Heidegger* (2011); *Strahlungen und Annäherungen: Die stereoskopische Phänomenologie Ernst Jüngers* (2016); and *Il trionfo di Proteo: Tecnica e metamorfosi dell'umano* (2021).

Francesco Marchesi is postdoc fellow at the University of Pisa. He has been also postdoctoral fellow at Fondazione Luigi Einaudi di Torino and at Scuola Normale Superiore, Pisa. He is the author of *Riscontro: Pratica politica e congiuntura storica in Niccolò Machiavelli* (2017), *Cartografia politica: Spazi e soggetti del conflitto in Niccolò Machiavelli* (2018), *Geometria del conflitto: Saggio sulla non-corrispondenza* (2020), *Ritorno ai princìpi: Concezioni della storia da Machiavelli alla Rivoluzione francese* (2023), and *Machiavellian Ontology: Politics as Conflict* (2024). He founded, with Roberto Esposito and Mattia Di Pierro, the Almanacco di Filosofia e politica.

Alberto Martinengo is associate professor of aesthetics at the University of Turin, Italy. He has taught philosophy at the University of Milan and at the Scuola Normale Superiore. He has published essays in German, English, French, and Spanish, on different aspects of the hermeneutical tradition. His most recent research deals with the philosophy of images and their political relevance. Martinengo is the author of a book on Martin Heidegger and Reiner Schürmann, *Un pensiero anarchico: Filosofia, azione e storia in Reiner Schürmann* (2021); a volume on Paul Ricoeur, *Il pensiero incompiuto: Ermeneutica, ragione, ricostruzione in Paul Ricoeur* (2008); and two books on the relations between language and images, *Filosofie della metafora* (2015) and *Prospettive sull'ermeneutica dell'immagine* (2021). His edited books include *Beyond Deconstruction: From Hermeneutics to Reconstruction* (2010).

Valentina Surace was a research fellow (theoretical philosophy) within the framework of the FISR project "The Refunctionalisation of the Contemporary" and holds a PhD in methodologies of philosophy (University of Messina). She is a member of several national and international research groups. Her research focuses on German and French twentieth-century philosophy and contemporary philosophy in particular: Martin Heidegger's ontology of life and its Lutheran roots; Judith Butler's social ontology; Jacques Derrida's deconstruction, in its ethical-political implications; and the question of human habitation on Earth from a geophilosophical perspective. Among her publications are *L'inquietudine dell'esistenza: Le* *radici luterane dell'ontologia della vita di Martin Heidegger* (2014); *Soggetti precari: L'ontologia sociale di Judith Butler* (2023); "Messianismo e politica: Il frammento teologico-politico di Walter Benjamin" and "Messianismi e cosmopolitica: Derrida oltre Kant," in *Schegge messianiche: Filosofia, religione, politica*, ed. C. Resta (2017); V. Surace, ed., *Anacronie: L'inattualità del contemporaneo* (2022); V. Surace and A. Reid, eds., *Just in Time: Theorising the Contemporary / Giusto in tempo: Pensare il contemporaneo* (2023); V. Surace and A. Reid, eds., *Pained Screams from Camps: The Human Condition of Exception: Collected Essays and Aldo Quarisa's Diary: An Italian-English Edition* (2024); and "Abitare la Terra: Un percorso geofilosofico da Martin Heidegger ad Augustin Berque," *Logoi.ph. Journal of Philosophy* 10, no. 24 (2024): 88–95.

Massimo Villani has a PhD in political philosophy. His studies concern modern political thinking, with an emphasis on the aesthetical aspect of politics. He is member of scientific/editorial staff of *Shift: International Journal of Philosophical Studies* and *Post-filosofie: Rivista di pratica filosofica e scienze umane*. He has translated and edited the Italian edition of several works of Jean-Luc Nancy and Jacques Rancière. He published the monographs *Arte della fuga. Estetica e democrazia nel pensiero di Jean-Luc Nancy* (2020); *On Extension: Jean-Luc Nancy in the Wake of Hannah Arendt* (2023); and *Time and History: Researches on the Ontology of the Present* (2023).

Index

Abensour, Miguel, 142n21, 143n42
Achella, Stefania, 7–8
Adinolfi, Massimo, 39, 196n68
Adorno, Theodor Ludwig Wiesengrund, 205
Agamben, Giorgio, 38n20, 45, 52, 55n19, 62, 69, 71n21–22, 107n8, 112, 128n1, 190n4, 191n18, 195n58
Anidjar, Gil, 191n7
Arendt, Hanna, 5, 7, 11, 12, 58, 61, 75–76, 79–90, 93n32–33, 93n39, 93n41, 132, 141n10, 164, 208, 212n56, 215, 223
Augustine, 86, 93n41

Bataille, Georges, 201
Bateson, Gregory, 72n39
Badiou, Alain, 144n52
Balakrishnan, Gopal, 106n3, 107n23
Baudrillard, Jean, 189n1
Bazzicalupo, Laura, 140, 144n42
Benso, Silvia, 92n23
Benveniste, Émile, 133, 142n14, 185, 187, 192n33
Bennington, Geoffrey, 191, 193n34, 195n58
Benjamin, Walter, 194n46, 221–222
Bergson, Henri, 31–32, 35, 39n39, 63

Blanchot, Maurice, 5, 18–19, 120, 135–137, 142n27, 143n35, 143n39, 197, 201–208, 210n19, 210n23, 210n25, 210n27–28, 211n30–33, 211n36–38, 212n44, 212n46, 212n50, 212n52
Bloch, Marc, 221
Borradori, Giovanna, 192n23
Buber, Martin, 134, 159n20
Butler, Judith, 132, 142n11, 190n3

Calabrò, Daniela, 14, 160n26, 212n51
Calcagno, Antonio, 92n28, 93n50, 194n53
Campbell, Timothy, 37n11, 38n29, 53n1, 56n37, 71n20, 92n28, 128n5, 141n3, 141n9, 158n8, 191n13, 191n15, 191n19, 209n6, 209n7
Carlson, David Gray, 194n46
Castoriadis, Cornelius, 70n11, 72n43
Caygill, Howard, 143n31
Chenavier, Robert, 92n26
Ciaramelli, Fabio, 141, 144n55
Ciccarelli, Roberto, 37n14, 38n21
Ciglia, Francesco Paolo, 143n34
Claverini, Corrado, 91n5
Cohen-Levinas, Danielle, 142n15

Cooper, Anthony, 190n2
Cornell, Drucilla, 194n46
Cremonesi, Laura, 2, 7–8, 55n26
Crépon, Marc, 193n34
Critchley, Simon, 143n39
Cuomo, Vincenzo, 141n1
Cusset, François, 54n10

Dadà, Silvia, 14–15, 143n34, 143n40, 144n47
De Libéra, Alain, 141n7
De Petro, Fausto, 160n26
Deleuze, Gilles, 5–11, 23–35, 36n1, 36n5–6, 36n9, 37n11–12, 37n14, 37n16, 37n17, 38n20, 38n26, 38n28, 38n30, 38n35, 39n37–38, 39n45, 42–44, 49, 52–53, 54n6, 54n8, 54n10, 54n13–14, 62–63, 65–66, 71n24–26, 75, 77–79, 91n10, 133, 135, 199, 201, 205, 208, 210n9, 210n17, 218–219
Derrida, Jacques, 5, 17–18, 43, 52, 78, 91n12, 126, 144n47, 182–189, 190n5, 191n6–12, 191n21–27, 192n32, 192n34, 193n35, 193n36–41, 194n46, 194n53, 195n58–60, 196n61–67, 196n69, 211n29, 226n7
Didi-Huberman, Georges, 221
Di Pierro, Mattia, 10–11, 70n12, 72n35, 72n41, 106n3, 144n56
Donis, Giacomo, 191n9
Duns Scotus, 27, 37n17
Duso, Guseppe, 106n1
Dutoit, Thomas, 193n34

Evans-Pritchard, Edward, 72n39
Ewald, François, 211n37

Ferraris, Maurizio, 37n12, 191n9
Flores D'Arcais, Paolo, 55n35

Flynn, Bernard, 72n41
Forti, Simona, 55n35, 92n24
Foucault, Michel, 4–13, 20, 24, 31, 36n1, 37n16, 38n29, 41–56, 59, 65, 72n35, 75, 78, 79, 82, 87, 88, 91n14, 133, 146, 190nn3–4, 195nn57–58, 199, 200, 205, 210n16, 213, 219, 220
Freud, Sigmund 2, 188, 189, 216
Fulco, Rita 1, 11, 12, 56n43, 91n14, 92n16, 92n23, 92nn26–27, 93n30, 93n48, 142n24, 144n56, 196n68

Galli, Carlo 55n35
Garritano, Francesco, 211n29
Gehlen, Arnold, 60
Gentili, Dario 36n2, 73n48, 91n5
Ginzburg, Carlo, 3, 221, 226n3
Girard, René, 194n45
Goria, Giulio, 212n51
Gramsci, Antonio, 8, 25, 34, 36n4
Greco, Tommaso, 93n48
Guattari, Félix, 38n28, 54n8, 71n26, 77, 78, 91n10, 210n9
Guercio, Francesco, 164

Habermas, Jurgen, 106n3, 107n15
Hayat, Pierre, 139, 144n48
Haraway, Donna, 129n21, 195n57
Hardt, Michael, 45, 55n19
Hartog, François, 72n39
Hegel, Georg Wilhelm Friedrich, 3, 6, 8, 18, 25, 27, 34, 36n3, 37n15, 58, 59, 63, 106, 119, 129n23, 175, 186, 193n43, 197–200, 203, 205, 209, 209nn1–2, 212nn58–59, 215, 220
Heidegger, Martin, 5, 15–17, 28, 34, 35, 42, 61–63, 66, 75, 77, 91, 136, 147–149, 151–152, 156–158, 158nn9–11, 159nn12–

18, 159n24, 160n25, 160n28,
161nn46–47, 161n49, 163–177,
177n6, 177nn10–11, 177nn13–15,
178nn16–24, 178n26, 179nn37–38,
203, 208, 218, 221
Heitz, Michael, 164
Herbrechter, Stefan, 192n32
Hobbes, Thomas, 59, 115, 143n42,
195n56, 215–216
Hölderlin, Johann Christian
Friedrich, 152, 159n24, 171, 176,
177n15, 178n15
Höfner, Markus, 159n17
Hume David, 39n38
Husserl, Edmund, 10, 42, 67,
120–122, 166, 203, 210n26

Iadicicco, Alessandra, 177n6

Jamieson, Michelle, 192n32
Jankélévitch, Vladimir, 134

Kalyvas, Andreas, 106n3, 107n23
Kant, Immanuel, 31, 59, 78, 86
Kervegan, Jean-François, 106n2,
107n14
Kirchmayr, Raul, 211n37
Kojève, Alexandre, 28, 193n43
Koselleck, Reinhart, 221–222

Labelle, Gilles, 72n41
Labriola, Antonio, 25
Lèbre, Jérôme, 212n50
Lefort, Claude, 5, 7, 10–11, 42, 52,
57–58, 60, 64–68, 70n11, 71nn32–
34, 72nn38–39, 72n41, 72n43,
72n46, 129n25, 140, 219–220,
224–225
Levinas, Emmanuel, 5, 14–15,
134–141, 142n15, 142nn20–24,
142nn28–30, 143nn31–44,
144nn45–46, 144n57, 203, 210n28,
211nn28–29
Lisciani-Petrini, Enrica, 39n35,
73n48, 128n9, 141n1, 196n68,
211n37
Loraux, Nicole, 221
Losurdo, Domenico, 160n25
Luhmann, Niklas, 224
Lyotard, Jean-François, 43

Machiavelli, Niccolò, 3, 6, 8, 11, 13,
31, 34, 58–59, 68, 75, 79, 91n16,
92n16, 95, 140, 209, 209n2, 216,
219–220, 223–225
Marcantonio, Erika, 160n26
Marchesi, Francesco, 12–13, 70n12;
144n56
Marcuse, Herbert, 65, 219
Marchart, Olivier, 144n52
Marx, Karl, 96
Mbembe, Achille, 223
McCormick, John P., 107n15
Mead, Margaret, 72n39
Meierhenrich, Jens 106n3
Mengue, Philippe, 40n49
Merleau-Ponty, Maurice, 7, 10–11,
52, 60, 66–67, 72n41, 118,
120–122, 129n25, 129n27,
211n37
Mitchell, Peta, 192n32
Montesquieu, Charles-Louis de
Secondat, 87
Moresco, Andrea, 92n, 229n
Mosès, Stéphane 142n15
Mouffe, Chantal 106n3, 107n23
Müller, Jan-Werner 106n3,
107n23

Nancy, Jean-Luc, 5, 11, 14, 16, 43,
52, 55n35, 62, 70–71n20, 76,
91n4–5, 111–128, 128n2–3, 128n7,

Nancy, Jean-Luc *(continued)*
  128n11, 129n23–24, 129n34,
  129n35–36, 129n38–39, 129n42,
  144n52, 147, 150–153, 155–156,
  159n21, 160n24, 160n26, 160n29,
  160n30–35, 161n37, 161n43–45,
  178–179n36, 193n38, 193–194n43,
  201, 205, 212n50
Negri, Antonio, 24, 33, 36n1, 39n45,
  45, 52, 55n19, 63, 69
Nietzsche, Friedrich, 24, 26, 27, 31,
  43, 52, 75, 78, 105–106, 112–113,
  146, 174, 190n5, 195, 220

Parmenides, 168, 174, 176, 177n11
Pavel, Thomas, 92n26
Plato, 32, 83, 193n36, 193n41
Poirier, Nicolas, 72n41, 72n43
Preterossi, Geminello, 107n15

Rajan, Tilottama, 92n28, 194n53
Rauch, Malte Fabian, 164
Reich, Wilhelm, 65
Resta, Caterina, 91n12, 92n23,
  189n2, 190n2, 196n67
Revel, Judith, 55n27
Ricoeur, Paul, 142n25, 219
Rodotà, Stefano, 128n8
Rogozinski, Jacob, 212n50
Romano, Santi, 60
Ronchi, Rocco, 143n39
Rosenfeld, Michel, 194n46
Rottenber, Elizabeth, 190n5
Rousseau, Jean-Jacques, 59

Sahlins, Marshall, 72n39
Sartre, Jean-Paul, 59, 204, 211n37,
  219
Schmitt, Carl, 5, 7, 12, 13, 61, 75,
  78, 95–106, 106n2–3, 106n6,
  106n7, 107n9–23, 216

Serratore, Costanza, 70n2
Schneider, Nicolas, 164
Schürmann, Reiner, 5, 16, 17, 163–
  177, 177n1–5, 177n7–9, 177n11,
  178n25
Simons, Oliver, 106n3
Somers-Hall, Henry, 36n3
Sophocles, 175
Specter, Matthew G., 106n3
Spinoza, Baruch, 3, 6, 24–25, 31, 35,
  58–59, 63, 75, 209n2, 220
Starobinski, Jean, 210n22
Stiegler, Bernard, 192n26
Stimilli, Elettra 73n48, 91n5, 91n12,
  196n67
Strummiello, Giusi 73n48, 91n5
Surace, Valentina, 3, 17–18, 190n3

Tarde, Gabriel, 36n6
Tarizzo, Davide, 133, 142n18
Tauber, Alfred, 117, 128n20, 154
Thiel, Udo, 141n8
Thucydides, 81
Tinning, Søren, 190n2
Tronti, Mario, 13, 95, 106n3, 107n23

Vatter, Miguel, 73n49
Viriasova, Inna, 92n28
Voltaire, François-Marie Arouet, 154,
  161n41

Webb, David, 191n9
Weber, Max, 107n23, 216
Weil, Simone, 5, 7, 11, 12, 61,
  75–90, 91n2–3, 91–92n16, 92n23,
  92n25–26, 93n30, 93n33, 93n48,
  93n50, 135, 215–218, 226n1
Wolfe, Cary, 194n53

Zarader, Marlène, 211n29
Žižek, Slavoj, 40n49, 71n24

www.ingramcontent.com/pod-product-compliance
Lightning Source LLC
Chambersburg PA
CBHW021839220426
43663CB00005B/314